PLAS

PITT
LATIN
AMERICAN
SERIES

Authoritarians and Democrats

Regime Transition in Latin America

James M. Malloy and Mitchell A. Seligson, Editors

University of Pittsburgh Press

For Cole Blasier, founder of the Center for Latin American Studies, and Carmelo Mesa-Lago, who nurtured its growth.

Published by the University of Pittsburgh Press, Pittsburgh, Pa. 15260
Copyright © 1987, University of Pittsburgh Press
All rights reserved
Feffer and Simons, Inc., London
Manufactured in the United States of America

Second printing 1988

Library of Congress Cataloging-in-Publication Data

Authoritarians and democrats.

(Pitt Latin American series)
  1. Latin America—Politics and government—1948–
2. Representative government and representation—Latin
America.   3. Authoritarianism—Latin America.   I. Malloy,
James M.   II. Seligson, Mitchell A.   III. Series.
JL966.A98   1987   321.09'098   86-25035
ISBN 0-8229-3551-1
ISBN 0-8229-5387-0 (pbk.)

Contents

Acknowledgments

The conference upon which this volume is based was organized to commemorate the twentieth anniversary of the founding of the Center for Latin American Studies at the University of Pittsburgh. The Center, therefore, provided major support for the conference through funds from the Andrew W. Mellon Foundation. We wish to acknowledge our deep debt to the people who run the Center, especially its former director, Carmelo Mesa-Lago and his staff, Associate Director Diana Velez, Assistant Director Shirley Kregar, and Research Director John Frechione. The Center's secretaries, Marci Valle and Linda Gaskill, were indispensable to us on many occasions. But the Center was not alone in its support. The University Center for International Studies and its Director, Burkart Holzner, and Assistant Director, Thomas McKechnie, helped secure additional funding for the conference. The Department of Political Science, especially its administrative assistant Mary Ann Salapa, helped in countless ways as well, including the preparation of the final manuscripts for publication, ably typed by Josie Raleigh. Finally, we would like to thank Jane Flanders, our editor at the University of Pittsburgh Press; who helped improve the final published product in countless ways.

Authoritarians and Democrats

Mitchell A. Seligson

1 Democratization in Latin America: The Current Cycle

The 1980s has been a decade of rapidly accelerating democratization in Latin America. Throughout the region there have emerged formal, constitutional democracies, replete with comparatively honest and open elections, active party competition, and a relatively uncensored press. By mid-decade, only Chile and Paraguay seemed largely impervious to the trend. The change from the preceding two decades has been dramatic; almost all nations of the region were ruled by military men for some, if not all, of that period. Of those Latin American and Caribbean countries that have been independent since at least 1960, only Costa Rica and Venezuela have enjoyed continuous constitutional rule, competitive party politics, and civilian supremacy.[1] Throughout much of the rest of the region, unconstitutional regimes, repressive and brutal even by Latin American standards, were the norm.

While there are those, especially in diplomatic circles, who point with great pride to the widespread emergence of democracy in Latin America, most scholars expert in the region remain skeptical regarding the long-term significance of this change. They quickly point to previous periods in Latin American history, such as the years immediately following World War II, the 1920s, and earlier periods, going all the way back to the 1820s, when democratic forms of government seemed to be taking hold. In each period, however, democracy proved ephemeral. Democratic governments were readily replaced by authoritarian regimes which often were more repressive than those that had preceded them. Indeed, the prevailing view among scholars is that democracy and authoritarian rule have oscillated throughout an extended series of cycles of roughly twenty

3

years' duration and that this pattern of oscillation, sometimes called a "pendular pattern," is likely to continue. The predominance of authoritarian rule in the 1960s and 1970s merely followed the earlier period of democratic rule in the 1940s and 1950s, and is currently being replaced by a cycle of democracy. If this pattern continues, the current cycle has only another fifteen or so years to run before it, too, will be repeated.

A complicating factor in the current cycle is that authoritarian regimes have left the scene at a time that, at first inspection, seems to be unusually inauspicious for the long-term stability of democracy. This is so because most Latin American nations are facing unprecedented economic challenges, and democratic governments have come to power saddled with international debt burdens that offer them little room for maneuver. On the international side, few private banks are willing to get in any deeper and therefore resist making new loans in the region. There is little chance, however, that the debts will be repaid without further infusions of new foreign capital. These loans are badly needed in order to help modernize and stimulate sagging economies. On the domestic side, the International Monetary Fund presses these debtor nations to improve their ability to meet their foreign obligations largely by restricting consumption. Such consumption-restricting measures, however, have their greatest impact on the urban working class and middle sectors, the very groups from whom continued political support is required if these elected regimes are to stay in power. In sum, there are strong grounds for predicting that the present cycle of democracy in Latin America will be ephemeral.

While it appears that the cyclical oscillation between democracy and authoritarian rule seems to be an unalterable pattern, each new cycle is not necessarily a carbon copy of the one that preceded it. Cyclical patterns can occur with evolutionary movement. Clearly, the last authoritarian cycle was fundamentally different from preceding ones in at least two ways. First, the new military regimes that dominated in the 1960s and 1970s were not merely caretaker governments ruling to bring order to societies ensnared in chaotic, inefficient, and immobilized civilian rule. Rather, during that cycle Latin American militaries came to power articulating explicit developmental goals. Second, these military regimes saw themselves as more or less permanent features of the political landscape. These new regimes were a far cry from the personalist dictatorships, à la Trujillo, Batista,

Somoza, and so on, that had typified the region for so many years. These were a new breed of professional, technocratic military men.

Guided by development programs and led by professional norms, these new "bureaucratic-authoritarian" military regimes were seen by many scholars as typical of the emerging pattern in the region.[2] Nevertheless, they too succumbed to the cyclical swings and were swept away by the current drive toward democratization. But there is no escaping the conclusion that the last cycle of military rule was different from those that had preceded it.

The democratic regimes now in power throughout Latin America may turn out to be no more than carbon copies of those of earlier periods, but this would be unlikely. Just as the bureaucratic-authoritarian regimes of the last cycle proved to be a new breed, so too the new democracies promise to differ substantially from those previously existing in Latin America. Two factors in particular, one arising directly out of the performance of the last military cycle and the other from broad socioeconomic trends, suggest that the democratic regimes of the current cycle will be different.

When the military regimes of the 1960s and 1970s left the scene in the 1980s, they left behind them a dual legacy that is shaping the democracies that have now come to power. First, their leaders demonstrated more profoundly than ever before their ultimate incompetence to rule. The old-time military regimes and personalist dictators of Latin America had made no special developmental claims. Their sole source of legitimization had been brute force and the power to coerce restive populations into quiescence. Hence, their frequent failures in economic matters had not undermined their claims to legitimacy. The new militaries promised much more and based their claims to legitimacy on those promises. They would have done away with politics and made decisions based upon rational, bureaucratic criteria. They convinced themselves, and exhorted the masses to believe, that only in this way could the obstacles to rapid economic growth be overcome.

Alas, by the time the Latin American militaries had left the scene, not even their staunchest supporters could believe in their claim to a superior calling to rule. While some of the regimes could point to areas of progress, none was able to transform the economy, and nearly all jeopardized long-term economic growth by debt crises for which they are ultimately responsible. In the 1970s Latin American governments became addicted to foreign borrowing at levels not previously experienced. Early in the decade foreign loans were justified by the hope that they would stimulate long-term economic development. Later, largely as a result of the failure of many of these investments to yield the expected dividends, and also as a result of spiraling interest rates on world credit markets, it became necessary for these governments to incur even larger debts in order to repay existing obligations. But these new loans were largely short-term, and carried extremely high interest rates. By the time the militaries had withdrawn, most of Latin America was drowning in a sea of unpaid international debts. Not that the civilian governments were doing any better (for example, Venezuela, Mexico, and Costa Rica), but the military's sanctimonious claims as to their superior ability to rule could not be sustained.

Another component of the legacy left by the last cycle of military rule is a deep distrust among the very groups which in the past have been most willing to see the military take over. Prior to the last cycle of military rule, civilian governments had often relied upon the military to bail them out of difficulties. When economic failures produced uncontrollable labor unrest, populist civilian governments would often privately call for the military to take over to calm the waters; the outcome has become known as the "middle-class military coup."[3] They would do so with the understanding that military rule would be brief and would not intrude into established political structures, especially political parties. But the militaries of the 1960s and 1970s had a very different agenda in mind. They came to power with the intention of ruling on a permanent basis, and while they ruled they made it their business to try to destroy the old-time party structures and political alliances. In so doing, the modern military regimes often used totalitarian terror tactics, including mass arrests, arbitrary imprisonment, "disappearances," and torture. This was certainly more than the traditional civilian political elite had bargained for and ultimately left them much less willing to resort to using the military as an escape hatch for their own political and economic failures. In short, the democracies of the present cycle are likely to be more tenacious in their grip on the reins of government and much more reluctant to step aside the next time there are rumblings in the streets or in the barracks.

The second factor favoring a transformed and possibly longer-lived set of democratic regimes in Latin America relates to the pattern of socioeconomic development that the region has experienced. According to a large body of comparative research on democracy, until relatively recently the minimum levels of socioeconomic development that are necessary to sustain democratic rule simply were not present in most of Latin America.[4] Several studies have led to the near-universal conclusion that underdevelopment and stable democracy do not mix. There appears to be a lower threshold of economic and sociocultural development beneath which stable democratic rule is unlikely to emerge. The income threshold appears to be around $250 per capita in 1957 dollars, and the sociocultural threshold, usually defined by educational achievement, seems to be the reduction of illiteracy to below 50 percent.

As late as the end of World War II, just when a new cycle of democratization was beginning, of the eleven nations covered in this volume, only Argentina, Chile, and Costa Rica had achieved both the levels of income and literacy that have been found elsewhere to be the minimum economic and sociocultural conditions necessary for promoting and sustaining democratic rule. All three of these nations had, by that time, known extended periods of democracy. All of the other nations covered in this volume, however, had far less experience with democratic rule, a fact that emphasizes the importance of the economic and socioeconomic thresholds just mentioned. Conversely, all three of the nations that had achieved the necessary conditions by 1945 saw their democracies break down in the years that followed. In both Chile and Argentina the breakdowns were protracted, with authoritarian rule still predominating in Chile as of this writing, whereas in Costa Rica it was much shorter-lived (1948–1949). These breakdowns emphasize that economic and sociocultural development seem to be merely necessary but not sufficient conditions for sustaining democratic regimes.

Slow but noticeable economic growth and improvements in sociocultural development did take place in the years following World War II. By 1957, however, the base year used in several key studies regarding the preconditions of democratic rule, only Brazil could have been added to the other three nations that had already achieved the necessary conditions.[5] By the mid-1950s Brazil's GNP per capita was moving above the $300 level, and illiteracy had dropped to slightly below 50 percent. In Ecuador and Peru, illiteracy levels declined below the 50 percent level by the 1950s, but their economic development still lagged below the income threshold. (See figures 1.1 and 1.2.)

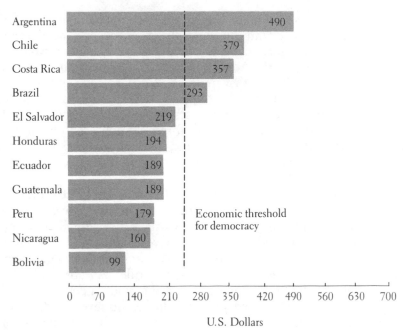

Figure 1.1   GNP Per Capita in Latin America, 1957 (in U.S. dollars)

Source: Bruce M. Russett, Hayward R. Alker, Jr., Karl W. Deutsch, and Harold D. Lasswell, *World Handbook of Political and Social Indicators* (New Haven, Conn.: Yale University Press, 1964), p. 156.

By the 1980s, however, considerable economic and social development had occurred in all of these countries. Even Bolivia and Honduras, the least developed countries treated in this volume, by 1982 were sending 86 percent and 95 percent, respectively, of their school-aged children to primary school, and had managed to reduce illiteracy to only about one-third of their population.[6] Nevertheless, Bolivia's economic development still lagged behind that of the others in the region, and probably fell below the established threshold, and Honduras was a borderline case.[7] By the beginning of the 1980s, then, nine or ten of the eleven nations covered in this book had achieved levels of both economic and social development that are considered to be minimal prerequisites for the emergence of stable democratic rule.

Meshing the empirical democratic theory with the data presented above leads one to the conclusion that with the exception of Bolivia, and possibly Honduras, the socioeconomic foundations for stable

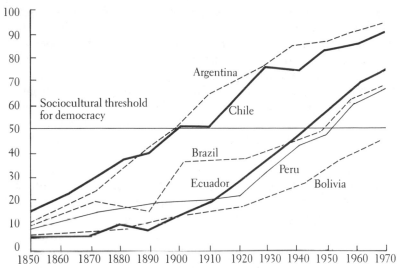

Figure 1.2   Literacy in Six South American Nations, 1850–1970

Source: Tatu Vanhanen, *Political and Social Structures,* Part 1: *American Countries 1850–1973* (Tampere, Finland: University of Tampere Institute of Political Science Research Reports, 1975), pp. 238–59.

democracy had finally been established among the nations treated in this volume. It does not, however, lead to the conclusion that democratic rule is somehow inevitable among these nations. Indeed, the long-term breakdown of democracy in Chile and Argentina emphasizes the fact that socioeconomic development is only a necessary, not both a necessary *and* sufficient condition for the development and maintenance of stable democracy.

Taken together, the factors just enumerated suggest that the present cycle of democracy is likely to be different in nature, potentially more robust in character, and probably more durable, than the ones that preceded it for three reasons. First, the recent record of the military has made civilian governments much less willing to consider the "military option" as a convenient way out of mounting economic and/or political problems. These governments have good reasons to suspect that, once invited to return to power, the generals will hold on to it for a protracted period. They also suspect that the military will on the one hand do considerable damage to the extant political power structure, and on the other hand engage in large-scale violations of human rights. Secondly, professionalized and bureaucratized though it now may be, the military establishment has shown itself to be as inept at running the economy as the civilians. Third, civilian governments have taken power in Latin America at a time when almost everywhere in the region the minimum necessary levels of socioeconomic development appear to have been attained.

There is yet another factor tending to favor a more permanent institutionalization of democratic rule. For many years the conventional wisdom among experts in Latin American studies has been that the political culture of the region is fundamentally authoritarian and therefore the "natural" state of affairs is authoritarian government. In an effort to understand why democracies were being replaced with authoritarian regimes in the 1960s and 1970s, Peter Smith has argued that it is authoritarianism and not democracy that is to be expected in Latin America: "The prevalence of nondemocratic, authoritarian ideals in Spanish America strongly suggests that dictatorship is not an aberration. It would seem to be a logical expression of the political culture."[8] According to this widely held point of view, authoritarian rule is legitimate in Latin America because "there is congruence between claims of the leaders and the values of the people."[9]

Recent research has challenged the notion that there is a political culture of authoritarianism in Latin America responsible for the prevalence of dictatorial regimes. In two recent studies, one on Mexico and another covering Argentina and Chile, extensive survey research data fails to offer evidence of a political culture of authoritarianism. The study of Mexico "uncovered a largely democratic political culture within an essentially authoritarian regime,"[10] while the study of Argentina and Chile found that the respondents "are much more likely to hold prodemocratic values than one might expect on the basis of their political circumstances."[11] In light of these studies, it is necessary to reconsider the view that contemporary political culture and regime type are closely linked in Latin America; the roots of authoritarian politics probably lie elsewhere.

There is a limit as to how far these generalizations can be stretched to cover the great variety of cases in the region. Not all military governments of the last cycle blatantly violated human rights, not all sought to eliminate politics, and not all were equally incompetent in running their economies. Each democracy that has emerged in the present cycle has its own particular origins and historical evolution. Each has emerged from a somewhat different political, social, and economic mix of conditions, and each has its own political culture. To do justice to this diversity, one would need to examine the cases one by one. That is what we propose to do in this volume.

We have organized the case studies geographically. The Southern Cone is represented by Aldo C. Vacs's contribution on Argentina, by John Markoff's and Silvio Duncan Baretta's study of Brazil, and by Silvia Borzutzky's chapter on Chile. The Andean republics are treated in the chapter by James M. Malloy and Eduardo Gamarra on Bolivia, in Luis Abugattas's analysis of Peru, and in Catherine M. Conaghan's chapter on Ecuador. The five Central American cases are treated by two chapters, one by Mark B. Rosenberg and another by Mitchell A. Seligson. The role of the United States in the process of political change in Latin America can never be far from one's consideration, and the chapter by Cole Blasier looks at that aspect of the problem. The book concludes with James M. Malloy's attempt to abstract from the wide range of countries covered the elements common to each. He finds in those elements a set of patterns that may help us understand the nature of democratic development in Latin America, and that might help predict its future.

Notes

1. Colombia held elections throughout this period, but frequent states of siege were declared whereby the military came to exercise extensive power, especially in the judicial system. Mexico also had regular elections, but opposition parties stood no chance of unseating the hand-picked successor of the incumbent president.

2. See Guillermo O'Donnell, *Modernization and Bureaucratic Authoritarianism: Studies in South American Politics* (Berkeley, Calif.: Institute of International Studies, 1973).

3. See José Nun, "The Middle-Class Military Coup," in *The Politics of Conformity in Latin America*, ed. Claudio Veliz (New York: Oxford University Press, 1967).

4. For a summary of this literature, see Myron Weiner, "Empirical Democratic Theory," in *Competitive Election in Developing Countries*, ed. Myron Weiner and Ergun Ozbudun (Durham, N.C.: Duke University Press, forthcoming). The major works are Robert Dahl, *Polyarchy: Participation and Opposition* (New Haven, Conn.: Yale University Press, 1971); Seymour Martin Lipset, "Social Requisites of Democracy: Economic Development and Political Legitimacy," *American Political Science Review* 53 (March 1959): 69–105; and Phillips Cutright, "National Political Development: Measurement and Analysis," *American Sociological Review* 28 (April 1963): 253–64.

5. GNP data for this early period are difficult to obtain and not particularly reliable. The data reported here are from Wendell C. Gordon, *The Economies of*

Latin America (New York: Columbia University Press, 1950), p. 335. Gordon presents GNP per capita data for the 1943–1946 period. He assigns, for example, a GNP of $61 to Nicaragua, $48 to Peru, and $34 to both Bolivia and Ecuador. Some literacy data for 1940 is contained in the United Nations *Statistical Yearbook, 1949–50* (New York: United Nations), p. 490. Additional and probably more reliable literacy data are found in James W. Wilkie and Maj-Brit Nilsson, "Projecting the HEC (Health, Education and Communications) Index for Latin America Back to 1940," in *Quantitative Latin American Studies: Methods and Findings*, ed. James W. Wilkie and Kenneth Ruddle (Los Angeles: UCLA Latin American Center Publications), p. 81. This source gives the following figures: Argentina, 89 percent; Chile, 71 percent; Costa Rica, 70 percent; El Salvador, 49 percent; Peru, 42 percent; Brazil, 40 percent; Nicaragua, 34 percent; Ecuador, 30 percent; Guatemala, 29 percent; Bolivia, 24 percent; Honduras, 22 percent. Harry Stark, *Social and Economic Frontiers in Latin America*, 2d ed. (Dubuque, Iowa: Wm. C. Brown, 1963) gives estimates for each of the countries which show that only Argentina, Chile, and Costa Rica exceeded the 50 percent level in 1948.

6. The World Bank, *World Bank Atlas, 1985* (Washington, D.C.: The World Bank, 1985), pp. 6–9, and World Bank, *World Development Report, 1982* (New York, Oxford University Press, 1982), pp. 150–51.

7. According to the figures from the World Bank, the GNP per capita of Bolivia in 1983 was $510; that of Honduras was $670. Reliable deflators of Bolivia's GNP to convert it to 1957 dollars are not available, but, as shown in chapter 8, Honduras was just below the threshold in 1982.

8. Peter H. Smith, "Political Legitimacy in Spanish America," in *New Approaches to Latin American History*, ed. Richard Graham and Peter H. Smith (Austin: University of Texas, 1974), p. 241.

9. Ibid.

10. John A. Booth and Mitchell A. Seligson, "The Political Culture of Authoritarianism in Mexico: A Reexamination," *Latin American Research Review* 19, no. 1 (1984): 118.

11. Susan Tiano, "Authoritarianism and Political Culture in Argentina and Chile in the Mid-1960s," *Latin American Research Review* 21, no. 1 (1986): 86.

I The Southern Cone

Aldo C. Vacs

2 Authoritarian Breakdown and Redemocratization in Argentina

This chapter analyzes the latest Argentine transition from authoritarianism to democracy placing it within the framework of the pattern followed by such processes since 1930. Redemocratization in Argentina has been characterized by some recurrent features: suddenness, lack of control, unexpected outcomes, and discontinuity. Among the explanations of this pattern of spasmodic shifts are: the question of legitimacy; the dilemma of capital accumulation versus redistribution; the problem of hegemony; social characteristics, especially of political parties; the unstable nature of military-civilian alliances; and the corruption of the military. This chapter analyzes the rise of military authoritarianism after 1976, its decline, the process of transition to democracy and the characteristics of the new democratic regime. In each case, the focus is on the political and socioeconomic elements that explain the dynamics of the Argentine process. Finally, the chapter explores the prospects for the consolidation of democratic stability in Argentina, stressing the importance of economic constraints, the praetorianization of society and the authoritarian features of its political culture as basic obstacles that need to be overcome.

The Pattern of Disruption

Many observers of the transitions from authoritarianism to democracy in Argentina have noted the suddenness of these shifts and the inability of the authoritarian rulers to steer these processes in an orderly way so as to safeguard their own interests. Since 1930, successive military governments have initially exhibited considerable strength and a certain degree of popular support; yet each has rapidly become unstable, finally being forced to call elections and transfer power to political groups that did not share their programs and objectives.[1]

General Uriburu's military government came to office with the intention of establishing a long-lasting corporatist regime in the mold of Italian fascism. However, in 1932 it was forced to stage rigged elections from which its conservative opponents emerged victorious. The military government established in 1943 cherished the dream of developing a falangist-style regime, but in 1945, amid domestic turmoil and external pressures, it was constrained to allow free elections that resulted in the first Peronist triumph. The Revolución Libertadora that overthrew Perón and tried to eliminate his influence was finally forced to hand over power to Arturo Frondizi, who was elected president with the support of the banned Peronistas. The military experience that followed the fall of Frondizi in 1962 was plagued by internal rifts and culminated in the 1963 elections won by the Radical candidate, Arturo Illia, while the military's favorite, General Aramburu, finished a distant third. General Onganía's Revolución Argentina, which was supposed to last for decades and to create a stable semicorporatist regime, collapsed after the urban mass explosions of the late 1960s, and in 1973 the military experience terminated with elections in which the reinvigorated Peronistas gathered 50 percent of the votes, while the military candidate obtained less than 3 percent. The last authoritarian experience inaugurated in 1976 began to falter in 1980 amid a generalized socioeconomic crisis; the Malvinas fiasco only accelerated an inevitable decline. A new call to elections followed and once again the military rulers were unable to control the process of transition and its outcome; this time they were surprised by a Radical landslide that overwhelmed the Peronistas, who had enjoyed the open or tacit support of various military sectors.

Thus, the transitions from authoritarianism to democracy in Argentina have been characterized throughout this century by certain recurrent features: suddeness, discontinuity, lack of control, and unexpected outcomes. Although in each case special circumstances contributed to these features, there are also general factors that explain this recurrent spasmodic pattern.

First, there is the question of legitimacy. If the legitimacy of a given political order can be guaranteed by a belief in its validity or by the expectation of specific benefits, or both,[2] Argentine authoritarian governments have clearly faced a difficult problem when trying to legitimize their rule. Notwithstanding the number of military

coups and the ephemeral quality of many prior democractic experiences, Argentine society traditionally ascribes legitimacy to governments elected through normal democratic procedures. It is true that
in most cases people grant such legitimacy more to an ideal than to
real elected governments. Nevertheless, the belief in the legitimacy
of democratically elected governments, however utopian, pervades
Argentine society to the extent that even those involved in military
coups feel obligated to proclaim that their ultimate objective is to
create the conditions in which a "perfected" democracy can be
established.

Confronted with the problem of building legitimacy in a context in
which they are seen as illegitimate, authoritarian governments have
followed a predictable pattern in Argentina. In the first phase after
the coup, they receive a certain degree of support for their declared
intention of restoring order and creating the basis for a renewed and
more stable democratic regime. Enjoying this political "honey-
moon," the military rulers try to implement policies designed to
promote economic growth and to gain the support of those sectors
favored by such policies. The hope is to build legitimacy by catering
to self-interest. However, as these policies fail to attain their goals,
this feeble base of legitimacy fades away before any belief in the
validity of the authoritarian regime has developed, and the military
begin to face a generalized opposition that demands elections. At this
point, military unity begins to crumble. Palace coups intended to
further the "revolution" occur, but owing to the stagnant economic
situation, the new rulers are unable to deliver anything in exchange
for the support they request, and their ultimate resource is to repress
demands. Finally, when it becomes clear that the repressive measures
only create more opposition, a "liberal" military group displaces the
"orthodox" sector and announces a gradual political relaxation. By
then, however, it is too late to proceed with an orderly transition.
The military government is so weak and the opposition so strong that
efforts toward liberalization rapidly go out of control. In the meantime, the retreating military try to impose conditions on the incom-
ing civilian government by negotiating with the main political
parties, but the attempt is generally rejected by those who consider
the authoritarian government an illegitimate usurper. A military-
civilian pact, when attained, has in fact been the kiss of death for
those parties that have accepted the military offer. Popular antimilitary feeling and the craving for an ideal democracy without restric-

tions result in the rejection of those "tarnished" by their alliance with the military rulers. As a consequence, outgoing military rulers are unable to secure the victory of their civilian allies or, at least, to impose effective constraints on their successors.

Second, Argentine military governments have been unable to stay in power or to guarantee an orderly transition to civilian rule because they have not been able to solve, in any meaningful way, the political-economic dilemma presented by the tensions between the economy's need to accumulate capital and popular demands for the redistribution of wealth. In each case, the military comes to power declaring (with various degrees of accuracy) that the country is passing through its most serious socioeconomic crisis and blames the previous administration's mismanagement for having produced such a situation. Then, in order to overcome the crisis, the military typically names a conservative economic team who rapidly formulate orthodox stabilization programs designed to increase savings and investment and to contain inflation and fiscal deficits. These strategies for economic accumulation imply a strict control of wages and salaries, and result, first, in the mounting opposition of low-income groups, and afterward, of the middle class and the economic sectors that produce for the domestic market. Thus, military governments have been unable to implement the kind of redistributionist policies that are necessary for the expansion of their support. Moreover, the armed forces usually inhibit the full application of the adjustment programs by opposing any measures that could adversely affect their interests: reductions in military salaries and expenditures, and divestiture of state enterprises controlled by military officers. This opposition not only ensures the failure of the stabilization program but also generates antimilitary feeling among those negatively affected by government's income policies. Finally, when the accumulationist strategies fail to produce the announced "economic miracle," the military rulers are confronted with an explosive socioeconomic situation without having established any meaningful base of support among the population. In these circumstances, lacking legitimacy and the capacity to implement any kind of satisfactory redistributionist policies, the only option available to the military in order to avoid further deterioration is to call for elections and a rapid transfer of power to the civilians.

Third, the relative acquiescence of the military to these swift retreats from power is explained by the fact that none of the major Argentine political parties seems to threaten the institutional survival of the armed forces.[3] The military government can favor the victory of one party because it is closer to its conservative position, or because it offers better guarantees of noninterference in the government's internal affairs. But, in any case, even if the favored party is defeated, the military make certain that the winners do not threaten the military institution as a whole. Retirements and transfers of personnel are expected, but these changes at the top do not affect the hierarchical organization of the services and are even welcomed by the remaining officers as an opportunity for rapid promotions. Moreover, in many cases, the retreat to the barracks is considered only a temporary withdrawal that offers the chance to reorganize the cadres and to regain some prestige, while waiting for circumstances to develop that will favor a new coup.

Fourth, the inability of military regimes to organize orderly transitions and to use elections as a means to put their political allies in power arises from the characteristics of the Argentine sociopolitical arena. This arena is occupied by large populist and reformist parties, such as the Peronists and the Radicals, and by well-organized socioeconomic groups—trade unions, industrial, rural, commercial, and financial associations—that preempt the political space in which the military have tried to create their own organizations.[4] Popular reluctance to abandon their parties and associations and the inability of military rulers to create attractive alternatives have undermined all authoritarian attempts to eliminate and replace the traditional organizations. Typically, most of these groups have dwindled under the pressure exerted by the nascent authoritarian regimes, only to reappear with new strength as crises mount and the military loses control of the situation. On the other hand, the attempts of authoritarian governments to use existing organizations—generally small conservative and provincial parties, and isolated trade unions—to develop their own base of political and social power have consistently failed due to the limited support of these groups, their fragmentation at the national level, and the added unpopularity stemming from their collaboration with the regime. As a consequence, each time the authoritarian rulers call elections, they find themselves isolated and unable to steer the process of transition by manipulating any of the most powerful political or socioeconomic groups.

Fifth, the suddenness of Argentine transitions is also related to the fact that the military and civilians have always been linked in intrinsically unstable alliances.[5] At various times, practically all political partics and socioeconomic organizations have tried to obtain military support for their own objectives. Similarly, the military have always sought the political support of some of these groups before embarking upon a coup. As a result of being at the same time important political actors and potential instruments of these sectors, the armed forces typically have been engulfed by the same political and socioeconomic environment and have been affected by the same tensions and contradictions that affect Argentine civilian society. In this context, the military have been able to preserve their unity as long as the most powerful of these groups expect a profitable partnership with the new regime and continue to support it. But as military governments demonstrate their reluctance or inability to satisfy the political and economic demands of all their early supporters, important sectors of the coalition transfer their support to the opposition and, using their military contacts, transform the armed forces into an arena for confrontation. As crises develop and each group mobilizes its allies, military unity crumbles, and the increasingly isolated government becomes progressively paralyzed. Thus, when the time comes to make the transition to civilian rule, a military divided by internal disputes cannot avoid the disorderly and rapid transitions that are characteristic of Argentina.

Sixth, the absence in Argentina of a class or group that might be regarded as incontestably hegemonic is another factor that reinforces the trend toward unmanageable transitions.[6] There are groups that exert domination, but none of them has been capable of developing the kind of political, ideological, and cultural leadership over the rest of the society that constitutes real hegemony. This circumstance, which partially explains the nation's continuous political instability, also accounts for the unmanageability of the transitions from authoritarianism to democracy. The vacuum created by the military's inability to steer the transition in an orderly way is not filled by any other group capable of performing such a role. Be it a stalemate or simply the absence of any hegemonic group, the lack of this unifying factor means that no clear agreement is possible between the declining authoritarian rulers and the reinvigorated opposition. As a consequence, sudden shifts, unexpected outcomes, and clear discontinuities become the rule in the transfer of power in Argentina.

Finally, the enormous distance between the Argentine military governments' stated ideals and the behavior of their members also helps to explain the dramatic characteristics of the transitions to civilian rule. Since 1930, all military governments have come to power as crusaders against corruption and immorality. And all of them, once in power, have provided examples of the most blatant corruption. As a result, popular antimilitary feeling has rapidly increased, and the armed forces have confronted the periods of transition to democracy with their prestige and credibility so damaged that their capacity to negotiate a conditioned transfer of power is tangibly diminished.

We should consider the latest transition from authoritarian to democratic rule in Argentina in this context. In fact, this essay argues that the most recent transitional period provides one of the clearest examples of Argentina's characteristically disorderly transition to democracy.

The Rise of Military Authoritarianism (1976–1980)

On March 24, 1976, the Argentine armed forces overthrew the constitutional government headed by María E. (Isabel) Martínez de Perón. The second Peronista government had lasted less than three years. After the coup, the armed forces closed the national Congress and the provincial legislatures, removed the municipal mayors, provincial governors, and justices of the Supreme Court from their posts, placed labor and some of the entrepreneurs' federations under military control, and enacted a host of other measures aimed at controlling political life.[7] All political activity was banned and a number of leftist parties and groups were outlawed. The new regime was characterized by its tough policies that surpassed previous levels of military repression of the opposition. In short, a full-blown system of state terror and violence was implemented. Carried out by many different military and paramilitary groups, the repression succeeded in destroying all structured opposition to military rule. To achieve this end, multiple forms of state terrorism were implemented, including murder, "disappearance," imprisonment, torture, incarceration in clandestine concentration camps, exile, and the looting and destruction of political opponents' property.

The armed forces were also interested, however, in producing some fundamental changes in Argentine society and politics to avoid the restoration of populist regimes such as that of the Peronists. They knew, because of the experience of previous military governments, that repression and political exclusion were not solid enough foundations for a new type of political regime. The attempt to create a new type of corporatist, conservative coalition on the part of the leaders of the Revolución Argentina between 1966 and 1970 had failed, demonstrating the strength of the populist coalition as long as economic factors favored an alliance between the workers, parts of the middle class, and national entrepreneurs. This time the military would not seek to create a new corporatist pact among these groups. It would destroy the structural conditions that made possible the growth of any corporatist experiment in the first place. It was on this point that the military agreed with the economic liberals.[8] This latter group has not had electoral weight in Argentina, but exerts great influence among sectors of the business community, the press, the judiciary, and the military. Their central belief is that the free market, acting without restraint, is not only the most efficient allocator of resources but also the best instrument of social discipline.[9] Thus, loosening market forces would not only reshape the economy by modernizing it, but also destroy the basis for the praetorianism that characterizes Argentine society and has in the past led to populist and corporatist experiments. All social classes and groups would perceive the uselessness of trying to influence state policies in their favor, because impersonal market forces and not the state would allocate resources and distribute income and wealth. Once the connection between politics and economics had been broken, the argument went, the main reason for political unrest would be removed and the military and their liberal allies would be able to design a less participatory but more stable political regime in which political competition and elections would be allowed.

Thus the strategy formulated by the economic team and defended by the military was designed to reestablish the Argentine economy in the global economic system while dramatically altering its internal structure. The import-substitution phase was declared to be finished and was denounced as an irrational experiment responsible for most of the country's current economic problems. Protectionist barriers were lifted and the economy was totally opened to the world market in the expectation that the comparative advantages for the production of certain goods would give Argentina a better position in the international division of labor. Domestic price controls were totally removed, while wages were frozen and then slowly adjusted according to increases in productivity. A strategy of lagging the exchange rate was adopted in order to diminish inflationary expectations and to favor savings and productive investment while discouraging speculation with foreign currencies. State intervention in certain sectors of the economy—especially the financial one—was diminished. And, in an attempt to remove corporatist obstacles to the free play of market forces, trade unions were placed under military control and strikes outlawed.

The liberal economic program was designed to overcome the tension between accumulation requirements and redistribution demands that had caused a pendulum swing in Argentine economic politics, from orthodox stabilization programs to populist redistributionist policies, without any adequate strategy of economic development as a result. The radical deregulation of the economy was designed to overcome this impasse by effecting deep structural changes. In the meantime, as the program was implemented and in order to avoid intolerable social tensions, the reordering action of the market was to be accompanied by generous amounts of foreign credit that would provide a certain "trickle-down effect" buffering the full impact of the liberal policies on workers, the middle class, and industrial sectors. On the other hand, the long-standing political problems caused by the demands for redistributive policies and the inability of political institutions to deal with them would be temporarily neutralized by widespread repression. Meanwhile, because of the transformation of the country's socioeconomic structures, the state would no longer be the target of these demands, and a new type of legitimate rule would appear in which the market's new strength as an instrument of social control would mean that political stability would come from consensus rather than coercion.

For a brief period, this strategy seemed to succeed. Positive trade balances, growing international reserves, a decrease in the inflation rate, revaluation of the national currency, the easy availability of imported goods and raw materials, and high employment were some of the signals that the government hailed as proof of its accomplishments. During this time a stifled opposition was barred from protesting other, dangerous developments such as the closing of factories, a growing external debt, regressive redistribution patterns, high rates of interest, and financial speculation. The government's prestige in some business circles increased and it began to gather some open support among middle-class sectors that were favored by its policies. At the end of 1978, the military rulers were so confident in their ultimate triumph that they began to look for a way to establish the long-term political legitimacy of the regime. In a document about "the political basis for national reorganization" they discarded the possibility of a sudden "electoral adventure," proposing instead the creation of an officialist party. This party would be the essential element in a gradual transfer of some offices (first, at the local level; then, at the provincial; and, finally, at the national level) to their civilian allies through carefully controlled elections in which none of the traditional parties would be allowed to participate.

Authoritarian Breakdown and Political Transition (1980–1983)

The project of legitimizing a kind of semiauthoritarian regime with limited political participation rapidly manifested its main weakness: it could succeed only if the economic situation continued to improve. By focusing their hopes on a liberal economic program designed to transform the structural elements of the economy that nurtured the corporatist coalitions and their populist offsprings, the military had inextricably tied the fate of their government to the results of its economic policies. Only a satisfactory economic performance would provide the opportunity to achieve the desired goals: in the short term, to obtain some degree of popularity among key sectors of Argentine society; in the long term, to establish solid foundations for the legitimacy of a new type of political regime.

It will be impossible here to analyze in depth all the economic and social factors that caused the failure of the military's economic policies, but at the beginning of 1980 it was clear that a serious economic crisis was developing.[10] The reduction of import tariffs and the overvaluation of the peso favored the entry of cheap imports and created serious problems for the hitherto protected industrial sector; industrial output in 1980 was lower than it was in 1970. The exchange rate lag that resulted in the overvaluation of the peso not only negatively affected the industrial sector but also reduced the purchasing power of farmers by distorting the relative prices of their export crops. Workers not only were affected by the decline in their real salaries but also suffered the consequences of the loss of jobs in the manufacturing sector (a 26 percent decrease between 1976 and 1980). The middle classes, which at first were spared the worst aspects of the income policies and enjoyed buying imported goods and traveling abroad, gradually lost purchasing power as their real incomes dropped. Inflation, which had slowed, began to increase again. In the financial sphere, the liberalization of the market did not bring about the expected results: instead of being used for productive investment, domestic savings and foreign loans were used for speculation, as consumers and investors took advantage of the high real rates of interest and the exchange rate lag. As a consequence, while consumption, investment, and exports began to decline, middle-class groups became more vocal, demanding changes in economic policies. In this context of mounting tension, the intensified repression directed at selected targets, especially trade union activists, was not enough to neutralize the growing discontent.

Moreover, the economic experiment also confronted obstacles established by the military itself. Military salaries continued to grow during this period, and conspicuous consumption was widely observed among the officer corps. High military budgets were maintained: defense and security expenditures increased more than 60 percent in real terms between 1976 and 1980. (In contrast, health expenditures decreased 70 percent in real terms, while the education budget dropped 50 percent in the same period.) Finally, blatant military corruption multiplied. These abuses, perpetrated by the same individuals who had come to power proclaiming their revulsion at Peronista corruption, generated growing antimilitary feeling among the population.

The brewing socioeconomic crisis finally exploded in March 1980 when a financial crash closed several of the most important banks and credit institutions. Most of these institutions were new ones that because of the deregulation of financial markets had overextended themselves, had taken speculative risks in the financial and exchange markets, and had got involved in illegal operations. When one of the most important of these banks was unable to meet its obligations and was taken over by the Central Bank, the public reacted with a run on many other banks and credit institutions that resulted in the closing of more than thirty of them. The crisis rapidly spread to other sectors, causing numerous industrial, commercial, and agricultural bankruptcies and a rush on the exchange market. Contributing to this climax were the expectations raised by the planned transfer of power, scheduled for the beginning of 1981, from General Videla to another army general, Roberto Viola. However, the general perception was that Viola's assumption of power would represent a turning point in both the economic and political strategies of the military government.

In fact, this perception was accurate. When the government changed hands in March 1981, the country was confronting such severe external pressures as well as an acute domestic recession that the market-centered project of economic, social, and political restructuring was abandoned by the new rulers. The new team attempted to solve the crisis by applying several Keynesian anticyclical measures that disavowed the orthodox strategy designed by their predecessors. A two-tier exchange market was established, import controls were imposed, the Central Bank intervened in the financial market in an attempt to lower interest rates, and an industrial reactivation policy began to be implemented. The ban on political activity was not lifted but it was not strictly enforced either. As this timid liberalization process was undertaken, the government tried to establish closer ties with conservative groups in order to coopt their support.

Nevertheless, these steps were not enough to guarantee the stability of Viola's administration. On one hand, the military hard-liners were bitterly opposed to any kind of political opening, while the liberal economic right resented the abandonment of its program. The hard-liners began to persecute politicians and trade unionists in order to obstruct the liberalization while preparing a palace coup to overthrow Viola. The liberals severely criticized the program of the new economic team and gave their support to the military hard-liners hoping to return to power after Viola's fall. On the other hand, most of the important socioeconomic groups and political parties refused to support the new government. These groups considered the government's economic measures inadequate to cope with the crisis and made demands that the government was unable to satisfy. The political parties gained momentum and asked for a faster pace of liberalization and the establishment of electoral deadlines, but the Viola administration, still committed to the success of the military experience and faced with the hard-liners' opposition, was not ready to take such steps. Caught between these contradictory pressures, the government gradually lost its capacity to take the initiative and finally became a passive entity.

Meanwhile, the economic situation worsened: devaluations multiplied (by 500 percent in 1981); the external debt increased; the flow of foreign credit stopped; reserves dropped; inflation began to climb (by 156 percent in 1981); and the main economic indicators declined—the GNP declined by 5.9 percent, investments were down by 19.2 percent, and average real salaries were down by 11.2 percent in 1981. At the same time, the internal division of the armed forces became clear when an ailing Viola refused to resign graciously, as his military adversaries suggested he do. Thus a protracted military crisis developed and after three months of discussion, the military junta made up of the commanders in chief of the three forces merely removed Viola and replaced him with General Galtieri in December 1981.

The basic objectives of this consolidating palace coup were to prevent the continuation of the type of political opening that Viola had tried to implement, and to restore the economic policies set up by the first leg of the military regime. The hard-liners' analysis of the situation was that Viola lacked the strength and will necessary to resist the mounting pressures, but that a stronger government would be in condition to stay the course, achieving the objectives stated in 1976. It was believed that the economic crisis was only temporary, and maintaining the original strategy would soon be rewarded with economic recovery and social peace. Consequently, the suspension of political activities was once again strictly enforced by the security forces. Nevertheless, while attempting to destroy the political opposition, Galtieri tried to expand his base of support by maintaining contacts with some small provincial and conservative parties and trying to create for himself the kind of caudillo image that both Videla and Viola had lacked. Meanwhile, the new economic team headed by orthodox liberals began to apply stabilization policies: exchange controls were lifted, public wages were frozen, monetary expansion was reduced, and public investment decreased. As a result of these measures, the rhythms of devaluation and inflation slowed down, but unemployment rose, real wages fell another 15 percent, interest rates remained extremely high and bankruptcies multiplied.

In this context, the government's room for political maneuver became practically nil, and popular discontent mounted. Disregarding the renewed enforcement of the ban on their activities, political parties continued to actively oppose the government and, in a clear challenge, a multiparty coalition—the Multipartidaria, that included Peronists, Radicals, and other minor groups—was formed to demand changes in economic policy and a rapid return to democracy. Trade unions began to mobilize their members against governmental policies. Middle-class sectors took an increasingly strong stand against the military. For the first time, the demands for explanations about the fate of the "disappeared persons" and for the restoration of civil liberties could not be suppressed and grew every day. The charges of widespread corruption in the higher military and governmental circles began to be publicized in the press. Finally, on March 30, 1982, the first general strike in the years of military rule was called by the clandestine General Confederation of Labor. The strike paralyzed the country.

In this situation, the military seems to have decided that there were only two ways to save the regime: to rapidly solve the economic and social crisis, or to find an issue around which to unify the nation behind the government. Because the first alternative was impossible in the short term, the military chose the second. An issue was readily available: the Malvinas Islands, occupied by the British since 1833, could arouse nationalistic feelings. The assertion that sooner or later these islands should be recovered was one of the few points of agreement in a country sharply divided by internal quarrels.[11]

By recovering the islands, the military not only would generate a sense of national unity and gain a respite from social and political pressures, but would also preserve their institutional role and prestige that had so seriously deteriorated. The military establishment was so deeply involved in governmental mismanagement that the government's fate was its own. For the first time in the history of Argentine military regimes, the armed forces' institutional survival, at least in the traditional form, was not totally guaranteed. Moreover, the brutal repression of the last years had heavily relied on tactics of anonymous terror immune to public discussion, to the extreme that the military themselves called it a "dirty war." This "war" had been won, but its "battles" of murder, torture, and looting could not be told. So there was an urgent need for the military to find a way to erase the memory of the terrorist actions of the past and achieve victory in a patriotic crusade, a "clean war." Finally, this alternative also offered the possibility of institutionalizing and legitimizing the regime by using its newly gained popularity to arrange a plebiscite. As Galtieri remarked, after being ousted from power, his intention had been to call elections after the final victory over the British—elections in which he would have been a presidential candidate and that he "was sure to win."

Between April 2 and June 14, as the confrontation with Great Britain grew into an all-out war, it seemed that the military government would be able to achieve its goals. The population reacted to the recovery of the archipelago with an outburst of nationalism and strongly backed the military action. Dissent practically disappeared, and most of the political parties, labor, entrepreneurs, and religious organizations manifested their support of the military. But all these developments rested on only one point of support: the conviction that the war could be won.

Thus, when the conflict ended with the surrender of the Argentine forces on the islands, the backlash against the military drove their prestige to an all-time low. Popular unrest exploded and led to a wave of violent street demonstrations directed against the government and the armed forces in general. Galtieri was obliged to resign, but the military junta that succeeded him split and could not agree on his successor or on the economic and political programs to be implemented. Finally, the air force and the navy withdrew from the junta, leaving all the political responsibility to the army, which in turn named a retired general, Reynaldo Bignone, as president. Once again, in a moment of authoritarian decline, the armed forces became a political arena in which insiders and outsiders tried to advance their own political projects. The air force, with the support of ultrarightist nationalist politicians, attempted to place its commander in chief as president, underscoring the point that of the members of the three branches of the armed services, only the pilots performed adequately. The navy was internally split among those who, supported by some populist and center-right politicians, tried to advance the cause of the former Commander in Chief Massera and those who rejected him. Both services were unable to overcome the opposition of the army to their projects, but by formally withdrawing from governmental responsibilities, they further weakened the regime in its transitional period.

The first political actions of the new president were to lift the ban on political party activities and to promise elections before the end of 1983.[12] In the economic sphere, the stated objective of the new administration was to keep the situation under control, avoiding socioeconomic explosions in order to allow an orderly transfer of power to the elected authorities. It is important to note that the market-centered economic project was discarded, and with it vanished the regime's hope of eliminating a situation in which all socioeconomic groups directed their demands to the state. As in previous periods of transition, the lack of reliable political channels able to articulate and mediate these demands placed the state at the center of a continuous struggle among groups. The attempt to withdraw the state from the economic arena had failed, and once again all sectors asked for the formulation and implementation of the state-led programs of reactivation and redistribution better suited to their interests and goals.

In this framework, the capacity of the military rulers to negotiate with the civilian opposition an orderly and conditioned transfer of power was practically nil. They tried, however, to get the agreement of the political parties on three negative conditions: not to investigate the state-terrorist actions; not to investigate the sources of economic mismanagement and corruption; and not to reorganize the armed forces or curtail their power in matters related to external defense and internal security. The attempt to impose these restrictions on the next civilian government was rejected by the multipartidaria, and some parties declared their intention to investigate these issues, dismantle the repressive machinery, and put the military under total civilian control.

Unable to obtain the general agreement that they had hoped for, the military tried other methods of safeguarding their position. First, they unilaterally promulgated an amnesty that covered all crimes committed by armed forces personnel during the "period of exception." This action generated an immediate rejection on the part of the human rights groups that by that time had gathered important numerical strength. The law was judicially challenged by the relatives of the "disappeared" on the grounds that a self-amnesty granted by the criminals to themselves represented a legal aberration, and some parties—including the Radical—announced their intention of repealing such a law if they came to power.

Faced with this unexpectedly strong resistance, the military tried to guarantee that the so-called law of national pacification would not be repealed by the constitutional government, establishing what was called a "corporatist pact" with some sectors of the Peronista party and labor movement. Convinced that in free elections the Peronistas would win, the military returned the trade union organizations—the real backbone of the Peronista movement—to the same labor leaders who had been displaced after the coup and lifted the prohibition on the political activities of Isabel Perón and other important members of the party whose political rights had been suspended in 1976. In exchange, they received what were considered satisfactory assurances that the amnesty law would not be derogated and that no investigations would be undertaken. In fact, some Peronista sectors had their own reasons to accept this deal: terrorist acts against the opposition

had been encouraged by certain members of the Peronista government before the coup, and their record regarding corruption and
mismanagement was not much better than that of the military. Thus,
any thorough investigation of such acts could lead to embarrassing
questions and would be detrimental to their own interests. Reassured
by explicit and implicit agreements with the Peronistas on these matters, and remembering that they had never lost an election in which
they were allowed to participate, the military ignored the positions
assumed by other parties on these issues and continued with a process
of transition that would extricate themselves from power under relatively agreeable terms.

The Return to Democracy: Unexpected Outcomes and New Developments

The national elections of October 30, 1983, had a largely unexpected
outcome—the victory, by a wide margin, of the Radical presidential
candidate over the Peronista one. The elections transformed what
had been seen by the military as a relatively safe retreat into a leap
into unknown territory. In many aspects, the situation that developed
was unprecedented in Argentine political history. For the first time,
the Peronistas had been defeated in free elections. The Radical presidential candidate Raúl Alfonsín, a politician who until a few years
ago had been unable to gain control of his own party, obtained a
landslide victory against all odds. The Radical party that for a long
time had gathered no more than 25 percent of the vote, obtained 52
percent of the presidential ballots. The Argentine political arena became truly bipartisan, with Peronistas and Radicals together collect-
ing more than 92 percent of the votes. The smaller parties, which
had performed an important role in Argentine politics in previous
periods, either competing for the support of the proscribed Peronistas
or trying to erode the middle-class constituency of the Radicals, practically vanished from the scene, with a few provincial exceptions.
More important, the military leaders had retreated from power without obtaining any guarantees from the Radicals and were in such
disarray that it seemed impossible for them to attempt a comeback in
the near future.

The surprising victory of the Radicals came as a result of a series of
events that increased its electoral chances while eroding the Peronista
base of support. The Unión Cívica Radical, one of the most tradi-

tional Argentine parties, was the first vehicle for the political mobilization and participation of the middle classes.[13] After being the most important political party in the first half of this century, it lost its electoral preeminence after the appearance of Peronismo. However, the death of Perón in 1974, the surge of a more dynamic leadership embodied in the person of Raúl Alfonsín, the popular rejection of the authoritarian tendencies of the Peronista movement and the memory of Isabel Perón's chaotic administration favored the Radical victory. Thus in the October elections the Radicals not only maintained their traditional electoral base among middle-class sectors but also captured a good proportion of votes among those who in previous contests had supported the Peronista, center-left, and center-right parties. The party that came to power through this realignment of the Argentine electorate can be defined as a center-left organization whose program calls for the construction of a "social democracy." It maintains a relatively nationalistic stand and assumes the defense of a pluralistic democratic regime, human rights, federalism, and an active participation of the state in the economy in order to achieve developmental and redistributionist objectives.

Once the elections were over, the Radicals began to demand a rapid transfer of power. The military government tried to resist such pressures and to maintain the original schedule that called for the inauguration of the new administration in March 1984. In the meantime, they expected to negotiate with the politicians in order to ensure the acceptance of at least one of their conditions—namely, no investigation of human rights violations. However, amid a mounting socioeconomic crisis, the lame-duck military government was unable to negotiate from a solid position. The hard-liners' threats of implementing an internal coup and nullifying the elections if an agreement were not reached lacked substance because of the weakness of their position after the Malvinas defeat. Thus, the military were forced to accelerate the process of transition and finally, on December 10, 1983, the new constitutional authorities were inaugurated without having offered any explicit guarantees to the armed forces.

Besides the military's distrust regarding their intentions, the Radical government faced other severe problems when trying to guarantee its stability and solve the economic crisis that plagued the country. It had to confront the opposition of the Peronist party and the Peronist-dominated trade unions; the business sector's distrust of their interventionist and redistributionist program; the opposition of the Catholic church to liberalization in social and cultural matters; and the pressures exerted by the foreign banks, the IMF, and their domestic associates to implement stabilization measures that could result in mounting popular opposition.

Coming to power under these conditions, the Radical administration tried to consolidate and expand its base of support and to guarantee its stability by confronting a number of urgent tasks. In the military sphere, the government tried to develop a strategy designed to attain civilian control over the armed forces. To achieve this end, several measures, some of them unprecedented in Argentine political history, were implemented: rapid removal of the military leadership; detention and trial of the members of the military juntas and of some of the high-ranking officers who had been involved in illegal activities; complete removal of military officers from civilian posts, including state enterprises; drastic reduction of the military budget; decrease in the number of draftees and officers; elimination of the commanders in chief and concentration of decision-making power in the hands of the president and the minister of defense; and investigation into who was responsible for the repression, corruption, and mismanagement of the years of military rule.

Although these initiatives were much more severe than any implemented regarding the military in previous processes of redemocratization, the radicals' conciliatory style and their reluctance to be involved in an all-out confrontation with the armed forces resulted in a number of setbacks. The displacement of the old military leadership was a relatively superficial operation that allowed the promotion of officers who shared many of the antidemocratic views held by those whom they replaced and who had been involved in similar objectionable activities during the previous period. Thus, even if more discreetly because of the extreme weakness and unpopularity of the armed forces in the current circumstances, the new military chiefs tried to obstruct any organic restructuring of the services, opposed budget cuts and the imprisonment of their retired colleagues, stated their concern about the "leftward drift" of some governmental sectors, and reactivated their close contacts with ultrarightist groups.

The government's reaction to these military probes has been extremely cautious. Very few officers have been punished for these oppositionist activities. The prosecution of the crimes committed during the authoritarian period was assigned to military tribunals, and only after they refused to indict anyone were cases transferred to the civilian judiciary. The reorganization of the services has proceeded at a slow pace: budget reductions have resulted in some voluntary retirements but also in stronger demands for higher salaries. The removal of important garrisons from the Buenos Aires area—the garrisons that have been instrumental to implement the coups—has not been realized yet. Replacing the drafted army with a volunteer one is still being discussed. Finally, the concentration of decision-making power in the president and defense minister has not prevented high-ranking officers from trying to interfere with governmental decisions. In fact, it seems that the Radical administration lost its opportunity to implement deeper military transformations during its first months in office and that it became more difficult to act in this direction as time passed. However, an important circumstance continues to protect the government against any military temptation to mount a destabilizing offensive: the armed forces' prestige remains very low and is likely to continue to be low as new revelations about crimes and corruption are made public.

The political opposition, for its part, has not endangered the stability of the government. It is true that the difficulties faced by the Radical administration have been compounded by the fact that they must operate in a limited political setting. They control the executive, the Chamber of Deputies, and some of the most populous provinces, but not the Senate nor the majority of the provinces, which are governed by the Peronistas. The Radicals were unable to obtain Senate approval for a law designed to democratize the trade unions, and thus to reduce the Peronists' ability to engage in antigovernment actions. Nevertheless, although the law that remains in force favors the current Peronista leadership in hope of controlling the trade unions, the new political circumstances have resulted in some setbacks for the entrenched leaders. The General Confederation of Labor has divided itself into separate groups, some of them disposed to collaborate with the government. Politically the Radicals have also been assisted by the surge of internal rifts in the Peronista movement that culminated in a division between two sectors, each of which claims to be the legitimate heir of the party. Involved in this internal struggle, the principal opposition party has been unable to structure a united front to obstruct governmental policies. A clear demonstration of the Peronists' inability to mobilize their followers against governmental intiatives came even before the formal division of the party. In the November 1984 referendum, Argentine voters overwhelmingly approved (by 81 percent of the vote) the peace treaty with Chile. The Peronista call for abstention went unheard, and more than 70 percent of the eligible voters participated in this nonobligatory election.

It is in the economic and social spheres that the Radical administration has been facing the most severe challenges and where destabilizing pressures could become more dangerous. The enormous foreign debt accumulated during the years of military rule places a number of difficult constraints on the possibility of combining satisfactory economic growth with redistribution. Coupled with it are domestic economic problems of great magnitude: the partial destruction of the industrial sector; underemployment and unemployment; financial disorder; and declines in productivity, investment and real salaries. These produce socioeconomic and political tensions that represent a serious challenge to the government and cannot be solved in the short term. In part, the government's lack of success in dealing with these problems has been due to the catastrophic dimensions of the crisis. But, in part, the Radicals' economic policies have lacked clear direction. Adopting a conciliatory style, they lost the opportunity to formulate and implement some drastic policies during their first months in power. In particular, the government did not take advantage of the favorable political situation to try to reorganize the financial system and the fiscal sector, to modernize agriculture, and to reactivate industry, as contemplated in its program. As a consequence, financial groups have continued to speculate, the fiscal deficit has increased, the productivity of the agricultural sector remains very low, and industry has been unable to operate at full capacity. The time has been spent trying to obtain the agreement of labor and capital for a "social pact" guaranteed by the state, but the government has not forcefully advanced any clear proposal. As the agreement became more difficult to achieve, strikes multiplied and prices went out of control. The crisis was aggravated by the existence of conflicting views between the Ministry of Economics and the Central Bank, making impossible the formulation of a coherent strategy for adjustment and recovery. Finally, in February 1985, the continued division of the economic team led to the resignation of the minister of economics and the president of the Central Bank, and their replacement by what was announced as a more coherent team of economists.

Meanwhile, the administration has been under continuous pressure from the international banks and the IMF to adopt an orthodox adjustment program designed to solve the economic crisis and to meet Argentina's external obligations. The government's attempt to circumvent these pressures and to politicize the debt issue by establishing a common front with other Latin American debtor countries has been, thus far, not very successful. Some timid redistributionist measures have failed to achieve their targets. These measures include: wage raises, food, health, and housing programs, price controls, and easier access to personal credit, as well as reactivation initiatives: preferential credit lines for depressed activities, tax reform, and import and exchange controls. High inflation has neutralized the effect of wage raises; price controls have been ineffective; increased financial liquidity has been diverted to the speculative circuit and the black exchange market; productive investment has not increased as expected; and tax evasion and illegal import-export practices have proliferated. The only bright aspects of the picture are represented by some noneconomic factors that tend to moderate socioeconomic tensions: the general agreement on the fact that the Radical administration had inherited and had not generated the crisis; the lack of any clear options for solving it in the short term; the conviction that the destabilization of the current government would only mean a worsening of the crisis and the application of unpopular measures of adjustment; and the confidence that Alfonsín continues to enjoy among a large part of the population.

The Prospects for Democratic Stability

The prospects for establishing a stable democratic regime in Argentina depend upon permanent features of the system that in the past have caused the breakdown of constitutional experiments. Among such features are economic constraint, praetorianism, and the lack of a democratic political culture.

Argentina's economic constraints are clearly illustrated by the continuing tensions between the accumulation requirements for economic development—savings, investments, financial deepening—and the popular demands for redistribution, which imply increasing consumption and a more equitable pattern of economic growth. Democratic governments, and the Radical administration is not an exception, are always caught in the dilemma of trying to satisfy and harmonize these contradictory pressures. They can try to promote accumulation through the application of orthodox economic policies, but they cannot ignore popular demands for redistribution, especially in a country such as Argentina, where trade unions are extremely organized and powerful. But if incentives for investment are not provided, after a while demand-led economic growth begins to decline, inflationary pressures and shortages appear, and it becomes impossible to continue with redistributive policies. Moreover, the international situation makes it difficult to attract foreign capital, in the form of economic aid, loans, and direct investment, to complement scarce domestic savings. As such a situation develops, the democratic government's basis of support is eroded to such an extent that democracy tends to be equated with chaos, and its legitimacy declines. It is then that the military see the opportunity to intervene, and they have done so many times under the pretext of restoring order and establishing the basis for a "perfected" democratic regime.

The Radical administration can avoid this fate, especially if it mobilizes some of its major assets in order to develop a program designed to satisfy popular demands and to harmonize contradictory economic pressures. Politically, the undeniable legitimacy of its authority, the disastrous effect of the recent military experience, which temporarily eliminated any longing for a new coup, its genuine concern for improving the circumstances of lower-income groups, and its rejection of corruption, tend to provide time and a margin for maneuver in which to restructure the economic apparatus. Economically, the country continues to enjoy several favorable conditions— large food surpluses, oil, underutilized industrial capacity, competitive exports—that can be exploited to generate economic growth, especially if some adjustment of the external debt situation can be achieved.

The praetorianization of Argentine society is a long-standing problem whose most negative manifestations are the politicization of the military and the absence of a representative and solid party system.[14] Even though all Argentine groups are extremely politicized, the most dangerous for the survival of a democratic regime is the military establishment. Other groups can destabilize a constitutional government, but the coup de grace has always been administered by the military. Moreover, in Argentina the military have repeatedly demonstrated that many factors that favor their intervention are present.[15] They believe in their "manifest destiny" and hold a messianic self-image as the last defenders of "Western and Christian civilization" and as the proponents of the most cherished traditions of the Argentine nation. They have middle- and upper-class positions to defend and important corporate interests to promote. And they display a morbidly high self-esteem that leads them to react with determination against any attempt to impose civilian supremacy.

Even so, the new democratic government has the opportunity to depoliticize the military and to demilitarize politics. Some such measures have been implemented, even if in a hesitant way. Deeper reforms are necessary regarding the internal structure of the armed forces, and stricter controls should be imposed on their members to avoid a new surge of military politicization. Although some opportunities have been lost, the government still enjoys sufficient popular support as to be able to implement measures of this type. The defiant attitude still adopted by many high-ranking officers gives the administration a chance to act before it loses support and the military begins to strenthen its position. In any case, if the principle of civilian supremacy is to be upheld and the opportunity for military intervention eliminated, longer-term policies are needed to change the ideological and doctrinal tendencies of the armed forces—and more important yet, to remove the basis for their praetorian activities.

A solid and representative party system, able to channel the demands of all important socioeconomic and ideological groups, is necessary to create an environment in which military or civilian putschists cannot succeed. Because there are no real hegemonic groups and important sectors cannot create solid political organizations, there are no political parties that effectively represent the interests and demands of the economic right and the ideological left. The parties that once represented these constituencies, the Conservatives and the Socialists, have been replaced in the political arena by reformist "catch-all" parties (the Radicals) and populist movements (the Peronists) that have preempted their electoral space. These multiform, multiclass coalitions have absorbed most Argentine voters, leaving both right and left in very marginal positions.

At various times in Argentine history, the rightist upper class has abandoned any hope of gaining power through free elections and has established close ties with the military, offering them their support, technobureaucratic skills, and orthodox economic programs. In return, they ask the armed forces to become their political tool—the so-called military party—in order to establish regimes favorable to their interests, either through rigged elections or outright military coups. When the left also has found itself without electoral channels, it has recurrently appealed, especially in the 1960s and 1970s, to elitist and violent means to achieve power. Even if leftist violence does not succeed, it contributes to the disarray that seems to justify military coups. At the same time, it nullifies the possibilities of creating more democratic leftist parties, whose potential membership is absorbed by the violent groups and the populist movements, languishes into numerical insignificance, or is directly destroyed by the military.

Obviously, it is impossible for a democratic government to create from above parties that represent the interests and ideologies of particular sectors, integrating them into their institutional framework. But the Radical government can promote a pluralistic environment in which these groups can pursue their ends through party channels. They will do so especially if they are convinced that the government will not obstruct their organizational attempts, will respect their rights as political minorities, and will accept them as valid partners in the quest for political, economic, and social solutions.

Third, Argentina's political culture must be modified in order to help guarantee the stability of Argentine democracy. It is obvious that Argentine society has never been politically pluralistic. The rights of different groups to participate in government have been constantly curtailed or challenged by other groups; key sectors have not been integrated into the democratic mainstream; and public opinion has not always opposed military intervention. Many of the economic, social and political factors that help to explain this lack of respect for the rules of the democratic game, already mentioned, constitute a fertile ground in which authoritarian values and ideologies prosper. From the corporatist-ultrareactionary, through the economically liberal–politically dictatorial, to the leftist-authoritarian positions, a wide spectrum of antidemocratic groups have attacked the basis of pluralistic coexistence with different degrees of success. Some of them have attempted to eliminate opposition by establishing corporatist military-trade union agreements; others have used the military to impose their programs by force; still others have engaged in armed resistance. And all of them have diffused their beliefs and methods into political parties, socioeconomic organizations, civilian and military bureaucracies, educational, cultural, and religious organizations. This has created situations in which the authoritarianism of one sector justifies the growing authoritarianism of others, destroying any hope of strengthening democratic values.

A more pluralistic political culture in Argentina partially depends on the determination and ability of the democratic forces to expand democratization to new areas while eliminating their own authoritarian leanings. Greatly favored by the popular revulsion created by the last authoritarian experience, other spheres of Argentine life besides politics have been liberalized, such as the social, cultural, educational, and scientific spheres. Attempts to redemocratize labor organizations are under way. Projects to restructure and depoliticize the military have begun to be implemented. The censorship of cultural and artistic activities has been lifted. Authoritarian elements have been removed from educational programs, and the universities have been democratized allowing the active participation of all their members. And the failure of the authoritarian factions to gather electoral support has engendered rank-and-file movements favoring their removal from the leadership of the Peronist and other minor parties. If these processes continue, an adequate environment for the growth and consolidation of democratic values can be created, and political forces can agree on how best to defend the stability of the constitutional regime.

In conclusion, the prospects for consolidating Argentine democracy are not brilliant but at least relatively encouraging. The main hope for stability rests on the assumption that democratic regimes in part represent the outcome of a long process. Its participants must learn to value an environment in which human rights and civil liberties are respected, to accept the uncertainty of electoral results with no restrictions on participation, and to take for granted the accountability of those elected. People willingly defend such a regime when they share a rational and strongly felt conviction that the benefits of democracy outweigh its problems, especially when compared with the tragic outcomes of authoritarian regimes. In the Argentine case, the last period of military rule had such terrible consequences for the country that there is a real basis for hope that the people will unite to stop the pendulum swings between military dictatorships and civilian governments.

Notes

1. On the characteristics of the successive Argentine transitions from military to civilian rule since 1930, see, for instance, Robert Potash, *El Ejército y la Política en la Argentina, 1928–1943* (Buenos Aires: Sudamericana, 1971), and *The Army and*

Politics in Argentina, 1945–1962 (Stanford, Calif.: Stanford University Press, 1980); Alain Rouquie, *Pouvoir Militaire et Société Politique en République Argentine* (Paris: Presses de la Fondation Nationale des Sciences Politiques, 1978); and Marcelo Cavarozzi, *Autoritarismo y Democracia (1955–1983)* (Buenos Aires: Centro Editor de América Latina, 1983).

2. See Max Weber, *Economy and Society* (Berkeley and Los Angeles: University of California Press, 1978), 1:31–36.

3. The importance of this fact has been underscored by, among others, Guillermo O'Donnell in his *Notas Para el Estudio de Procesos de Democratización Política a Partir del Estado Burocrático Autoritario* (Buenos Aires: CEDES, 1979). About political parties and electoral results in contemporary Argentina, see Darío Cantón, *Elecciones y Partidos Políticos en la Argentina: Historia, Interpretación y Balance, 1910–1966* (Buenos Aires: Siglo XXI, 1973).

4. On the features of the Argentine socioeconomic and political configuration that set obstacles to these authoritarian attempts, see Marcelo Cavarozzi, *Autoritarismo y Democracia*; Alain Rouquie, "Hegemonía Militar, Estado y Dominación Social," in *Argentina Hoy*, ed. Rouquie (Mexico City: Siglo XXI, 1982), pp. 11–50; and Gary Wynia, *Argentina in the Postwar Era: Politics and Economic Policy Making in a Divided Society* (Albuquerque: University of New Mexico Press, 1978).

5. In this respect, see Darío Cantón, *La Política de los Militares Argentinos, 1900–1971* (Buenos Aires: Siglo XXI, 1971); Alain Rouquie, "Hegemonía Militar"; and P. Waldmann and E. Garzon Valdez, eds., *El Poder Militar en la Argentina, 1976–1981* (Buenos Aires: Galerna, 1983).

6. On the absence of hegemonic groups or the existence of a "hegemonic stalemate" in Argentina, see Oscar Braun, ed., *El Capitalismo Argentino en Crisis* (Buenos Aires: Siglo XXI, 1973); Alain Rouquie, "Hegemonía Militar"; and J. Sabato and J. Schvarzer, "Funcionamiento de la Economía y Poder Político en la Argentina: Trabas para la Democracia," *Ibero Americana* 13, no. 2 (1983), 11–38.

7. The economic and social policies of the military government are analyzed in Adolfo Canitrot, *Orden Social y Monetarismo* (Buenos Aires: Estudios CEDES, 1981), vol. 4, no.7; and by the same author, "Teoría y Práctica del Liberalismo: Política Antiinflacionaria y Apertura Económica en la Argentina, 1976–1981," *Desarrollo Económico* 82 (1981), 131–89; Aldo Ferrer, "El Retorno del Liberalismo," *Desarrollo Económico* 72 (1979), 485–510, and "La Economía Argentina bajo una Estrategia 'Preindustrial,' 1976 1980," in *Argentina Hoy*, ed. Alain Rouquie, pp. 105–28; and Jorge Schvarzer, *Martínez de Hoz: La Lógica Política de la Política Económica* (Buenos Aires: CISEA, 1983). Its political and ideological characteristics are analyzed in the articles included in *Argentina Hoy*, ed. Alain Rouquie; and *El Poder Militar*, ed. P. Waldmann and E. Garzon Valdez.

8. In Argentina, the words "liberalism" and "liberals" make reference to neoclassical economic doctrines and their supporters, and do not resemble the usage common in the English-speaking countries. In fact, Argentine "liberals" are generally politically conservative, and many of them have promoted and supported rightist military coups.

9. On the capacity of the market to perform such a role in a very different setting, see Karl Polanyi, *The Great Transformation* (Boston: Beacon Press, 1957). About state authority and market exchange as two different mechanisms of social control, Charles Lindblom, *Politics and Markets: The World's Political-Economic*

Systems (New York: Basic Books, 1977). The best analysis of the extent and limits of the liberal project is in Canitrot, *Orden Social*.

10. The crisis and breakdown of the economic model are analyzed in Schvarzer, *Martínez de Hoz*; Aldo Ferrer, "Monetarismo en el Cono Sur: El Caso Argentino," *Pensamiento Iberoamericano* 1 (January–June, 1982), 109–15; Roque Fernandez, "La Crisis Financiera Argentina: 1980–1982," *Desarrollo Económico* 89 (1983), 79–97, and "La Crisis Financiera Argentina, 1980–82. Réplica," *Desarrollo Económico* 91 (1983), 456–59; and Ernesto Feldman, "La Crisis Financiera Argentina: 1980–82. Algunos Comentarios," *Desarrollo Económico* 91 (1983), 449–55.

11. The best account of the Argentine side of the Malvinas-Falklands crisis, its background and consequences, is found in O. R. Cardoso, R. Kirschbaum, and E. Van der Kooy, *Malvinas. La Trama Secreta* (Buenos Aires: Sudamericana/Planeta, 1983).

12. The events from the fall of Galtieri to the present have been followed through different issues of CISEA, *El Bimestre Político y Económico* (a bimonthly chronological publication that summarizes the information published by nine Argentine newspapers and twelve magazines), *Information Service on Latin America—ISLA* (which reproduces news published in U.S., British and French sources), the newspapers *Clarín* and *La Prensa*, and the periodical publications *Humor* and *El Periodista de Buenos Aires*.

13. On the evolution, support, organization, and ideology of Argentine Radicalism, see David Rock, *Politics in Argentina, 1890–1930: The Rise and Fall of Radicalism* (Cambridge: Cambridge University Press, 1975); Luis A. Romero, ed., *El Radicalismo* (Buenos Aires: Carlos Pérez, 1969); and Peter Snow, *Radicalismo Argentino* (Buenos Aires: Francisco de Aguirre, 1972).

14. For the notions of praetorianism and mass praetorianism, see Samuel P. Huntington, *Political Order in Changing Societies* (New Haven, Conn.: Yale University Press, 1968), pp. 79–82, 192–263. A refinement and application of these notions to the Argentine case is found in Guillermo O'Donnell, "Modernización y Golpes Militares: Teoría, Comparación y el Caso Argentino," *Desarrollo Económico* 47 (1972), 519–66.

15. A general analysis of the motivations, modes, and opportunities that favor military interventions is found in S. E. Finer, *The Man on Horseback: The Role of Military in Politics* (New York: Praeger, 1962).

Silvio R. Duncan Baretta and John Markoff

3 Brazil's *Abertura*: A Transition from What to What?

Following the Second World War, the extended authoritarian period under President Getúlio Vargas gave way to electoral politics and competitive parties in Brazil. The legacy of the Vargas era has often been described as a state of compromise in which coffee planters, union officials, army officers, industrialists, and civil servants managed to avoid trampling on one another's vital concerns. The Brazilian version of populism was noted for its pragmatic management of conflict rather than the formulation of coherent visions; its leaders were more noted for their accommodating style than for their charisma. Brazilian intellectuals saw a pattern of muted social antagonisms in contrast to the starker divisions evident in the ideologically more coherent parties of Chilean democracy or the personal following of Argentina's Perón.

Elite accommodations, however, proved inadequate in the face of the tensions of an industrializing Brazil. The relationship of Brazilian industry to the international economic order, the financing of development projects, the intractable inflation, the problem of politically incorporating an economically marginalized rural and urban underclass (swollen by extraordinary population growth), the self-assertion of the armed forces, many of whose officers saw themselves as the vanguard of a glorious (and industrial) future—these problems strained the system to its limits. A series of coups and attempted coups, a president's resignation, and a president's suicide were only the most dramatically visible indicators of an increasing paralysis. In a climate of extreme tension that some on the political right held to foreshadow revolution and many in the middle classes experienced as a slide into chaos, the military assumed power in 1964. To the dismay of their

43

many civilian supporters, it gradually became clear in the months
and years that followed that the generals were not about to step down,
as they had typically done, once they had thrown out an unacceptable president; rather than quickly restoring what the civilian leaders
took to be normalcy, the military were, it became clear, going to be
in power for an indefinite period. But for all their staying power, as
Juan Linz notes, the military rulers still had not managed to institutionalize the regime after a decade of rule.[1] A clear sign of this,
argues Linz, was the extreme fluidity of the formal rules of the
political game, as shown by an apparently endless succession of Institutional Acts and Complementary Acts, constitutional modifications,
shifting electoral laws, and the continual making and remaking of
political forms.

   Against this background, we shall try to understand the broad out-
lines of the reopening of Brazil's political system that began in 1974
when the fourth military president, General Geisel, announced a
new political direction.[2] Recent Brazilian politics have been governed
by a continuous struggle, and sometimes cooperation, between forces
committed to a more or less authoritarian order and forces committed
to something resembling democracy. The regime has oscillated between authoritarian and democratic poles, but this fluid and contradictory situation has given rise to highly experimental, pragmatic
political arrangements. While these arrangements may well have approached full authoritarianism in the first decade of military rule,
although even within the dark period of closing there were many
moments of opening, since 1974 they have been moving toward the
democratic pole.
   The Brazilian experience demonstrates that authoritarianism and
democracy are not necessarily radically distinct. While in many instances a transition from one to the other is precisely demarcated by a
dramatic rupture, in other cases the movement is subtle, the distinc-
tion is blurry, and the nature of the situation is uncertain. Sometimes
political tactics and political discourse have become finely attuned to
this ambiguity and, at least in the case of Brazil, have helped to
sustain it.
   Probably the most fundamental observation one can make about
Brazil's political *abertura* is that it has lasted for such a long time.
Compared to other processes of democratic opening, it would be hard
to imagine anything more dissimilar from the recurrent pattern in
Argentina depicted by Aldo Vacs in this volume. In this pattern, the

military hang on until internal dissension and general hostility lead to a precipitous, uncontrolled withdrawal on terms wholly unacceptable to the military, who then nurse their wounds, recover some minimal unity, and await the inevitable crisis of civilian politics to try—and fail—again. Not that the Brazilian military withdrawal was problem-free. Tensions and even crises were inherent in the amalgam of democratic and authoritarian forms that constituted the structure of Brazilian politics. But what is striking is that in spite of almost continuous tension, the political opening advanced nonetheless. Again and again, politically active Brazilians experienced minutes, hours, and days in which rumors circulated that a coup might be imminent; after many such occasions, sighs of relief were reported in the press. And yet the feared coup never came; "decompression," "relaxation," or "opening," as the process had been variously called, was not aborted; and the game continued. How are we to understand the capacity of Brazilian politics to sustain such a slow opening of the system? And why is the process so radically different from that experienced in Argentina?

A good point of reference for analyzing the nature of Brazil's political process is to be found in the public statements in which General Geisel outlined the nature of the political relaxation he intended to sponsor. Shortly after assuming office in 1974, Geisel indicated the aims of the coming political opening. In the short run, he expected that emergency measures would be utilized infrequently, although the potential for vigorous repressive action would be maintained. But in the longer run he hoped that even this situation would be "superseded by a creative political imagination, capable of instituting . . . effective safeguards within a constitutional framework." This transformation of Brazilian political life, Geisel continued, would not and could not be brought about by executive decree alone; rather, "It demands to a great extent the most sincere and effective collaboration of the other powers of the nation." In particular, this project required a "general repudiation" of the "adversarial spirit" of intransigent minorities. This was in no sense a project for the establishment or reestablishment of a democratic order; it was, as the opposition has frequently insisted since, a project for the stabilization of an authoritarian one. Open brutality was to cease, but only to the extent that the opposition cooperated in disciplining itself. Of course, it was not to be expected that the entire gamut of oppositional sentiment could be enlisted, but sufficiently broad support had to be brought into "most sincere and effective collaboration" so that the diehards became politically isolated. Under those circumstances, the rule of emergency decrees and state violence was to be brought to an end.[3]

Institutionally, what we shall call the Geisel project meant the harnessing of democratic forms, not their elimination. To point to three prominent arenas in particular: The legislature had to be revitalized (although it was hoped that it would not be too effective in thwarting the will of the executive). There had to be competitive elections (but it was hoped that the opposition forces would not do so well as to call the system into question). Finally, restrictions on free expression were to be relaxed—including eventually the freedom for those in prison or exile to reenter political life—but it was hoped that those now permitted to speak and write would accept certain limits in their challenge to the status quo. All of these issues converged in the attempt to give new life to the party system that the military had attempted to organize early in their rule. There was a progovernment party whose electoral successes were to be matched by its parliamentary docility. The military also provided for the existence of an opposition party to legitimate the system; if its members were too oppositional, they could be removed from office. If it was collectively too successful, the election laws could be rewritten. In short, the Geisel project was a mix of democratic and authoritarian elements whose interplay we are going to examine and whose tensions we are going to explore.

There are two very deep sources of challenge to the realization of the Geisel project. There was, in the first place, what we may loosely speak of as the "opposition," those for whom an *abertura* was an opportunity to be exploited, not so much in the interests of institutionalizing an authoritarian situation, as for dismantling it. The nature of this opposition was diverse and has included different groups at different times; the projects of these groups have been correspondingly diverse: if we refer to them as "the democratic forces," it is not at all because they were united in desiring something approximating political democracy, but because the effect of their challenge to the regime was to move it closer to the democratic pole. Some of the most noteworthy components of this opposition are the following:

–Elements of the business community: Many industrialists were dismayed at the extent to which the state had penetrated the economy under the generals.

–What we may call the "political class": Brazilians active in formally
competitive politics, past or present, found the untrammeled sway
of the executive to be anathema. It is of the greatest significance for
the evolution of the transitional process that, as expected, not only
were the official opposition politicians at odds with the military and
their civilian allies in control of the executive, but also, significant
elements of the deliberately created establishment party frequently
found themselves in agreement with their congressional opponents
in challenging unrestrained and arbitrary executive power.

–The leftists: Brazil's various lefts were in agreement on little more
than their dismay at the increasingly inegalitarian distribution of the
benefits of economic development as carried out (at points with
great success by some criteria) by the economic managers of the
military regime. These groups all desired an opening, but the purposes of such an opening differed for each persuasion. The cautious
mainstream of the Communist party, who hoped that liberalization
in a climate of revulsion against authoritarian excesses would lead to
their acceptance as a legitimate part of the political order, had little
in common with the Catholic radicals who were extremely active in
an intense and widespread mobilization of the rural poor. These
radicals, in turn, differed deeply from those on the left who felt that
the lesson of the repressive nightmare that followed the wholly ineffectual radicalism of the 1960s was that there was much to be said
for liberal democracy, after all, as a desirable state in itself and not
just as an arena for organizing the revolution.

–A significant portion of the church hierarchy: Already critical of
social injustice before 1964, church leaders had been drawn more
deeply into the most bitter and uncompromising opposition by their
solidarity with radical priests subject to brutal treatment.

–The Brazilian Bar Association: Because of its intellectual orientation
and its attempts to act as if Brazil were governed by the rule of law,
the bar association became a center of criticism of the regime for its
arbitrary actions.

–The community of academic social scientists: Scholars quite effectively demonstrated the distribution of the social costs of the dramatic changes Brazil had undergone since 1964, as a largely rural,
illiterate, and agricultural country became a largely urban, literate,
and semi-industrial one. The flourishing of empirical social research in Brazil made it impossible for the regime to dismiss these
people as mere leftist ideologues.

–A new pattern of industrial unionism: Workers in the modern large-scale industries attempted to assert their claims on what they saw as the fruits of their own productivity. But the older unions were hardly happier with a regime whose central labor policy was to deny them the benefits of the traditional corporatism.

The extent to which these groups succeeded in seizing the opportunities presented by the *abertura* may be measured by the extent to which the Brazilian case today, for all its ambiguities, enters into discussions of transitions to democracy rather than discussions of authoritarian stabilization. Measured against its original intentions, it would seem that the Geisel project has been profoundly altered, even democratically perverted.

There was a second and extremely dangerous challenge facing Geisel's program, coming largely from within the military itself. Some officers found that Geisel's program was in itself threatening; others held that Geisel's vision of a stabilized, authoritarian state was acceptable, but pursuing it too precipitously would open the door to the unacceptable, and any step was too precipitous for somebody. Broadly speaking, these officers fell into two groups.

First, there were those who feared the possibility of a return to the undesirable conditions of politics before 1964. Their specific apprehensions varied: fear of communism, of chaos, of corruption, and fear that their plans for a greater Brazil could not survive electoral politics. The "hard-line" component of the military, who not merely supported the coup, but also delighted in the end of the Castello Branco administration and the fall from power of those whose political program was oriented to the authoritarian imposition of democratic reforms, were at the heart of this group. We might speak of them as principled antidemocrats. Some among them combined an antipathy to popular mobilization (carried out through either parliamentary or extraparliamentary channels) with a developmentalist nationalism. This "right-wing developmentalism," which had some support outside the military, has converged in several important ways with the developmentalism of the moderate left, a convergence that we shall argue below places an important brake on political polarization at the moment.

Second, there were those who enjoyed the opportunities that had opened for them since 1964 and who feared losing their positions.

Quite apart from civilian *situacionistas*, we have in mind particularly the personnel of the military's security apparatus, the "information service." At the height of the repressive period, this had become a closed and semiautonomous world, making its own rules, of questionable subordination to the high command and strategically placed throughout the formal organs of government. Far from being fully identified with the hard line, the information service was initially a creation of the reformers close to Castello Branco. *Abertura*, even in General Geisel's version, let alone the projects of the democratic forces, was very threatening to them—for whatever else it was, the promise of reducing the scope of exceptional measures was a program directed against their autonomy.

Roughly speaking, then, the battle waged first by Geisel and then by Figueiredo for a controlled and limited opening was a struggle against diverse groups (and eventually the overwhelming majority of the politically active) who in various ways desired a more open political system and a process of opening far less under the control of the military. A second, no less difficult, struggle was going on within the military against those who waged a covert and determined battle to subvert the whole process. This second struggle was complicated (on both sides) by the need to maintain sufficient military unity so that the latent threat of coercion, so central to Geisel's demands of self-discipline from the opposition, would continue to be credible.

It is no wonder then that there have been many sources of tension and crisis: the mix of democratic and authoritarian forms, the deep and quite opposed challenges to the stability of the process of slow and controlled decompression, and the climate of serious social and economic tension within which the *abertura* was played out. The outcomes of the major confrontations were simple. The opposition did better at the polls than the generals wished. In the executive's confrontations with the legislature, whether the subject was the latest economic crisis or the pace of *abertura* itself, the establishment party was far less uniformly docile than Geisel had envisioned. Freedom of discussion sometimes went beyond the military's tolerance and the freedom to organize—in the factory, in the countryside, and in the streets—was pushed far beyond what anyone imagined in 1974. Finally, the internal military opposition, which had resorted to terrorism, got caught in public. The government could not easily pretend to ignore bomb throwers under its nominal command. The wonder is that in the eleven years of political opening, the process has not been aborted: it is this stability in the processes of political change that we wish to elucidate.

The Survival of *Abertura*

Roots

We stress the problem of the survival of *abertura*, not its genesis. *Abertura* has been present as an idea since the first days of the first military presidency of the 1960s, that of Marshal Castello Branco. The military, or at least their dominant faction in those early months, had no intention of remaining twenty years in power, even less of building an authoritarian regime.[4] The early military view was still constrained by what Alfred Stepan calls the "moderator model": after removing a president who had exceeded the bounds of constitutional behavior, the military would step down and allow the resumption of democratic politics.[5] Castello and his supporters definitely wanted the prompt restoration of democracy following some political house-cleaning. Their intervention was aimed primarily at the left, both legal and illegal,[6] and at political corruption, which was held to thwart Brazil's potential greatness in the interests of a narrow and venal elite. However, the house-cleaning task posed a more formidable challenge than at any time since World War II. When the military did not step down, many observers concluded that some dramatic and decisive change of mentality must have taken place. With the perspective of time, however, it seems that the military's attempt to govern Brazil rather than merely restore its political balance was the result of a political process rather than the fulfillment of a coherent pre-coup vision.

While the leftist factions could be controlled and even destroyed by brutality, it was less easy to root out corruption, as the military defined it. This objective brought the most intellectually consistent sectors of the military into conflict with the profoundly clientelistic structure of Brazilian political life. By the end of 1965, the congressional left had been severely weakened by military purges. It was harder to deal with the conservative elements that had supported the coup.

With the possible exception of the war against the left, the most important political goal of the Castelistas was to regenerate Brazilian democracy so as to prevent the populist coalition forged by Vargas from gaining power. This coalition found its major expression in an alliance between the PSD (Partido Social-Democrático) and the PTB (Partido Trabalhista Brasileiro) in every presidential election since 1950.[7] Both of these parties were targets of the anticorruption mentality. The PSD had inherited the rural elite's long tradition of dominating an impoverished rural electorate through favor and fraud, while the PTB's considerable resources, primarily jobs, came from its control of political appointments, particularly in the Labor Ministry. One might have opposed the pre-coup regime because one favored an authoritarian regime; but one might well have favored democracy *and therefore* found both the PSD and the PTB abominable (to confine ourselves only to the major parties). At first, Brazil's military leaders were of the special sort of liberal democrats who flourished in Brazil, namely, those who contended, with some plausibility, that antidemocratic means were necessary to make liberal democracy work properly.[8] On the civilian side, this tendency was associated with the UDN (União Democrática Nacional), the political organ of the anti-Vargas forces; in its military aspect, this was the group associated with the ESG (Escola Superior de Guerra). In addition, of course, there were powerful sectors within the military that wanted to establish an authoritarian order.[9]

It proved impossible to regenerate democracy using the moderator model, which called for the prompt restoration of civilian democratic rule. That failure, and the pressure of the thoroughly antidemocratic sectors of the military, explains why the armed forces gradually tightened their grip over Brazil's economy and society and maintained power for twenty years.

The idea of *abertura*, then, already existed on the day Castello Branco took office. It would have been virtually impossible to create a legitimate nondemocratic order in this milieu. The dominant visions of Brazilian political life since 1945 could probably be summarized as follows: For the "democratic purists," civilian and military, democracy as it existed in Brazil was repulsive and needed reform. Next, there were the politicians, for whom democracy enabled a narrow elite stratum to perpetuate and exploit the clientelism that gave them power. Third, the radical left criticized democracy for its inability to transform Brazilian society. Finally, the radical right, especially in the military, feared that the weaknesses of democracy threatened to deliver Brazilian society into the hands of a communist minority.

These four broad orientations were complemented by a fifth and very potent group: those who were indifferent toward democratic forms. For many who were politically active, left and right, officers and civilians, democratic forms were not important in themselves, but were to be opportunistically embraced or rejected in the pursuit of other goals. Thus, generals who championed democracy in 1945 in order to remove a Vargas who had become too close to labor, terminated democracy in 1964 to remove a Vargas protege who was again too close to labor.[10] Or, to look at a different part of the pre-coup political spectrum, labor leaders who criticized democratic forms as bourgeois before 1964 have been consistent champions of redemocratization since the mid-1970s.

Conflicts regarding democratic structures continued after the coup. In this sense, there is a continuity in Brazil's political history. But in the pre-coup period of competitive politics, formal, explicit democratic rules coexisted with—and conflicted with—both the informal patterns of clientelism and the recurrent civilian attempts, and occasional successes, at inducing the military to intervene. After 1964, however, the explicit democratic rules were simply done away with—gradually at first, and more rapidly after the promulgation of Institutional Act No. 5 in late 1968. But while some were committed to a clean break, others hoped for a democratic restoration of some sort. Although the civilian backers of the coup tended to favor a limited action against the left, many in the military who saw themselves as democrats insisted on a more thorough reform. The major characteristic of the 1964–1984 period is therefore the fluid and experimental character of all political rules and institutions. The conflict now seemed not so much one between explicit rules and political realities, since even the rules were pragmatic, experimental, and provisional. Brazilian politics after 1964 can best be described as a groping for definition—of rules, of institutional forms, of a legitimacy principle. (Perhaps one ought to speak of an *experimental authoritarianism*.) The great achievement of the political initiative launched under Geisel was to discover a source of legitimacy in this very groping. The evident impermanence of institutions, the transitory character of the rules of the game, furthered the acceptability of a political process designed to change the current structures. For most participants, the goal was some formally democratic structure, while a minority hoped to create a legitimate authoritarianism.

Given this broad respect for some model of democracy, it was almost inevitable that a serious *abertura* project would be launched by someone. What is remarkable is that it has survived.

The Creation of a "Clean Democracy"

There was a profound contradiction between the ideal of creating a "clean democracy" and the ideal of promptly restoring formal democratic rules. A "clean democracy," as defined by the Castelistas and their civilian allies, was far more than a set of procedural rules. It assumed a certain type of social and economic organization, usually designated by the amorphous but emotionally resonant term "development." It assumed a citizenry free of clientelistic ties to powerful political bosses. This meant, in the cities, ending elected officials' control over bureaucratic jobs; it meant ending the interpenetration of the state and the unions. This latter arrangement ensured the containment of working-class demands by preempting them. At the same time, it gave the workers (or more accurately, the government-sponsored stratum that claimed to speak for labor) political power out of proportion to their real organizational achievements.[11] In the countryside, the task was to end the rule of powerful country bosses who delivered the rural vote. An anticorruption program that had, or came to have, such a sense of its task would take on a far more arduous mission than merely eliminating politicians held to be personally unworthy. It was not individual thieves but Brazil's central institutions that the reformers took on.

This view of a "clean democracy" provided the military rulers with a benchmark to gauge the success of their regime: a clean democracy would have been achieved when elections no longer returned the wrong groups to power. To this end, quite early in their rule the military reorganized the party system into two camps, their supporters in the Aliança Renovadora Nacional (ARENA) and their opponents in the Movimento Democrático Brasileiro (MDB). But no matter how the executive altered the game, the wrong people continued to play an active part on the public stage. Legislators could be purged and elections quashed, electoral rules could be manipulated to favor ARENA, increasingly rigid rules could prevent the opposition from voicing their objections, and the electoral representation of various regions of the country could be altered. Such devices could tame the MDB, but they had the perverse result of ensuring that the wrong people would now be found in ARENA as well. The more the military asserted its authority, the more its erstwhile civilian allies who wanted politics restructured in their favor turned into critics of the system. The more the military worked its will, regardless of Congress, the more visible was the solidarity of *arenistas* and *emedebistas*, despite opposition on specific policies.[12] The more the military actively combated corruption, the more they encroached on the traditional political resources of ARENA, which far more than the MDB recruited from those pre-1964 parties dependent on rural clientelism. The more it appeared that the MDB might be totally decimated, the more uncomfortable the thoughtful members of ARENA became, for without at least a weak opposition to hold up as a threat, how could they defend their autonomy to the military?

The great crises between the military and the Congress in the early years, in short, grew from the executive's difficulties in dealing with its own party.[13] The thoroughly antidemocratic component of the military found it increasingly easy to contend that the wrong people dominated ARENA as well as the increasingly paralyzed opposition. Those who favored a clean democracy found themselves repeatedly having to agree. The purges, the harsh authoritarianism, and military domination of even the minute details of decision making continued to increase. The immediate cause of Institutional Act No. 5, the formal charter of virtually limitless executive authority, to take a crucial instance, was the refusal of many in ARENA to go along with the prosecution of an MDB legislator who had offended the military hard-liners.

Even authoritarian successes, however, were judged by large sectors of the military against the background of some form of democratic ideal. The very success of an authoritarian order in removing undesirables from the political scene would be for some an indication that it was now time to restore civilian rule. This is why authoritarianism failed to institutionalize itself in Brazil. If the present analysis is correct, economic performance was hardly the only means through which the regime laid claim to support (as is often asserted). There was also a political form of legitimation, however provisional, which consisted of evaluating all reforms against their success in bringing Brazil closer to a clean democracy.

We can summarize the argument, in short, by saying that the task of democratic house-cleaning proved to be much more difficult than the liberal sectors among the military had expected. The groups and individuals to be excluded from office were gradually redefined more and more inclusively, making success ever more elusive, and this very lack of success only served to justify military continuation in power. Although the regime lasted for years, it was fundamentally a regime of exception, a period of emergency rule.

Why was the halting movement toward a deeper authoritarianism reversed in the early 1970s? The crucial circumstance was the change in the behavior of the Brazilian opposition.[14] The left had been devastated after ten years of repression that became especially brutal after the promulgation of the Institutional Act No. 5. Leftist parties had been totally dismembered and the revolutionaries among them imprisoned, exiled, or killed. The officially sponsored opposition party—the MDB—faced a hopeless dilemma. The military hard-liners interpreted any electoral successes for the opposition as a reason to change the rules yet again. By the early 1970s, the Brazilian opposition had totally abandoned its former adversary attitude. The "moderates" rather than the "authentic oppositionists" dominated the MDB, which now appeared to accept the regime and to act within the narrow space assigned to it by the government. Of course it struggled, as Brazilians put it, to at least preserve and eventually expand that space.

The disappearance of the more uncompromising sectors of the opposition was seconded by the ejection of the urban working class from Brazil's ruling coalition. Before 1964, urban workers had been accepted as minor partners in a broad alliance that included industrialists, rural bosses, state managers, and certain sectors of the middle class, all groups carefully avoiding infringing on each other's essential interests. The political exclusion of workers after 1964 dramatically changed the context within which the opposition, adversarial or not, exerted its activities.

The change in the opposition, and especially in its left wing, marked a major change from the ideological polarization of the 1960s to the pragmatic convergence that has been developing in Brazil since the early 1970s. Free of the revolutionary threat, sectors of the right have advanced proposals that in the 1960s had been put forward by the moderate left. By Figueiredo's presidency, we find that many rightists favored extending social welfare to the rural poor, giving minimal social benefits to avert disruption, tolerating a new and radical union movement, and taking a tougher line on the IMF. In foreign policy, the idea of Brazil serving as a junior partner in the United States' worldwide battle against communism—championed by the military intellectuals of the Escola Superior de Guerra—has altogether evaporated. Rightist Brazil has had dealings with Cuba, has refused to boycott the Moscow Olympics, snubbed an American president, failed to support the United States in Central America, refused the presence of the U.S. Peace Corps, halted the purchase of American weapons, armed American enemies (notably Libya), and gone ahead with developing nuclear technology. Respectable, responsible Brazilians now talk about repudiation of the foreign debt or at least a unilateral moratorium. What was once not merely a leftist proposition, but also identified with the extreme left in particular, is now an option to be seriously considered by all.

The left has also shifted its ideological ground. Much of the current program of those who had constituted the pre-'64 left sounds remarkably moderate. The shift in the rhetoric of the formerly fiery Brizola is only the most dramatic instance. The Communist party (PCB) is pursuing a very cautious policy; for example, it repudiated the "new unionism" and supported abertura. The strength of their current insistence on moderation was demonstrated by their expulsion of their great hero and certainly leading potential votegetter, Luis Carlos Prestes, in a dispute over this issue. And what of the "far left" of independent Marxists, radical Catholics, and intransigent enemies of the existing order? They too have been transformed, and for reasons that go far beyond purely Brazilian developments. Many independent radicals and dissident communists were stirred when Che called for "one, two, many Vietnams." In the wake of the boat people, the battles of Vietnamese and Chinese armed forces, and the Cambodian nightmare, Che's call to armed struggle is less inspiring. If the right no longer identifies itself with the United States in a worldwide Manichean struggle, the left's international identifications are even murkier, if they exist at all.

The change in the opposition, the rise of an ideological climate in which pragmatic convergence became predominant, and the end of the threat of populism, all contributed to the abertura. Certain sectors of the military—notably, those who favored reestablishing some sort of democratic regime and those who favored a withdrawal from power for institutional reasons (i.e., to preserve institutional unity from the divisive or corrupting consequences of a deep involvement in the political realm)—were convinced that democratic house-cleaning had been accomplished and the time had come to reopen the political system. Moreover, by the mid-1970s for many senior officers the greatest threats to their vision of Brazil, their sense of the social role of the military within Brazil and their personal authority within the military, were the autonomy of the apparatus of coercion and the ideas of the hard-liners rather than the actions of revolutionaries and the dreams of the left.

The Economic Crisis

To say that Brazil's growing economic problems have contributed to the survival of the *abertura* sounds puzzling. Were not similar problems—high rates of inflation, frustrating negotiations with the International Monetary Fund and rising working-class demands, among others—among the major reasons for the coup of 1964? Were not "bureaucratic-authoritarian" regimes in the more industrialized nations of South America rooted in the economic crises of the 1960s and 1970s?[15]

The response to the economic crisis of the sixties differed from that of the eighties in a number of important ways. First, creating a "clean democracy" was only one of the goals of the civilian and military coup makers. An economic goal (seen as a precondition, in fact, for the development of a properly functioning democracy) was the renewal of Brazilian capitalism. To this end, agriculture was to be modernized and a class of independent farmers created. Industry was to be reoriented toward exports and consumer durables. Major development projects would simultaneously open up the interior, integrate the nation, and demonstrate the glory of modern Brazil. The state was to become a bastion of rational management through the application of technical knowledge.

Apparent economic successes (the "Brazilian miracle") seemed to prove that the government had accomplished the feasible socioeconomic transformations. But when the old economic difficulties re-emerged, these problems seemed insoluble because they were rooted in an international order that could not be manipulated by a single government. Such a view was nurtured by the left-right convergence, and added to it. And why not let civilians deal with these intractable issues? In this sense, the economic crisis of the eighties encouraged the military to further withdraw from politics, rather than to intensify their involvement.

Second, the economic crises of the sixties and of the eighties represent very different types of economic disruption. In the sixties, as O'Donnell emphasized, it was the growing political power of the popular sectors that posed the challenge.[16] The threat, perhaps more

imaginary than real, was seen as affecting the very social foundation
of the Brazilian capitalist order. The economic crisis of the eighties
does not seem to challenge Brazil's place in the capitalist world
economy. Strikes and demonstrations have been common events in
Brazil in the last few years, but, whatever their intensity, they appear
less threatening than those that took place during Jango Goulart's
government. They are manifestations of a politically excluded class,
and one that, by itself, cannot at this moment challenge the existing
social order. In short, what has been missing in the eighties is the
prospect of an alliance between the state apparatus and the popular
forces, such as existed before 1964. In this situation, the major political actors can afford to react to present economic difficulties in a very
different way from their response in Jango Goulart's time.

Third, there has been a significant shift in elite thinking about
fruitful directions for future economic growth. In the highly polarized 1960s, proposals for growth through development of the internal
market by redistributing wealth were largely the monopoly of the left
and closely tied to a series of highly explosive political issues. More
recently, the precariousness of the international market and the already achieved successes of Brazil's industrial exports have led to a
new appraisal of future options.

Much of the recent rhetoric of Brazilian entrepreneurial groups
invokes a new model of development, one relying on the internal
market. Concerns about redistribution are again being heard. Emphasis is placed on the need to increase the number of jobs[17] as well as the
productivity of enterprises. Hope is expressed that agricultural growth
will help Brazil out of its present difficulties.[18] To the extent that the
leading economic actors (the state and the national and the interna-
tionalized sectors of the Brazilian bourgeoisie) agree on redistribution
and on the expansion of the market as solutions to the economic crisis,
their support for redemocratization becomes understandable.

Moreover, while the business community may have been initially
grateful to the military for eliminating the threats of the 1960s, now
that the left has been tamed, many in the business community identify the military's own economic policies as a menace. In particular,
the enormous expansion of state management of the economy is
greeted by the Brazilian bourgeoisie with no greater love than would
be the case had it been carried out by planners and bureaucrats
identified with the left. Extreme confidence in the power of the free
market does not carry nearly the same force in Brazil as it does in

Chile; nevertheless, state policies are now seen rather widely as a major source of inefficiency, but the problem can no longer be laid at the door of left ideologues. Indeed, many in industrial circles feel such disdain for the political management of the economy that they are remarkably indulgent toward the most radical union movement in Brazil's history since the strike waves led by anarchists after the First World War. Because the "New Unionism" attempts to repudiate the system of state management of labor relations, to organize on the shop floor and to engage in direct negotiations with employers rather than dealing with state bureaucrats and legislators, some industrialists see these labor militants as allies rather than adversaries in a common battle against central economic control. And if the unions are to be autonomous from government manipulation, what can better assure workers representation in a high-technology future in which a great deal of expensive machinery is subject to sabotage than a genuinely representative group of union leaders? The "New Unionism" in this view may more effectively demand higher wages, but it also promises more stable labor peace. This is another curious point of convergence of left and right against the continuation of the military's policies.

Last, but not least, the political context of the crisis of the eighties is totally different from that of the sixties. We have already mentioned that today's economic problems are not seen, as they were in the pre-1964 years, as part of a context of threat to the national capitalist order. This change has occurred for several reasons: because of the absence of prospects of alliance between the state and the underclasses, because of the changed nature of the Brazilian opposition, and because of the pragmatic convergence of points of view between left and right. All of these factors have contributed to the steady support among sectors of the military for a gradual withdrawal from power. Economic problems are therefore interpreted in the context of the desire of significant groups of officers to relinquish power. The very conditions that had once been held to explain their assuming power are now turned into justifications for relinquishing it. The generals of the eighties are no longer willing to pay the price of power, particularly its costs to institutional unity and to their own professional standards. The aggravation of economic difficulties and social tensions is interpreted, not as requiring further involvement, but as raising the costs of governing the country. Hence, the new attitude: authoritarian moves are seen as accentuating social tensions;

economic problems can be lived with if need be. Democracy is now seen as a desirable means of controlling social conflict, even if it requires a few economic concessions to the popular sector. In short, a new and different political mentality has emerged, to which we now turn.

The Mentality of Transition

One major characteristic of a transitional regime as we define it is the emergence of a mentality—to follow Juan Linz's usage—that sustains the regime by defining it as *temporary*. Failures and difficulties that would lead rather rapidly to the delegitimation of fully institutionalized regimes, authoritarian or democratic, may be acceptable if the regime is seen as a transition to democracy. Difficulties and failures are tolerated for the sake of attaining a higher goal—that is, full redemocratization. However, the transitional regime, although publicly defined as transitional, may in fact become a nearly permanent situation. Brazil's passage into full democracy was initiated in the early seventies. At the moment of this writing (May 1985), President José Sarney has announced the election of a Constituent Assembly (to write a new, democratic constitution) for 1986, and that he will stay in office until 1988. Only after 1988, therefore, will a new president—directly elected and presumably serving under a new constitution—operate within what may become a fully institutionalized democracy. Meanwhile, the Sarney government appears to be generating constitutional amendments and shifting the rules of the game—that is to say, continuing the institutional pattern (but not, of course, the specific content) of the previous decade. Brazilians have given themselves at least three more years of transition, institutional fluidity, and a regime that is evaluated at least as much by its promises of a brighter political future as by its accomplishments in the economic and social spheres.

The mentality of transition may be illustrated by comparing two very similar situations: the deadlocks in Congress over wage bills in the early eighties and in the early sixties. In the earlier situation, congressional failure to conform to the guidelines that Goulart's finance minister, Santiago Dantas, hoped would provide a basis for negotiations with the IMF led to the collapse of the government's plans. This collapse was seen as one more example of the inability of democratic mechanisms to break out of impasses.[19] In the view of the critics, especially within the military, it was impossible to govern efficiently when dealing with the multiplicity of interests represented in Congress. In the early eighties, a very similar situation was interpreted in a totally different vein: the impasse was attributed to a lack of sufficient negotiation, to the breakdown of political channels between the executive and the legislature—in short, to the insufficiently democratic character of the regime.[20] In the sixties, democracy was the problem and authoritarianism the solution; in the eighties, the problem was located in the remaining authoritarian features of the regime, and redemocratization was seen as the solution.

Authoritarian forces, of course, made a vigorous effort to define the issue in the opposite fashion, attributing the impasse regarding the wage bill to democratic inefficiency.[21] Had they succeeded, Brazil might have reverted to a somewhat more repressive order or, at least, delayed a full political opening. But the major point is that the transitional regime made the success of authoritarian elements difficult. Transitional regimes are much less vulnerable than fully established democracies to the charge that democratic institutional mechanisms may lead to paralysis and to an inability to overcome conflicts of interest, precisely because these democratic mechanisms are not implemented in their entirety. The charge lacks credibility, and a mentality develops that sees in democratization not the cause, but the solution to the national problems. This mentality can, of course, create unrealistic expectations that will eventually bring serious difficulties to the regime to come.

Prospects

When assessing the prospects for democracy in Brazil, one must distinguish between the short-term and the long-term prospects. We will say something very definite about the short term, more precisely about the prospects until 1988. We will then very briefly speculate about developments in the more remote future.

The immediate outlook is less the institutionalization of an unambiguously democratic regime than the continuation of a transitional one, along the lines described before. A Constituent Assembly will be chosen in 1986, and only two years later will a new president be directly elected. Meanwhile, it is reasonable to expect that rules and institutions will remain highly fluid and experimental, as Brazilians try to discover the formulas that will ensure future political stability and/or the electoral victory of their parties. The question of the fundamental political structure of Brazil will likely remain at the center of national politics, and this centrality will often be used to divert popular attention, as much as possible, from the urgent social and economic problems of the nation. The military will no doubt continue to intervene in politics, not directly, but through statements suggesting the boundaries of acceptable behavior. Finally, the transitional mentality, in which the regime is accepted on the basis of its future goal of full redemocratization, will probably remain predominant. In short, returning to an analogy made before: if we accept Linz's characterization of Brazil in the sixties and early seventies as an authoritarian "situation," Brazil's democratic present should also be seen as a democratic "situation," rather than a regime. We suggest that both situations be encompassed under a regime type that we call "transitional."

In the longer run, a fully democratic regime can survive only if it is able to promote economic growth, minimize Brazil's enormous social inequalities, and meet other pressing questions, such as the astronomical international debt and rate of inflation. Failure is possible, and would bring with it a renewal of political radicalization and the destruction of the pragmatic convergence of right and left. Other changes, both political and economic—such as a newly vigorous international market that would increase the demand for Brazilian products and destroy the present national consensus on the need to promote income redistribution—could also contribute to a resumption of political radicalization. Would these changing conditions require adjustments of Brazil's dependent capitalism, adjustments that would again demand an authoritarian order?

Not necessarily, we would say. Bureaucratic-authoritarianism represented one response to the problem posed to the ruling classes by a mobilized popular sector and its potential disruption of the economic and social order. Another response would be a broad alliance between the moderate left, the political enter, and the moderate right, all united for the purpose of controlling a potentially revolutionary labor movement. This alliance would be fueled by the threat, always lurking in the background, of military intervention: if the politicians are incapable of restoring order, the armed forces will. Twenty years of bureaucratic authoritarianism might be the foundation enabling a centrist democracy to survive, the politicians taking action to preempt military intervention. In this sense, General Geisel's vision of an opposition that disciplines itself, because it has learned that the club can be taken off the shelf if it goes too far, might be seen as a rather consensually accepted reality. (One must add that in many particulars the present situation is also far more open than Geisel had envisioned.) In such a situation, the dominant, prodemocratic military find it vital to be able to point to their hard-line antagonists as bogeys to keep such a democracy within acceptable restraints. This is a role recently performed magnificently by General Newton Cruz, who, if he had not existed, would probably have had to be invented. In understanding the political behavior of his prodemocratic superior officers, we find it significant that the Brazilian press was always well apprised of his hostility to democracy in any form. We know of no term that encapsulates such a political system, but in Spain, observers speak of *democracia vigilada*, democracy under scrutiny.

This peculiar democracy—this "semi-authoritarian democracy"—would alternate phases of authentic popular participation and a broadening of the political arena with phases in which emergency measures would be declared and repressive controls upon certain social sectors (especially the labor movement) would be established. It would be, in fact, a continuation for years to come of the push-and-pull of democratic and authoritarian forces that characterized the transitional regime—now, however, without direct military participation.

If these projections are accurate, the transitional regime, such as we have described it, may represent a long-term situation, one possible political adaptation to the enormous social and political tensions inherent in a dependent capitalist society. Instead of the breakdowns and the bloodshed of constant military coups, the transitional regime proposes an alternative. It would be a regime in a constant state of institutional flux, in which military threats are preempted by a hardening of the regime, in which popular threats are preempted by its relaxation, and in which contradictory demands of all kinds can confidently wait their turn in the sun. Justifying it all is the mentality of transition, according to which true democracy is just around the corner.

The very ambiguity of this system has become its strength. As it became increasingly clear that a peaceful transfer of power to a civilian president would actually take place, many Brazilians had a sense of a world of unlimited possibilities and unbounded enthusiasm. With that transfer achieved, the limitations of the political situation have come to the fore, and the intractability of the international economic order has dampened the optimism. For an increasing number of Brazilians, the complaint of the labor militant Waldemar Rossi applies as well to the present civilian presidency as to the military government, about which he commented, "You can marry whom you like, as long as it's Maria."[22]

Notes

1. Juan J. Linz, "The Future of an Authoritarian Situation or the Institutional-ization of an Authoritarian Regime: The Case of Brazil," in *Authoritarian Brazil: Origins, Policies, and Future*, ed. Alfred Stepan (New Haven, Conn., and London: Yale University Press, 1973).

2. For a sample of the extensive literature on the *abertura*, see Bolivar Lamounier and José Eduardo Faria, *O Futuro da Abertura: Um Debate* (São Paulo: Cortez Editora, 1981); Bernardo Sorj and Maria Herminia T. de Almeida, eds., *Sociedade e Política no Brasil Pós-64* (São Paulo, Editora Brasiliense, 1983); Margaret J. Sarles, "Maintaining Political Control Through Parties: The Brazilian Stategy," *Comparative Politics* 15 (1982), 41–72; Scott Mainwaring and Eduardo J. Viola, "Transitions to Democracy: Brazil and Argentina in the 1980s," *Journal of International Affairs* 38 (1985), 193–219; and Fernando Henrique Cardoso, "Os Impasses do Regime Autoritário: O Caso Brasileiro," *Estudos CEBRAP* 26 (1980), 170–94.

3. This revealing speech is brilliantly analyzed in Sebastião C. Velasco e Cruz and Carlos Estevam Martins, "De Castello a Figueiredo: Uma incursão na pré-história da abertura," in Sorj and T. de Almeida, *Sociedade e Política*, pp. 45–47.

4. Ibid.; Ronald Schneider, *The Political System of Brazil: Emergence of a "Modernizing Authoritarian" Regime, 1966–1970* (New York: Columbia University Press, 1971).

5. Alfred Stepan, *The Military in Politics—Changing Patterns in Brazil* (Princeton, N.J.: Princeton University Press, 1971), chs. 4 and 5.

6. Margaret Sarles Jenks, "Political Parties in Authoritarian Brazil," Ph.D. diss., Duke University, 1979.

7. Thomas E. Skidmore, *Politics in Brazil, 1930–1964: An Experiment in Democracy* (Oxford: Oxford University Press, 1967), pp. 77, 146–49, 189–90.

8. Ibid., pp. 57–60. Even among those intellectuals whose hostility to the oligarchical electoral politics of the Old Republic led them to elaborate an authoritarian vision, we find striking evidence of respect for liberal democracy. See Jarbas Medeiros, "Introdução ao estudo do pensamento político autoritário brasileiro, 1914/1945," *Revista de Ciência Política* 17 (2), 1974.

9. Velasco e Cruz and Martins, "De Castello a Figueiredo," p. 16ff.

10. As a case in point, we offer the recollections of Marshal Cordeiro de Farias. An arch-conspirator against Goulart, Cordeiro had been involved in almost every politically significant action of the military over half a century from the *tenantismo* of the 1920s, through the construction of the authoritarian order under Vargas, the ouster of Vargas, and the founding of the Escola Superior de Guerra. In extensive interviews shortly before his death, he expressed himself with great lucidity on many aspects of Brazilian politics, economic development, and culture. Yet he has little to say on the subject of democracy—the question of democratic institutions does not

seem to have engaged this highly intelligent general's interest. See Aspásia Camargo and Walder de Goes, *Meio século de combate: Diálogo com Cordeiro de Farias* (Rio de Janeiro: Editora Nova Fronteira, 1981).

11. See Francisco Weffort's important book, *O populismo na política brasileira* (Rio de Janeiro: Paz e Terra, 1978).

12. On the sense of solidarity shared by members of ARENA and MDB, see the revealing interviews in Peter McDonough, *Power and Ideology in Brazil* (Princeton, N.J.: Princeton University Press, 1981).

13. The executive's difficulties with ARENA are nicely chronicled in Jenks, "Political Parties."

14. This is nowhere better discussed than in Velasco e Cruz and Martin's "De Castello a Figueiredo," p. 48ff.

15. The seminal work is Guillermo O'Donnell's *Modernization and Bureaucratic-Authoritarianism: Studies in South American Politics* (Berkeley: Institute of International Studies, University of California, 1973). For debates on the topic, see, for instance *The New Authoritarianism in Latin America*, ed. David Collier (Princeton, N.J.: Princeton University Press, 1979).

16. See, for instance, Guillermo O'Donnell, *1966–1973, El Estado burocrático-autoritário: Triunfos, derrotas y crisis* (Buenos Aires: Editorial de Belgrano, 1982).

17. In actual practice, Brazil's recent industrial development, particularly in the 1970s, has absorbed far more labor than the standard view of recent capital intensive peripheral industrialization suggests. See Vilmar Faria, "Desenvolvimento, urbanização e mudanças na estrutura do emprêgo: A Experiência Brasileira dos ultimos trinta anos," in Sorj and T. de Almeida, *Sociedade e Política*, pp. 118–63.

18. *Latin American Reports*, April 11, 1983, p. 14; May 25, 1983, pp. 23–25: August 10, 1983, pp. 2–4.

19. Skidmore, *Politics in Brazil*, p. 248ff.

20. *Latin American Reports*, November 14, 1979, p. 12ff.; January 21, 1981, p. 34ff.; August 5, 1983, p. 33ff.; 'January 11, 1984, p. 65ff.

21. Ibid., December 1, 1983, p. 48ff.

22. Waldemar Rossi, *Brazil: State and Struggle* (London: Latin American Bureau, 1982), p. 97.

Silvia T. Borzutzky

4 The Pinochet Regime: Crisis and Consolidation

This chapter does not deal with a process of redemocratization, but with a process of consolidation of a highly personalistic regime. Why is Chile, in spite of its democratic past, still living under a nondemocratic regime? Why is Chile not undergoing the kind of transition that its South American neighbors are experiencing? What are the prospects for redemocratization? To answer these questions, we must understand the goals of the regime and the reasons for its recent failures.

The nature of the Chilean regime of General Augusto Pinochet is clearly different from that of the bureaucratic-authoritarian regimes of the Southern Cone and, consequently, the process of return to democracy will have to be different. The consolidation of General Pinochet's power, beginning in 1978 and continuing until 1984, was accomplished through the use of politics—such as the 1978 plebiscite and the 1980 constitution—economics, and repression. Consolidation has been achieved, however, at the cost of the atomization of society and the establishment of an environment in which the political opposition is not viable. Moreover, the country is now in a state of profound crisis. The economic crisis is at least as severe as that of 1973, when the regime took power; politically, the society is deeply divided, and the regime has become increasingly more isolated from other sectors of the society. General Pinochet has responded by increasing repression, establishing strict press censorship, and banning all political activities.

Neither the economic crisis nor the deep socioeconomic and political divisions augur well for a return to democracy.

The Objectives of the 1973 Coup

The coup of September 11, 1973, had a clear set of political and economic goals, and both the state and the society would be transformed to achieve them. In the political arena, the military government faced two fundamental tasks: dismantling the previous political system and reorganizing the society along new lines. The representative nature of the political parties, the intertwining of unions and parties, and the mobilization of the electorate formed a tightly interconnected political structure that required massive repression and violence to dismember. The military government, following the principles of the National Security Doctrine (which gave the military the role of protecting the nation from its internal enemies), pursued a violent campaign against all those who in any way represented the deposed order.

During the first three years of military rule, the democratic system that had taken years to build was completely destroyed. As a result, not only was the pluralist political regime eliminated—as well as those organizations that formed the core of that regime—but also the role and functions of the state were changed. In the new regime, power was concentrated in the Junta de Gobierno, which was comprised of the commander in chief of the army, navy, and air force and by the director general of the police.

Initially, the government legitimized its actions on the basis of the state of internal war and the need to eliminate the Marxist threat. But, having achieved its short-term goal, the government needed to build a more permanent legitimacy based on the achievement of long-range goals. These goals were specified as the elimination of politics and the construction of a new social order led by a subsidiary state and market forces. The elimination of politics and politicians was to involve the permanent replacement of politicians, as the conductors of the nation's businesses, by technocrats who, according to government rhetoric, were not to act in response to narrow partisan or class interests but as *técnicos*, applying scientific knowledge in the best interests of the entire nation. Pinochet argued that before his advent all political ideologies had been tried and had all failed because of the ineptitude of the politicians and the narrowness of their interests.

The enactment of the Constitutional Acts of 1976 was the first step in institutionalizing the regime. And while the acts succeeded in giving constitutional validity to the junta, they did not solve the problem of the formulation of a new "apolitical" political system. During the following year, the regime began to move toward the formulation and implementation of this system. It eliminated those political parties that had been only temporarily suspended and imposed new legal restrictions on the already battered freedom of the press. These measures were aimed principally at the Christian Democratic party but involved the elimination of all existing political parties, including a transfer of their properties to the state. The new press restrictions included a ban on printing and distributing new publications and importing foreign publications without prior authorization of the military.[1]

These measures were followed by Pinochet's Chacarillas Speech in July 1977, where he announced a long-term flexible timetable for a return to democracy around 1990. Until then, the essence of political power was to remain in the hands of the armed forces.[2] However, Pinochet failed to make clear how the "protected democracy" he was proposing to the Chilean people would operate, particularly after 1985, when two-thirds of the legislature was to be elected by popular vote. He did make clear, however, that the old political parties would have no role in the process. As Garretón argues, this plan appears to have been inspired mainly by the need to improve the regime's tainted image with the U.S. government and in other international quarters and by the necessity of reordering the internal debate within the administration.[3]

According to this plan, the long return to civilian rule was to be achieved in three stages. First was the "recuperation" period that would last until 1980, during which the country would continue to be ruled according to Pinochet's will. The second stage was to begin in 1981 with the appointment of a legislative chamber formed by prominent citizens and representatives of regional organizations named by General Pinochet. Throughout this period, executive power would remain in the hands of the president, and the junta would retain veto power over any proposal that it considered threatening to national security. After four or five years, if all was going well, two-thirds of the Chamber would be elected and one-third would continue to be nominated by the president.[4] The final stage would begin in 1991, with the election of a president.

At the same time, and also because of the need to improve its external image, the government dissolved the infamous DINA (the

National Directorate of Intelligence) and replaced it with a new body, the Central Nacional de Informaciones (CNI), charged with the same functions.

This first attempt at establishing a timetable for the return to democracy was instrumental in improving the regime's international image, and secured General Pinochet's participation in the ceremonies that followed the signing of the Panama Canal Treaties in Washington. But on the home front, the situation did not improve. In fact, students, labor organizations, and political leaders began to speak out against the plan, with the excluded Christian Democrats leading the attack.

In December 1977, in view of the increasing labor unrest and the continuing internal debate, Pinochet reacted by taking tough measures against union leaders and increasing his own power. A first step toward the institutionalization of his personal leadership was the plebiscite of January 1978. Invoking external aggression and conspiracy against the fatherland, Pinochet, in spite of the opposition of the other members of the junta, called upon the people of Chile to show their support for his administration.[5] the result of the referendum was used by General Pinochet as a new source of legitimacy and as the basis for Pinochet's transformation into the undisputed leader. The plebiscite allowed General Pinochet to root his personal leadership in "the will of the people," to eliminate the other members of the junta, and to increase his control over the military, as was demonstrated on July 24, 1978, when Pinochet removed General Leigh from both the junta and from the air force.

Leigh's dismissal, followed by the removal of the eighteen highest-ranking air force generals who supported Leigh's position regarding a prompt return to a more institutionalized political system, consolidated Pinochet's power for the years to come. In fact, Leigh's declarations to the Italian newspaper *Il Corriere della Sera*, which ostensibly provoked his downfall, did not contain anything that Leigh had not previously argued. However, according to one observer, on this occasion Leigh appeared to have the full support of the air force high command.[6] Nevertheless, Pinochet proved strong enough to eliminate the intragovernmental opposition. The replacement of Leigh by General Fernando Matthei, a close associate of Pinochet, allowed the president to effectively eliminate the junta from the governmental process.

From the end of 1978 until the end of 1979, the political debate within the government focused upon the constitutional process and specifically upon the report of the Constitutional Commission formed by the government. Given the ideological affinity between the members of the commission (hand-picked by Pinochet) and the government, debate did not center upon the nature of the political regime—which continued to be authoritarian, military, and personalistic—but upon the need to institutionalize the personalistic leadership and to set guidelines for its future transformation—basically the same two issues that the government had been trying to resolve since 1976.[7] Faced with the culmination of the constitutional process he himself had set in motion, with a polarization of the internal debate, with the growing decomposition of his security apparatus, and with his personal reluctance to institutionalize the regime, Pinochet, assisted only by his personal advisors, secretly elaborated a new constitution bill. Furthermore, Pinochet effectively eliminated the possibility of any thorough analysis or debate of the bill by simultaneously announcing it to the public and setting the date for a plebiscite in which the population would approve or reject the little-known constitution.

The 1980 constitution should be analyzed from two different dimensions: as part of the ongoing process of legitimization of the Pinochet government and as the establishment of a new political model. Regarding the first, the plebiscite and the constitution constituted a new source of legitimacy for the regime, adding to the endorsement received in the 1978 plebiscite. In relation to the second, the constitution represented a compromise between the more moderate elements within the government (who argued for a clear limitation of the military regime's life and for the creation of political institutions that would replace them) and the hard-liners who opposed these moves.

The problem was solved through the establishment of two different political models, to be applied in two different periods: the transitional model, to be applied between 1980 and 1989 but that could be extended until 1997; and the authoritarian model, that would follow the transitional one.

The transitional period, a concession to the hard-liners, involved the institutionalization of the regime, maintaining and even increasing the personalist, repressive nature of the present government. In the words of Garretón: "It is a military regime in which there are no mechanisms of representation; in which "political spaces" are not created; in which the decentralizing mechanisms . . . reinforce a strictly vertical chain of command; in which there are no systems to channel demands."[8]

The second model, which the constitution calls "democratic," but which rather resembles an authoritarian regime, has a very strong executive branch, a congress deprived of its most basic functions, a judiciary dependent on the executive for its nomination and deprived of its role during the state of siege, and an armed forces empowered to supervise the political system.[9] Moreover, the constitution rejects even the most basic notions of ideological pluralism and leaves to the constitutional court, a body dependent on the president, the determination of future political rights, the functions of the political parties, and the nature of the other intermediate groups to be created in the second period.

Individual rights are dependent upon Article 24 (transitional). This article establishes that, during the period 1981–1989, the president can order arrests, restrict the freedom of the press and information, restrict the right to hold meetings, prohibit people from entering the country, and send people into exile for alleged threats to the peace of the nation or acts against the public order. Since the adoption of the constitution, the uninterrupted use of this prerogative on the part of Pinochet has resulted in continuous violations of basic civil and political liberties.[10]

The impact of the 1980 constitution went beyond the institutionalization of the existing political reality: it gave constitutional backing and structure to the neoliberal economic model through (1) the reduction of the state's economic functions, (2) the enhancement of individual economic rights, and (3) the integration of the neoliberal economic model as an intrinsic part of the constitutional makeup of the country. As a result, the entire constitution bears the imprint of the neoliberal economists, and especially the influence of the former minister of finance, Sergio de Castro. As General Pinochet and de Castro have repeatedly argued, the economic strategy and the political system "are indivisible parts of the social fabric, and both of them have served as the source that inspire the new institutionality."[11] Nowhere does the juncture of the political and economic systems become clearer than in the establishment of an eight-year transitional period, a duration that serves the needs of both.

length of the transitional period was determined by economic considerations. Thus, according to the projections of de Castro, by 1989, after ten years of high rates of economic growth, the shape and nature of the Chilean economy would be totally transformed. In fact, the market economy would not only have made every Chilean a property owner, but also would have eliminated poverty from the face of Chile. This, in turn, would eliminate forever the threat of Marxism. In the words of de Castro, "This, and none other, is the motive behind the eight-year transitional period."[12] Or, as the former minister of labor, José Piñera, argued, "By 1990 . . . Chile will be a developed country. In other words, by the end of the president's period, the military government and the Chilean people will have transformed a destroyed Chile into a developed country."[13]

Therefore, according to the forecasts of the policymakers, by 1990 the Chilean population would have acquired such a large stake in the economic system that it would naturally reject the calls of the Marxist parties—eliminating forever the Marxist threat—and achieving, simultaneously, economic and political stability, maturity, and development.

The Economic Model

The anti-Marxist conviction of the leaders of Chilean armed forces did not provide any guidelines for the reconstruction of the battered Chilean economy,[14] and, as a result, they had to rely on the neoliberal model presented to them by a group of well-known Chilean economists trained in the Catholic University of Chile and the University of Chicago.

The process of economic reorganization was initiated in 1974 when the government announced that the import substitution model and Keynesian fiscal policies would be replaced by those designed by the monetarist school of Chicago. The monetarists' policies would bring inflation, the endemic problem of the Chilean economy, under control; produce high rates of economic growth; and change the nature of Chile's relationship to the international economic system. The new policies converged at the state level, which was key to the entire policy.

The state's new role, based on the principle of subsidiarity of the state, argued that the state should perform only those activities that could not be performed by the private sector—either because they were related to the security of the country or because they involved an effort beyond the capability of the private entrepreneur. In practice, the application of this principle involved a drastic reorientation of the role of the state, particularly in investment, regulation, and ownership of commercial or industrial enterprises (the government returned to the private sector 455 of the 479 public enterprises). This process was followed by a large reduction in the social and economic sectors of the bureaucracy, which decreased 5 percent per year between 1974 and 1979.[15]

The so-called Chicago Boys followed a very orthodox set of monetary policies, based on a strict control of the money supply, which was deemed essential both to eliminating inflation and to generating rapid economic growth. Furthermore, both controlling inflation and the development model were based on the eradication of the protectionist system created in the 1930s.

This policy of economic *apertura* (opening the economy to the external market) had a trade and financial dimension. In its trade aspect, *apertura* involved the gradual elimination of tariffs. In its financial aspect, its goal was the creation of a large, solid, capital market formed mainly with international capital. The absence of a capital market was a major deficiency of the Chilean economy. In the view of the neoliberal economists, its development was essential to revitalize production structure and to guarantee consumers access to a large number of goods and services, while correcting distortions in the price structure.[16] Furthermore, the creation of a strong capital market and the decontrol of interest rates were to increase savings and allow a better allocation of those savings, promoting a financial deepening of the economy.

A final emphasis of the economic program was the universality of neoliberal policies. In contrast to previous attempts that favored either specific sectors of the economy or a given social class, neoliberal theorists argued that the program would benefit the whole society. Thus, the constrained and limited economic system that had resulted from state involvement in the past would be replaced by an open, universal system guided by the market—a neutral agent capable of reaching the entire nation.

The Rise and Decline of the Chicago Boys

By mid-1979, a new economic scenario had been constructed in Chile. While the monetarist economists and the executive insisted on presenting a rosy picture of the Chilean economy, a more impartial view saw some successes and many problems. On the positive side was the elimination of the fiscal deficit and the reduction of the inflation rate to about 30 percent per year. On the negative side was very high unemployment, a very large foreign debt, and mixed rates of economic growth (on the average only 1 percent per year).[17] Furthermore, a closer analysis indicated that the only sector experiencing growth was the service sector—already overdeveloped—while the industrial sector declined as a result of the *política de apertura*.

Monetarist policies also restructured the pattern of ownership and control within the private sector. In the privatization process that followed the coup, a few economic conglomerates or "economic groups," as they are called in Chile, were formed. In a short time, they acquired control of a large proportion of the banking and industrial sectors. By 1978, the five largest groups controlled the 250 largest economic enterprises in the country.[18]

The Chicago Boys, now at the peak of their power, launched what Minister Piñera called the "silent revolution," or the drive to adapt the society to the needs of the market economy. This revolution was carried out through the seven modernization laws that changed the structure of labor relations and labor organizations; the health, social security, and educational systems, and the organization of the professional associations. These laws not only replaced the old statist-oriented system with the new market approaches, but also destroyed important foci of opposition (such as the remnants of the labor organizations and the *colegios profesionales*). Moreover, they would change the value and belief systems of future generations.

Of all the existing problems, only one captured the attention of government economists: the inflation rate. Rising by 30 percent per year, the rate of inflation was unacceptable to the dogmatic monetarists. In fact, during the next three years, government economists fought an unremitting battle against inflation. And although they were successful in reducing inflation, by 1982 they also produced the most severe economic depression in the country's history and their own political downfall.

Given the impact of these monetarist policies both on the consolidation of General Pinochet's power and the crisis that followed, it is important to analyze these anti-inflationary measures.[19] Two interrelated issues deserve attention: the government economists' decision to rely on automatic adjustments to bring down the price of the overvalued peso, and the role played by foreign loans.

According to monetarist principles, domestic inflation can be brought into line with international inflation levels simply by fixing the exchange rate. During the initial stage, this policy should generate a trade deficit through the overvaluation of the currency and a rise in domestic interest rates, which would attract foreign capital. Theoretically, this stage should be brief, and the infusion of foreign capital should not be sufficient to cancel the negative effects of the deficit; in the second stage, inflation should fall below the world rate, compensating for the competitiveness lost during the period of overvaluation.[20] Thus, when the third stage is reached, the recession will be overcome, and the inflation rate will equal that of the nation's trading partners.

In practice, the consequences of the policy of pegging the peso to the dollar, implemented in 1979, were actually very different. The overvalued currency allowed the financial enterprises to borrow massively abroad, bringing in a large amount of foreign capital, which undermined the process of automatic adjustment. This capital increased liquidity and domestic demand. Furthermore, since domestic interest rates were very high, a large differential between domestic and external rates was created.[21] This increased the incentive to borrow abroad, locking the economy into a pseudo–growth spiral that encouraged consumption and imports and fueled financial speculation. During this period, inflation remained high and, by the end of 1982, the peso was overvalued by about 52 percent.[22] At the same time, the external debt increased at an average of 36 percent per year, rising from 5.9 billion in 1978 to 12.5 billion at the beginning of 1982 and to 18 billion in 1984. At the end of 1982, the foreign debt amounted to 80 percent of GNP as compared to 8.2 percent in 1970. The bulk of these loans (65–70 percent) were short- and medium-term credits to the private sector.[23] Nonetheless, the overvalued currency was generating high rates of economic growth, which Pinochet used to consolidate his personal power.

The combination of high interest rates and an overvalued currency produced catastrophic consequences in the domestic economy. In the agricultural sector, these two economic problems increased the price of exports, limiting their capacity to compete in an already depressed international market. Thus, the export-led subsector—the only growing agricultural subsector—began to decline rapidly. The industrial sector, which after a profound slump in 1975 was just beginning to return to 1973 levels, was also affected. In this sector, the new decline in growth was the result of high interest rates and the import boom. The full impact was felt in 1982, when the sector shrank by 21.6 percent.[24]

In early 1981, the government economists assessed the situation and again concluded that inflation was the distorting factor. This belief prompted them to reduce the money supply by 10 percent in the first quarter of 1981 and by 5 percent in the second quarter.[25] Given the depressed nature of the economy to which these measures were applied, they did not produce the mild recession (enfriamiento de la economía—cooling down of the economy) expected by the Chilean economists, but the deepest depression in the country's history.

The first signs of the economic crisis were manifested in May 1981 when CRAV (a monopoly producer of sugar owned by the largest economic group) went bankrupt. In the following months, many businesses were unable to meet their financial obligations. This brought the entire financial system to the verge of collapse and forced the government to assume the management of eight financial institutions.

The dogmatism of the Chicago Boys did not allow them to recognize either the depth of the crisis or the need to change the model. Confidence in the policies was undoubtedly boosted by Milton Friedman's declaration in mid-1981 that "the country [Chile] is in the midst of an economic boom. What you observe there is comparable to the economic miracle experienced by Germany in the postwar years."[26] The Chilean monetarists, in turn, continued to argue that the economy would take care of its own problems, that "the best thing the government can do is nothing." As Minister de Castro, the dean of the Chilean monetarists, said, "Profits and losses are only important to the individual entrepreneur."[27]

In the meantime, the combined effects of the massive foreign borrowing and the high interest rates had deepened the process of concentration of economic power in the hands of a few financial enterprises. By mid-1981, the banks owned by the two largest groups had issued 40 percent of total bank credit. In turn, more than 40 percent of their loan portfolio was concentrated in their top thirty clients.[28] By September, overdue repayments to these banks were growing rapidly, creating somber economic forecasts, and affecting the inflow of foreign currency. It was only a small step from this situation to the largest financial crisis that the country had ever experienced. Particularly troublesome was the situation of the largest private bank, the Banco de Chile (owned by the Vial group), which held a debt of US$2 billion.

The crisis that had begun in May with the bankruptcy of CRAV was followed by the decision of the government in November to take over the administration of the Banco Español, the second largest bank. The government also "intervened" (*intervinió*) by taking control of the administration of three smaller banks, which accounted for 22 percent of lending by private-sector banks and three financial enterprises (savings and loans), which accounted for 49.9 percent of all the loans of these enterprises. At the end of 1982, 34.3 percent of the financial sector was in the hands of the government.[29]

·Regardless of the political interpretation of these measures, they represented the first major departure from the orthodox approach, and marked the beginning of the end for the economic model and for the political role of its proponents. The next year and half saw the deepening of the crisis and the rather desperate attempts on the part of the Chicago Boys to treat the seriously ill economy with placebos.

By the end of 1982, the economy was in a shambles. The GNP fell 14.5 percent, private consumption decreased by 16.3 percent, and investment was reduced by 36.8 percent. Hardest hit by the recession were the industrial sector (which fell 21.6 percent) and construction (which decreased by 29 percent). Despite the recession, the inflation rate for 1982 was 20.7 percent.[30]

The most dramatic element in this rapidly deteriorating scenario was the unemployment rate, which had reached 30 percent by the end of 1982. Since its inception, Pinochet's administration had treated unemployment in purely monetarist terms, claiming that it was the result of rigidities in the price of labor and the high price of social security. The *plan laboral* and social security reform were designed to eliminate these problems and create a free labor market. They were, in fact, effective in reducing the price of labor, which fell 25 percent between 1974 and 1978 and another 12 percent between 1982 and 1983. By the end of 1983, real salaries were 14 percent below their 1970 level.[31]

Despite this decline in the price of labor, unemployment remained high simply because it was associated with the structural changes that had occurred in the economy—particularly the commercial opening, the reduction in the levels of investment, and the consequent reduction in the size of the industrial sector.[32]

As in the past, the government decided to assist only the financial sector. In order to prevent a total debacle, the government took control of the two largest banks in January 1983 and began to blame the now *intervenidos* economic groups for Chile's economic ills. At the same time, the government assumed full responsibility for the external debt, while guaranteeing only up to 70 percent of the deposits in the banks under the control of the government and rejecting any responsibility for money deposited in the savings and loans that were now under the control of the state.[33]

The Political Juncture of 1983

The political crisis of 1983 was a direct consequence of the failure of the Chicago model. This economic model had impinged directly on the political system, affecting its legitimacy, its relationship with society, and its future transformation. Particularly relevant was the model's long-term political role: it had been expected to generate an apolitical society in which consumption would replace political participation and a new generation of technocrats would lead the country under the protective eye of General Pinochet. In turn, Pinochet would rule this capitalist, apolitical society until 1989 or 1997.

There is no doubt that the failure of the monetarist experiment destroyed, at least temporarily, the internal cohesion of the regime and its basis of legitimacy. In order to restore both cohesion and legitimacy, General Pinochet proceeded, in August 1983, to form a new cabinet led by Sergio Onofre Jarpa. Jarpa was authorized to establish a dialogue with the illegal and vocal Democratic Alliance, one of the new political blocs. This policy, which many defined as *apertura*, allowed Pinochet to weather the crisis and to reconstitute his base of support, while not forcing him to compromise.

The Opposition

Chile's first political spring in ten years began to unfold in March 1983. This flourish of political activity was manifested in the formation of political coalitions, the establishment of a Comando Nacional de Trabajadores, and street demonstrations.

The reappearance of the old political parties is particularly interesting. These parties, which had been outlawed and deprived of their funds and any formal contact with the masses, managed to stage a rapid return to active political life under very difficult circumstances. In a study of Chilean political parties under Pinochet, Arturo Valenzuela and Julio Samuel Valenzuela argue that despite the regime's attempt to obliterate political parties, they have endured and continue to maintain their identity and autonomy regardless of the policies pursued by the state. These authors also suggest that limiting organizational and electoral activities, rather than undermining politics, freezes the positions of recognized leaders and shifts party activities to other outlets in civil society.[34] The events of 1983 proved this thesis to be correct.

The failure of the Chicago model, and Pinochet's failure to confront the many problems remaining from the experiment, enabled the opposition to question overall government performance in those areas Pinochet had defined as crucial for Chile's future. In early 1983, the Pinochet government was practically paralyzed. This paralysis was reflected in the government's inability to deal with the financial crisis, the public debt, massive unemployment, lack of investment, and increasing poverty and human misery.

Thus, beginning in March 1983, three processes began to unfold: the formation of political blocs, the revitalization of trade unions, and a popular protest movement. While these three processes are intimately interconnected, it is important to analyze each independently.

The process of political organization was manifested in the formation of three political blocs: (1) the Democratic Alliance formed by a sector of the political right, the Christian Democratic and the Radical parties, and factions of the old Socialist party; (2) the Socialist Bloc formed by a number of socialist factions; and (3) the Popular Democratic Movement dominated by the Communist party and yet another socialist faction (the old Socialist party was now divided into seven or eight factions). The Democratic Alliance, the largest of the three and the only one likely to have an impact on the armed forces, assumed leadership in the opposition movement. High on its agenda was to initiate a movement toward democracy. This was consistently rejected by Pinochet in the talks between the government and the opposition that took place in the second half of 1983. The Alliance proposed the establishment of a provisional government, formed by representatives of all political factions, which would reestablish a constitutional democracy in the next eighteen months. In the interim, the Alliance asked for a law that would legalize the activities of the political parties as well as the establishment of an electoral registry.

Before 1983, the union movement had been in disarray. The neoliberal labor laws and massive unemployment had limited the scope and effectiveness of the new, "apolitical" unions. Strikes were limited both by the law and by widespread unemployment. As was discussed above, the combined effect of the anti-inflationary policies, the reduction of the industrial sector, and the recessions of 1974–75 and 1982–83 had reduced real earnings to levels well below those of 1970.

From the point of view of the employed workers, their economic problems could be solved only after a total change in the direction of the economy. Given General Pinochet's identification with the economic model, this change also had to be political.[35] Under the leadership of the powerful Copper Workers' Confederation, a Comando Nacional de Trabajadores was formed. This Comando not only led the *protesta* movement, but was also instrumental in allaying the entrenched fear of political activity that was characteristic of most union leaders. Furthermore, the Comando aimed at providing an umbrella organization that would unite all anti-Pinochet forces, regardless of their political color.[36]

In the final analysis, the impact of the unions was limited by the structural conditions in which they were operating and the uncompromising posture of the government. It is important to keep in mind that national organizations were illegal because the neoliberal labor reform prohibited the formation of labor federations. This prohibition impinged upon their power and representativeness. Moreover, the economic conditions of both the employed and unemployed workers were such that their ability to withstand pressure was seriously impaired; finally, the right to strike was limited by the employer's right to hire during the strike. The government, in turn, responded to the unions' actions and demands with repression and violence. The leader of the Comando Nacional de Trabajadores, Rodolfo Seguel, and of the Coordinadora Nacional Sindical, Manuel Bustos, were imprisoned. Subsequently Bustos was forced to leave the country.

The third dimension of Chile's political awakening, the *protesta* movement, was first led by the Comando Nacional de Trabajadores and later on by the Democratic Alliance, with the support from other political blocs. The movement began in March 1983 and demonstrations were mounted on a monthly basis through March 1984. After a five-month interruption, the movement was renewed in September 1984 and continued until November.

In Santiago, there were two simultaneous but different *protesta* movements. The original movement was a pacifist movement, organized around the middle class and supported by syndical and religious organizations. The other movement was organized by the Democratic Popular Movement, led by the Communist party, and took place in the slums that encircle Santiago. The government responded to each of these movements with different forms of repression.

As stated above, the Pinochet regime had founded its legitimacy on two elements: the success of the economic model, and the maintenance of internal order. The collapse of the first element in 1982 resulted in the destruction of the second element. After a period of shock and surprise, the regime began to react to socioeconomic disintegration by constructing a new political alliance and by a combination of vague promises and repression to avert a crisis.

What was the real impact of the protest? Analysts and politicians were quick to attribute all sorts of consequences to the protest movement. In fact, it was argued that changes in the cabinet in mid-1983 and in early 1984 (and the few policy changes that followed) were due to the movement, and it could force Pinochet to compromise and speed up the return to democracy, and that it could also break the close alliance between Pinochet and the armed forces.

The *protesta* movement fell short of these goals. However, it did manage to break the political immobility that had characterized Chile for the past ten years, forcing Pinochet to abandon the fiction of an apolitical society and to react to the massive demonstrations both politically and militarily. In August 1983, he named a new cabinet that incorporated the nondemocratic sector of the Chilean right and, at the same time, he began to use massive military force to contain the *protestas.* A major political change was the appointment of Sergio Onofre Jarpa, a former member of the National Socialist Movement of Chile—the local Nazi party—and a former senator of the right-wing National party as head of the cabinet. Despite Jarpa's opposition, the ministries of finance and economy remained in the hands of the Chicago Boys.

Political analysts, particularly in the United States, interpreted Pinochet's decision to restructure the cabinet and to form a new political alliance as the beginning of a process of *apertura*. But neither Pinochet nor Jarpa ever declared that the government was ready to compromise with the opposition. The new cabinet's debut took place while the opposition was launching its fourth national day of protest. Jarpa's response was ominous: the deployment of 18,000 troops in Santiago, whose actions left a toll of at least thirty dead.[37] Simultaneously, he declared that the street demonstrations of the opposition should be followed by street marches of government supporters.

As mentioned above, the Democratic Alliance (AD), the most moderate of the opposition groups, had two sets of political goals. In the short term, they demanded from the government legal recognition of political parties and the return of some political exiles. The long-term agenda dealt with the return to democracy.

Under the auspices of Monsignor Juan Francisco Fresno, the outspoken archbishop of Santiago, Jarpa met officially with AD leaders three times to discuss the AD's political agenda. The conversations came to an end in October 1983 with the AD leaders venting their frustration over Pinochet's refusal to change the constitutional timetable, to recognize political parties and to let former politicians return to the country.[38] Moreover, throughout this period, Pinochet adamantly declared that he would stay in power until at least 1989 and that the planned democracy was going to be very different from the one that existed prior to 1970.[39]

A new antiterrorist law, enacted in 1984, was a step in the consolidation of a totalitarian political system. According to this law, terrorism involved any actions or omissions designed to create commotion or fear in a sector of the population, or any actions or omissions that had a subversive or revolutionary intent. Currently, the law is administered not by the civilian courts but by the military courts, and the penalties for its infringement range from five years in prison to death. The law authorizes the Central Nacional de Informaciones to detain and interrogate any person suspected of violating the law.[40] The 1984 law marked the beginning of a new period of legalized repression, since almost all forms of political actions and expressions fall within its definition of terrorism. Its impact was fully demonstrated after the imposition of the state of siege.

In the meantime, Jarpa promised that the new legislation to govern party activities would be in place by mid-1984. Throughout 1984, the so-called political laws were discussed by Pinochet and the legislative commission formed by the commanders in chief of the army, the navy, and the air force. The points of contention were a number of decisions made by General Pinochet. These decisions proposed to set a minimum of 150,000–200,000 signatures for the establishment of a political party, to create regional parties, and to establish the right of the executive to call for referendums. Furthermore, Pinochet refused to speed up the return to democracy. The commanders-in-chief of the navy and the air force, on the other hand, rejected both the attempt to establish the referendum and to modify the limits set on the organization of political parties.[41] The discussions ended in early November when Pinochet dismissed the entire issue as well as the so-called process of political opening.[42]

A few days thereafter, Minister Jarpa presided over one of the harshest repressive assaults since the opposition's protest movement started. On November 6, the state of siege was reimposed, along with a strict curfew in many cities. The crisis began on November 3 when Jarpa, invoking meetings in Rome between Chilean bishops and opposition leaders, claimed that collusion between the church and the Communists had rendered dialogue impossible. This was followed by the resignation of the cabinet and the decision of the government to ban the return to Chile of Reverend Ignacio Gutierrez, the director of the Vicariate of Solidarity (the church's human rights office) and an outspoken critic of the government. The decrees imposing the state of siege followed.[43] The police took over the offices of the Popular Democratic Front and the Socialist Bloc and arrested some of their leaders. In the following weeks, the police and military forces began to systematically raid shantytowns and poor neighborhoods. As a result, over 24,000 people were detained between November 1984 and January 1985,[44] and thousands were sent to internal exile because of violations of the antiterrorist law. Simultaneously, new press restrictions were established that prohibited the publication or broadcasting of any information of acts defined as terrorist, as well as any information that included any political content or impact, except for the official statements of the government.[45]

The government justified the imposition of the state of siege and other repressive measures, arguing that they were designed "to put an end to the criminal increase in terrorism" and in order to save democracy.[46] But, in fact, the decrees of November 5–7 were doing more than that: they were restructuring the position of the government and its relations with civil society.

It is clear that since early 1983, the government was besieged by growing opposition and its own lack of legitimacy. The cabinet change of mid-1983, an attempt to rebuild the internal coalition, and the softening of the regime with regard to political activities had not contained the opposition but, to the contrary, were eroding the government's already weakened base of support among the upper middle class. Of even greater significance was that the *protestas* and the political discussion were bringing the armed forces into the ongoing political processes.

The reinsertion of the armed forces was both political and military. From a political perspective, the commanders in chief had been asked to vote on the political laws. Instead of accepting Pinochet's proposal, the generals expressed their own dissenting views regarding these laws and Pinochet's refusal to return to democracy. Particularly important were the declarations of the air force's commander in chief General Fernando Matthei, one of Pinochet's closest allies. In October 1984, Matthei argued that "the transition should be completed before 1989 . . . and that the protests by themselves are legitimate."[47]

From another perspective, Pinochet had been forced to call on the military to contain the protests which, because of their massive and violent nature, could not be controlled by the police alone. This continuous military action was perceived as a threat to the military institutions. As General Matthei argued, "If the transition toward democracy is not initiated promptly, we shall ruin the armed forces in a way no Marxist infiltration could do."[48] It was publicly known that Matthei's views were supported by the commander in chief of the navy. Therefore, the political debate and the growing violence were threatening both the unity of the military institutions and their support for the regime.

On the other hand, terrorism was eroding the little support that Pinochet enjoyed among sectors of the middle and upper middle class. Repeatedly, Pinochet had claimed that he alone was capable of guaranteeing peace and order—indispensable conditions for Chile's prosperity and development. Since the beginning of 1983, a new terrorist movement, the Frente Patriótico Manuel Rodríguez, had been able to carry out a variety of terrorist activities throughout Santiago, including planting a small bomb in front of the presidential palace and attacks on water and electrical supplies. These actions, while not serious enough to threaten the stability of the regime, cast doubt in the minds of many Chileans over Pinochet's power and his ability to continue governing the country.

In conclusion, the reimposition of the state of siege, the suppression of political activities, strict press censorship, and the ensuing repression made perfect political sense for Pinochet. While these measures did not involve a solution to Chile's long-term political or economic problems, they allowed the Chilean ruler to weather the most serious crisis he has had to confront since he took office.

Conclusions: The Nature of the Regime and the Prospects for Democracy

As has been argued, the Pinochet regime is different from bureaucratic-authoritarian regimes in at least two respects: the lack of an institutionalized role for the army, and the nature of the relations between state and society. The Chilean regime is not a bureaucratic-authoritarian one because the army, as an institution, has played little or no role in politics since the coup. Since 1979, political power has been concentrated in the hands of General Pinochet. The institutionalization of his personal role, achieved both through the referendum and the constitution, has relegated the former junta to a legislative power with limited authority.

There is also a profound difference in the structure of relations between state and society. The Pinochet regime, unlike its Brazilian counterpart, did not approach the task of restructuring state/society relations from a point of institutional continuity, but rather based its policies on a total and absolute rejection of the past. Consequently, the regime committed itself to the destruction of all political organizations and the atomization of society.

The neoliberal economic model provided the ideological basis for the transformation of the economic role of the state, for the enactment of laws geared to disaggregate civil society, and for the foundation of Pinochet's legitimacy. Moreover, the model was expected to generate a powerful process of economic development, transforming Chile into a capitalistic society and eliminating Marxism forever. In the short run, the institutional framework created by the 1980 constitution and the "silent revolution" were designed to eliminate political parties, labor unions, professional associations, and other institutions of the past—creating a society ruled by *técnicos* who would act under the vigilant eye of General Pinochet. This model would allow the government to keep coercion at a low level. This would, in turn, improve the regime's tainted international image.

The collapse of the economy in 1982 destroyed this framework and forced the government to shift gears. The incorporation of the non-democratic political right wing into the regime in 1983 only made matters worse. It forced the regime onto the defensive, and threatened its existence by introducing devisive political issues into the agenda of the armed forces' leaders. Both issues began to impinge on the very existence of the regime. Pinochet reacted by reestablishing the state of siege and closing off political discussion.

Prospects for democratization, by and large, depend upon the nature of the regime and its relations with civil society. In the case of Chile, neither the political system created by Pinochet nor Pinochet's views will facilitate that transition. Regarding the system itself, what Pinochet has established in Chile is an amorphous political order with neopatrimonial characteristics. What is most striking about the Chilean political system is the concentration of power in the hands of Pinochet and a few trusted advisors, and the unrelenting use of repression to maintain control of the state and achieve the regime's goals. The increase in the power of the state was followed by the atomization and political disaggregation of civil society, which only enhanced General Pinochet's power.

The other chapters in this volume stress the nature and characteristics of the transitional regimes that have followed bureaucratic-authoritarian governments. In most cases, a decision has been made by the military to leave office and to transfer power to civilians. In Chile, on the other hand, the political spring of 1983–1984 has clearly shown that the Pinochet government is unlikely to follow that pattern. Furthermore, the events of 1984 also indicated that the power of the opposition is severely limited by the structural conditions created by a political order that has successfully atomized civil society and deprived political parties and unions of the power needed to challenge the regime.

Under these circumstances, one can draw both a general and a specific conclusion. From a general perspective, it seems fair to conclude that the very nature of bureaucratic-authoritarian regimes facilitates democratization through transitional regimes leading toward *apertura*. Conversely, in the case of Chile, the principal difficulty lies in the regime itself, and its very nature makes the prospects for the reestablishment of democracy very dim.

Notes

1. *Latin American Political Report*, March 18, 1977, p. 1.
2. Ibid., July 15, 1977, pp. 213–14.
3. Manuel A. Garretón, "La institucionalización política del régimen militar chileno 1973–1982," *Mensaje* 310 (July 1982), 329–33.
4. *Latin American Political Report*, July 1, 1977, p. 213.
5. The following statement appeared in the ballot: "In the face of the international aggression unleashed against our country, I support President Pinochet in his defense of the dignity of Chile, and I reaffirm the legitimacy of the government of the Republic as sovereign head of the process of institutionalization of the country." Under the text appeared the word "yes," followed by a Chilean flag, while the word "no" was accompanied by a black box.
6. *Latin American Political Report*, July 28, 1978, p. 226.
7. Garretón, "La institutionalización política."
8. Ibid., p. 332.
9. See Articles 90–96.
10. For an analysis, see Alejandro González, "La disposición Vigésimo Cuarta transitoria," *Mensaje* 300 (July 1981), 320–24.
11. Sergio de Castro, "Exposición sobre el estado de la hacienda pública," *Banco Central de Chile* 54 (August 1981), 1728.
12. Sergio de Castro, speech, Sesión Inaugural de la 2ª Reunión Conjunta del Comité Interempresarial Chile-Japón, September 8, 1980.
13. José Piñera, speech, *El Mercurio*, November 8, 1979, p. 12 (transcript).
14. For a discussion on this issue, see Silvia Borzutzky, "Chilean Politics and Social Security Policies," Ph.D. diss., University of Pittsburgh, 1983, ch. 7.
15. Pilar Vergara, "Las transformaciones de las funciones económicas del estado en Chile bajo el régimen militar," *Colección Estudios Cieplan* 5 (July 1981), 128–33. In the decentralized administration, the reductions are estimated at 10 percent per year. See H. Cortés and L. Sjaasted, "Protección y empleo," *Cuadernos de Economía* 54–55 (August–December 1981), 384.
16. Sergio de Castro, "Discurso en la Asociación Latinoamericana de Instituciones de Desarrollo," March 29, 1977, published in *Chilean Economic Policy*, ed. J. F. Mendez (Santiago: Budget Directorate, 1979), pp. 231–43.
17. The average rate for the Frei years was 4.5 percent.
18. Fernando Dahse, *El mapa de la extrema rigueza: Los Grupos Económicos y el proceso de concentración de capitales* (Santiago: Editorial Anconcagua), 1979, p. 22.
19. A. Garcia and H. Wells, "Chile: A Laboratory for Failed Experiments in Capitalist Political Economy," *Cambridge Journal of Economics* 7 (1983), 287–304.
20. Vincent Parkin, "Economic Liberalism in Chile, 1973–82: Model for Growth and Development of a Recipe for Stagnation and Impoverishment?" *Cambridge Journal of Economics* 7 (1983), 101–24. For an official statement on the nature of the "adjustment mechanisms," see Rolf Luders, *Towards Economic Recovery in Chile: A Report on the Economy and Public Finances of Chile by the Minister of Economy and Finance, Mr. Rolf Luder* (Santiago: Imprenta Ine, 1982).
21. Interest rates averaged 38.8 percent in 1981 and 35.1 percent in 1982.
22. Parkin, "Economic Liberalism in Chile," p. 110.

23. Garcia and Wells, "Chile: A Laboratory for Failed Experiments," p. 300; data for 1984, *Latin American Weekly Report*, March 19, 1982.

24. Banco Central de Chile, *Indicadores Económicos y Sociales, 1960–1982*, Santiago, April, 1983, p. 24.

25. Garcia and Wells, "Chile: A Laboratory for Failed Experiments," p. 299.

26. Milton Friedman, interview, *Hoy*, 1–7 July 1981, p. 6.

27. Alvaro Bardón, former minister of economics, cited by Aníbal Pinto, "Razones y sinarazones de la recesión," *Mensaje* 307 (March–April) 1982.

28. *Latin American Weekly Review (LAWR)*, September 11, 1983.

29. This process is known in Spanish as *intervención*. See Jaime Ruiz-Tagle, "La intervención estatal en los Bancos," *Mensaje* 305; Alejandro Foxley, "Alternativas para la política postautoritaria," *Desarrollo Económico* 25, no. 98 (July–September 1985).

30. Banco Central de Chile, *Indicadores económicos y sociales, 1960–1982*.

31. Patricio Meller, "Análisis del problema de la elevada tasa de desocupación en Chile," *Collección Estudios Cieplan* 14 (September 1984), 38.

32. See ibid.

33. See the speech by Minister of Finance Rolf Luders cited in note 20; see *LAWR*, June 25, 1982; and Jorge Leiva L., "Las etapas de la política económica frente a la crisis: 1981–1984," *Mensaje* 329 (June 1984), 253–56.

34. Arturo Valenzuela and J. Samuel Valenzuela, *Party Oppositions Under the Chilean Authoritarian Regime*, Wilson Center Working Papers (Washington, D.C., 1984), pp. 34–36.

35. Jaime Ruiz-Tagle, "El sindicalismo en situación de crisis prolongada," *Mensaje* 318 (May 1983), 168–71, and "El sindicalismo chileno mas allá de la crisis," *Mensaje* 331 (August 1984), 367–71.

36. Ruiz-Tagle, "El sindicalismo chileno," p. 369.

37. *LAWR*, November 25, 1983.

38. Ibid., October 21, 1983.

39. See, for instance, Pinochet's speech on March 11, 1983, published in the *Washington Post*, March 12, 1983.

40. For an excellent analysis, see Fernando Guzmán, "La militarización de la Justicia: Ley antiterrorista," *Mensaje* 327 (March–April 1984), 109–11.

41. *Hoy* 379 (October 22–28, 1984), 6–8.

42. *Hoy* 380 (October 29–November 4, 1984), 7.

43. *New York Times*, November 7, 1984, p. 184.

44. Patricio Verdugo, "Aires de tormenta," *Mensaje* 336 (January–February 1985), 37.

45. Decree 1200, November 7, 1984.

46. *New York Times*, November 7, 1984, p. 4.

47. *Hoy* 376 (October 1–7, 1984), 7.

48. Ibid.

II The Andean Region

James M. Malloy and Eduardo Gamarra

---

5   The Transition to Democracy in Bolivia

Like other Latin American countries, Bolivia has been attempting to move from repressive authoritarian modes of government to more open modes of rule organized within the framework of representational democracy. This process, which began in the late 1970s, however, has not been in any real sense redemocratization. The fact is that for most of this century Bolivia has not experienced any lengthy period of open democratic rule based on widespread citizen participation. Mass involvement in politics began only with the revolution of 1952; between that time and 1978, the country experienced twelve years of de facto single-party rule within a formal democratic framework followed by some fourteen years of military-based authoritarian and/or dictatorial rule. Since 1978, national political life has been rather chaotic as the country has lurched through three abortive elections and a variety of de facto regimes based on coups and countercoups. The present civil "democratic" government was installed in October 1982, but its authority to govern has been tenuous at best. At this writing, it is far from certain that civil democratic government will be able to establish itself firmly. In short, representative democracy remains more an aspiration than a reality in Bolivia.

There are, of course, many factors involved in Bolivia's problematic political situation. In this chapter we will emphasize structural political factors that have their main roots in the revolutionary process initiated by the Movimiento Nacionalista Revolucionario (MNR) in April 1952. Although it had formal control as a single-party regime for some twelve years, the elite of the MNR was unable to structure and contain the energies that surged forth with the revolution, and in November 1964, the MNR fell to a military coup. From

93

then until 1978, the armed forces were the dominant political force in Bolivia, and they have continued to be a crucial factor in the present transitional phase.

Like their counterparts in other developing countries, the MNR elite confronted at least two central problems from the outset of the 1952 revolution. The first was to reorganize the national economy so as to achieve the rapid economic development that was one of the primary stated goals of the revolution. The second was to create political institutions capable of channeling and controlling the demands and potential support of the various social sectors mobilized by the revolution.[1]

The core leadership of the MNR took as its inspiration the great Mexican revolution and particularly the model of social control elaborated by the Mexican Partido Revolucionario Institucional (PRI). As a result, it is important to note first that the MNR elite never aimed at establishing a pluralistic competitive system in the classic liberal democratic sense. Rather, like the PRI, the MNR sought a state-centered system based on de facto single-party control operating behind a formal facade of democratic institutions.

Second, like the PRI, the core MNR elite rejected a state-socialist model of development and sought to implement instead a state-capitalist model. Under state capitalism, the market would operate within a framework of rules set by the state and the state would be a major entrepreneur. The clear implication of this arrangement was that the costs of capital accumulation would have to fall mainly on those groups mobilized by the revolution, such as workers and peasants. Hence, the trick would be, as in Mexico, to mobilize and control these sectors even as surplus capital was extracted from them.[2]

One might argue that a major achievement in the institutionalization of the Mexican revolution was to make the left politically marginal and bring the labor movement into the corporatist structure of the PRI. In Bolivia, this was not to be the case. By accepting the Central Labor Confederation's (COB) claim to a *fuero sindical*, the MNR in effect granted the COB semisovereign status over the workers of Bolivia. Then, by granting the COB cogovernment, the MNR reinforced its status as an independent quasi-governmental entity in its own right. The consequences of these moves were substantial and long-lasting.

First, the COB evolved as an independent force outside party control. From this position, the COB over the years has challenged the principle of state capitalism either from the perspective of state socialism or in the interests of populist redistribution. More profoundly, the COB not only looked upon the MNR as a separate and essentially antagonistic political force, but also increasingly perceived the state itself in this way. Hence, the COB projected the state not as a "public" entity serving the people but as expressing only the interests of those groups that in effect captured it. The MNR by extension was viewed not as a multiclass coalition to be worked through but a vehicle by which particular classes or groups could control the state.

Hence, for the COB, the state (like the MNR) was to be either captured and used, or to be resisted so as to defend not only the interests of workers but also its own semisovereign authority over workers. The COB's relations with the MNR and the national state were more like interstate negotiations rather than those of groups within a single state structure. As such, the COB, through its demand for cogovernment, refused to accept the mediation of the MNR as a political party in its relations with the state and any specific government. This development prevented the MNR from assuming the role of structuring the relationship between social groups with the state and specific governments. It also established a precedent of unmediated relations with the state that was to be followed in later years by other class, sectoral, and regional entities.

By the late 1950s, the MNR found itself in open and often violent conflict with the COB as it sought to impose state capitalism on the nation. By then, Bolivia had, in effect, moved into the cycle of alternating populist and antipopulist politics that has characterized many Latin American countries since the 1950s, most particularly, its neighbor, Peru. (See chapter 6.) In their conflict with the more populist COB, subsequent MNR governments headed by Hernán Siles and Víctor Paz Estenssoro began to rebuild the Bolivian military. State power was needed to confront the workers' militias that gave the COB its semisovereign status. Again, however, unlike Mexico's PRI, the MNR had only minimal control over the military, and the revived Bolivian armed forces emerged as an independent source of institutional power.

Aside from these external developments, the MNR also began to disintegrate internally as personalistic factions began to overwhelm organizational or party unity. Like many other Bolivian political organizations before and since, the MNR drew support from the dependent bureaucratized middle class by offering them government jobs and contracts. As party membership swelled relative to the jobs in the expanding public sector, the party began to divide into clientelistic cliques formed around various party leaders. These cliques fostered a caudillo leadership style along with factionalism. By the late 1950s, intraparty struggles were as intense as conflicts among parties, classes, and groups.

Internal party conflict showed up dramatically in the legislative assembly. Ostensibly dominated by the MNR, the assembly was in fact an arena for increasingly intense rivalries. The assembly became less a body for enacting laws and representing the interests of civil society than a mechanism for circulating patronage and factional assaults on executive power. The MNR, in turn, also lost its interest-aggregating and incorporating functions and became an instrument through which factions could exploit the largesse of the state. Neither the party nor the legislature assumed a mediating role between the state and society at large. The state became associated almost exclusively with executive power. MNR executives, in turn, increasingly governed not through the party but through their own personalistic factions. These factions were as intensely opposed by other factions within the MNR as by opposition parties.

These multiple points of conflict and contradiction came to a head in 1964, when the MNR caudillo, Víctor Paz Estenssoro, made the fateful decision to rig the party convention and succeed himself as president. A contrast with Mexico is again instructive here. In Mexico, the PRI has been able to contain factional and patronage politics in part by guaranteeing that every six years the executive will change. Hence, there is an accepted built-in mechanism for rotating jobs and patronage among party factions on a regular and predictable basis. This tradition in Mexico not only reinforces the PRI dominance but also induces the party elite to play by the formal rules of democratic succession.

When Paz was reelected in Bolivia in 1964, there was immediately a wide range of groups arrayed against him. The left and the COB resisted the state-capitalist model he was pushing, while the factions behind other MNR caudillos were frustrated by the ruling faction's grip on executive-controlled patronage.

Thus, when the military moved against Paz in 1964, they did so with the extensive support of groups and factions both within and outside the MNR. This collusion was indicative of two important components of the political system that had developed in Bolivia. First, military intervention sprang as much from the inducement of civilian political leaders as from any motives internal to the armed forces. Second, it was clear that any commitment to democratic procedures for rotating political power among Bolivia's civil elite was, to say the least, rather tenuous. When push came to shove, Bolivia's civilian leaders were as inclined to seize power by a coup as by electoral means.

The new military-based regime quickly consolidated around the charismatic figure of Air Force General René Barrientos, and the somewhat less dramatic figure of Army General Alfredo Ovando. Barrientos became president while Ovando became commander of the armed forces. Thus, while the military had acted to a large extent as an institution, it did not act out of any institutional sense of mission but in support of dominant individuals or caudillos. Of the two, General Barrientos rapidly came to dominate the tone and substance of the new regime.[3]

The Barrientos government moved to impose by force the state-capitalist system that the MNR had been pushing since the late 1950s. As a result, Bolivia at one level manifested the general trend toward antipopulist military-backed regimes that swept through Latin America in the 1960s. The costs of development were imposed mainly on organized labor. Hence, as in other cases, the government moved to forcefully exclude labor from its previous position of power within the state and in general to break the back of organized labor.

While violently repressive toward labor, Barrientos sought to legitimate his regime by calling elections and promulgating a new constitution. The flamboyant general was popular with the Bolivian peasantry and the urban middle classes, and was easily elected president in 1966. However, Barrientos was unable to use his personal charisma to construct a new set of viable democratic institutions. The constitution of 1967 combined features of classic corporatism and liberal democracy. Barrientos was able to dominate the new legislative assembly through a new political party and an electoral front that he put together for the 1966 elections. However, the new institutions were in fact secondary to the real process of governance, and the president's party was little more than a personalistic clique whose members were more interested in state patronage than in providing a political base for stable governance.

Barrientos reverted to the classic mode of rule by manipulating clientelistic networks designed to coopt the leaders of the middle class and the peasantry. This fact had a number of important implications.

First, his style of rule effectively undercut the viability of the formal political institutions he was ostensibly pushing. In fact, the political infrastructure continued to disintegrate during the Barrientos period, as the fallen MNR, as well as his own electoral front, split into an increasingly perplexing array of personalistic factions. The legislature and the courts played little or no role in governance, and the executive had de facto power.

Given the dependent nature of political institutions, the real basis of executive and state power was military force. Barrientos's real claim to rule lay not in the electoral process carried out in 1966 but in his ability to hold onto the support of the armed forces, especially that of the army. Because the Bolivian military had not seized power with any coherent sense of mission or a doctrine to determine how it would use its power, Barrientos ruled not as an expression of the military as an institution but because he could count on the personal loyalty of the officer corps. To maintain that loyalty, Barrientos used the same mode of building personalistic patron-client ties that he used to manipulate civilian leaders.

Under Barrientos, the military were infected with the same strain of personalistic clientelism found in civil political organizations. The result was similar. The institutional coherence of the armed forces was undercut, and the military began to manifest the same kind of centrifugal factionalism that was pulling apart civilian society. Moreover, Barrientos found that simply to hold onto power he had to constantly arrange and rearrange an ever more byzantine set of personal and factional ties.

The political picture was extremely complex during Barrientos's brief period of dominance (1964 to 1969). However, this was a crucial time because it inaugurated a style of rule that was to come fully into play in the 1970s and explains why it is so difficult to establish formal democratic governance in Bolivia today.

Behind a formal institutional facade, Barrientos was in effect reverting to what we might call a neopatrimonial style of rule. Patrimonialism is a subtype of traditional rule developed in the work on systems of authority and rule by the noted political sociologist Max Weber. This style not only subverted the formal institutions of governance—whether authoritarian or democratic—but also created fundamental strains between the state and civil society, especially with regard to economic development.

Following the implicit logic of the state-capitalist model, Barrientos ostensibly sought to stimulate the private sector, to encourage foreign investment, and, most important, to rationalize (that is, curtail) and modernize the administration of the government. Again, however, this formal "modern developmentalist" logic was undercut by the traditional, personalistic logic of patrimonialism. Such logic pushed for the expansion of the state as the dispenser of patronage according to clientelistic rather than rational administrative criteria. Thus, until Barrientos's death, labor was repressed and interests associated with business and industry came to the fore. Yet the state remained a crucial, if not *the* crucial factor in structuring the Bolivian economy.

Resurgence of Populism

The practical irrelevance of constitutional procedures was made clear in April 1969 when General Barrientos was killed in a helicopter crash. The military high command "permitted" the civilian vice president, Luis Adolfo Siles, to fulfill his constitutional mandate as president. However, after a brief, hapless tenure of some four months, Siles was unceremoniously dumped, and General Alfredo Ovando assumed the presidency.

This particular coup initiated a fascinating and turbulent two-year period that deserves an extensive analysis that is beyond the confines of this chapter.[4] Suffice it to note for now that during two short-lived military presidencies (under General Ovando, September 1969–October 1970, and General Juan José Torres, October 1970–August 1971), Bolivia took a surprising turn to the left toward a form of "military populism." Developments in Bolivia were clearly influenced by the military-populist regime installed in Peru in 1968.

Aside from dramatic acts, such as the nationalization of Gulf Oil's holdings, these regimes were noteworthy for lifting the repression of the labor left and for a somewhat abortive attempt to mobilize labor behind a military-based national populist project. For our purposes, the 1969–1971 period manifested rather clearly some new tendencies and some old verities in Bolivian political life.

First and foremost was the fact that the armed forces as an institution were showing severe internal strain. It quickly became clear that the military were dividing into an array of personalistic and quasi-ideological factions vying for control of the institution as a stepping-stone to control of the state. Neither of the short-lived regimes represented anything like the military services acting as an institution. Rather, both governments were clearly pivoting around strong personalities who had some degree of control over the personal and ideological factions in the armed forces. Both Ovando and Torres, however, had to constantly juggle factional coalitions among the military and fend off a variety of coup attempts. In the end, both fell to actions led by rival officers and factions. Like the political parties of civil society, the armed forces were fracturing internally and succumbing to the decomposition process affecting all of the nation's institutions.

The actions of these two governments shifted the focus of policy to the populist left but, as in Peru, did not move toward any definitive state-socialist model. Moreover, while this change alienated those sectors that had benefited from enforced state capitalism under Barrientos, it did not produce a stable base of support on the left.

Under Ovando and Torres, the COB and the leftist parties surged forward again—demonstrating that, while they had been suppressed, they were far from destroyed. Indeed, so intact were their organizations that again they took up an independent position apart from that of the regime. As a result, neither Ovando nor Torres ever came close to mobilizing and controlling the popular sectors to the left. As in the early MNR period, the COB in particular refused to enter either regime. It assumed an independent position from which it offered only highly qualified support to either government. In fact, the COB and the left became a powerful source of demands pressuring these governments in a populist direction and offering support only as demands were met.

The government's complete lack of control over the left and the COB was made clear when, under Torres, the left formed a popular assembly (*asamblea popular*). Following in part the Trotskyist logic of dual power, the *asamblea* constituted itself as a separate government representing the people. But while the labor left represented a real power bloc in Bolivia that could under some circumstances extract concessions from a weak government, it had neither the will nor the capacity to underwrite a populist regime. Nor could it provide a power base from which to reorganize the state to fit some leftist ideological project.

Torres ended up caught between the forces of the right, whom he had alienated (the private sector, portions of the middle class, and to some extent the United States), and those of the left, who made prodigious demands on him but offered little or no real support for his government. An important development occurred when groups acting in the name of the popular assembly sought to convert young officers, and particularly noncommissioned officers, to the cause of radical transformation. This perceived threat to the armed forces was sufficient to instill some degree of coherence into the officer corps. The generals came to see Torres as a weak leader who could end by taking the armed forces to the kind of destruction that almost befell them in the revolution of 1952.

From a political point of view, the Ovando/Torres period provoked a clear polarization of forces in Bolivia. To the right stood business leaders, a substantial portion of the urban middle class, and new regional interests of the eastern departments that had gained political force in the 1960s. The United States, always influential in Bolivia, backed the right. Moreover, by this point, most of the factions associated with the MNR had also swung to the right. It was clear that economically the right wanted a return to the model of state capitalism pushed originally by the main-line MNR and enforced by the military under Barrientos. In formal political terms, the right stood for a constitution molded along the lines of pluralistic representational democracy that combined liberal and corporatist concepts of representation. In practical terms, the right was more than inclined to accept a military-backed authoritarian regime that enforced its preferred economic model.

The left was arrayed in a variety of "Marxist" parties, but pivoted fundamentally around the COB and organized labor. At this point, the peasantry (over 50 percent of the population) was still an inchoate and divided political force. Sectors of the peasantry were mobilized behind both the left and the right. The left did not project any clear economic model as an alternative to that of the right: some sectors stood for vague national populist projects, while others proffered more state-socialist alternatives. This ideological or programmatic confusion clearly weakened the left. In political terms, the *asamblea popular* spoke of an alternative model of direct democracy, but in practical terms the left too was inclined to accept some mode of military-backed authoritarianism.

At that stage, any real democratic regime was out of the question simply because none of the groups in civil society perceived a democratic regime as serving its interests. Real power lay with the military. The question was, on which side would the generals come down?

That was answered in August 1971 when a military uprising began in the eastern department of Santa Cruz. Openly backed by the right, the movement quickly mobilized the bulk of the officers behind it, and, after a series of bloody clashes, Torres was ousted on August 21, 1971.

Neopatrimonialism

The uprising of August 1971 brought Army Colonel Hugo Bánzer Suárez to power. The diminutive Bánzer was to rule Bolivia with a strong hand for some seven years. Bánzer's term also coincided with a relatively long period of growth and prosperity. Hence, the Bánzer regime can be fairly seen as having had more impact on the political economy of Bolivia than any government since the early days of the revolution. Most immediately, the *Banzerato* set both the political and economic stage upon which Bolivia has played out the drama of its "return to democracy."

Unlike the uprising of 1964, which was primarily directed at a single individual (Paz) and his faction, the action of 1971 was clearly aimed at crushing the political power of the labor left and making Bolivia safer for the private sector. Fear of the left was so virulent, especially among the military, that the violence directed at the left was also unprecedented. The level of bloodshed and repression, especially in the immediate wake of the coup, was such that the left and labor were indeed cowed. These actions also left a bitter legacy of hatred that has helped to poison the atmosphere surrounding all subsequent attempts to move toward democracy.

In many respects, the Bánzer regime was part of the general trend toward "right-oriented" authoritarian rule that developed in Latin America during the 1960s and 1970s. Moreover, the regime at some levels had the characteristics of what many analysts viewed as a new type of authoritarianism dubbed the "bureaucratic-authoritarian regime."[5]

The regime was based at least in part on an alliance between a development-oriented military establishment and young technocrats drawn from civil society. Under this group of leaders, Bolivia was set firmly back on the path of state capitalism. As in Brazil and other countries, the regime reinstated the state-capitalist model by forcefully excluding the left and organized labor from political participation. Through less than gentle means, it imposed the costs of state capitalism on labor and the huge masses of traditional Indian peasants. At the same time, entrepreneurial interests from the private sector had enhanced access to the regime. They and the urban middle class were the main beneficiaries of the developments that occurred.

The resemblance to the bureaucratic-authoritarian regime type was, however, only superficial. One of the hallmarks of bureaucratic authoritarianism is that it develops as a bureaucratized regime based on institutionalized military rule with a relatively coherent sense of mission. This was hardly the case in Bolivia under Bánzer. Indeed, one of the ironies was that even as Bolivia developed economically, it regressed politically. If political development, at the least, involves the coordination of a variety of modern institutions, Bolivia in the 1970s actually decayed. In a sense, the political decomposition that began in the early 1960s was completed in the 1970s. This fact is crucial to understanding the immense difficulties Bolivia faces in trying to build a democratic system in the 1980s.

At the beginning, Bánzer sought to base his regime on three pillars of support: (1) the private sector, represented by key appointments to his cabinet, (2) the military, and (3) a seemingly grand alliance between the center-right of the MNR led by Paz and the party's oldest and most bitter rival, the Falange Socialista Boliviana (FSB). In addition to a base of military support, the coalition seemed to give the regime stable and institutionalized political links with civil society through the nation's two most important parties.

By 1974, however, Bánzer ousted both parties and openly based his tenure on military power. Behind the collapse of the coalition were some important realities. In dealing with the parties, Bánzer discovered that they were rump factions who represented little more than cliques whose primary purpose was to lay claim to public-sector jobs. Moreover, in those circumstances, party leaders acted as intermediaries in the patronage flow through which they built their own support. This support was then rendered to Bánzer only indirectly. As always, party factions not cut into the action split from the main body and backed the opposition. In sum, while they drained off resources, the parties offered little in the way of support and actually helped produce opposition.

In ousting the parties, Bánzer eliminated the middlemen and consolidated patronage into his own hands. In so doing, he also affirmed that beneath the surface the primary mode of rule in Bolivia was the manipulation of byzantine clientelistic networks. These were in turn rooted in the fundamentally dependent urban middle class that continued to look to the state as the primary source of its well-being. The power of clientelism was so strong that the Bánzer regime, despite its modern veneer, was for all practical purposes a contemporary version of the traditional mode of rule that Max Weber called patrimonialism.

Bolivia, during this period, could well be described as a "neopatrimonial" society pursuing economic growth according to a state-centered "neomercantilistic" model. The point is that both political and economic life came to pivot around the central state, not as a public institution expressing some abstract concept of nationhood, but as the particularistic extension of personalized executive power in the hands of a modern quasi-prince, Bánzer.

Neopatrimonialism brought with it traditional political dynamics and cleavages that cut through and at times subverted more modern ones: specifically, personalistic patron-client relations that often were more important, or at least as important, as contemporary bonds of group, class, and ideology. This is not to say that modern dynamics did not exist. Rather, Bolivia epitomized the "living museum" in which modern and traditional forces are blended into dense and complex patterns of cleavage and conflict. Under Bánzer, more often than not, traditional neopatrimonial dynamics provided the inner-core logic and set the tone for the entire system.

The complexities of the situation stand out in Bánzer's relations with the private sector and the relationship between the state and civil society in the state-capitalist formula. In the first instance, it is clear that Bánzer guaranteed some mode of capitalism in Bolivia, and commercial interests surely benefited during his tenure. But it would be inaccurate to see his regime as dominated by some national or international bourgeoisie or as expressing the coherent interests of any real capitalist class in Bolivia.

During the Bánzer era, a capitalist class in Bolivia was at best only incipient. And, as with all else, Bánzer built relations not with a class as such but with individuals and groups who became his personal retainers. Elements of the private sector benefited through their personal access to the executive and/or by paying bribes, commissions, and other "fees" for contracts, concessions, and low-interest loans. As the years went on, therefore, Bánzer engaged somewhat less than the enthusiastic support of the "capitalist class." First, his style of rule undercut the ability of the private sector to act as a class. Second, those private-sector elements not tied into the patronage nets came to resent and oppose Bánzer. The point is that the deterioration in the state's relations with the private sector came to resemble the disintegration pervading all aspects of Bolivian society: instead of large, coherent groups capable of acting on the basis of common interests, there was increasing division and particularism reflecting the underlying dynamics of personalized patron-clientelism.

Deinstitutionalization continued apace under Bánzer, owing to his neopatrimonial style of rule. Most particularly, clientelism continued to invade the military establishment, sapping its institutional vitality and undermining its organizational coherence.[6] In a sense, the military paid dearly for their role in repressing civil politics, by importing politics into the military institution. Thus, by the mid-1970s Bánzer ruled almost exclusively by manipulating complex alliances of civil and military cliques. As a result, his hold on power was always tenuous, and he constantly had to fend off the putschist plots of rival civil and military factions.

The neopatrimonial mode of rule also engendered contradictions in the state-capitalist economic model. What developed in Bolivia was a kind of prebendal capitalism wherein, although individual capitalists benefited, the state was less and less synchronized with modern capitalism.

Because of the clientelism underlying neopatrimonial rule, any such regime is pushed in two directions: (1) The ruler must constantly expand his support networks, and, therefore, constantly expands the pool of patronage resources. (2) Because the central state becomes the main patrimonial resource, increasingly the executive tends to view the state not as a public phenomenon but as his personal property, by which to maintain his rule. Hence, there is a built-in tendency for the state to expand and to increase the range of its functions. At the same time, the state's behavior comes to reflect the personal political needs of the ruler and his entourage more than any modern framework of rational, legal norms.

Thus, while the state in a real sense guarantees the capitalist system by "disciplining" and imposing the costs of capital accumulation on labor and the masses, its own maintenance needs inevitably bring the state into conflict with the capitalist sector over how the surplus should be distributed. Moreover, the "irrationalities" of state behavior caused by neopatrimonial rule create problems for the private sectors because they introduce unpredictability into the system and raise the costs of doing business in a variety of ways.

Thus, owing to the voracious maintenance needs of the neopatrimonial regime, the state of necessity becomes a parasite in relation to the productive sectors and civil society as a whole. Moreover, those who enjoy the prebends distributed by the state likewise become part of the parasitic weight of an increasingly arbitrary regime. In a context like Bolivia, neopatrimonialism means that the state becomes a predator, as the patrimonial ruler and his ever growing entourage prey on society at large.

This was the pattern during the seven-year rule of Hugo Bánzer. Under Bánzer the state grew in size, weight, and economic impact to a degree unprecedented in Bolivian history. The public bureaucracy grew from some 66,000 employees in 1970 to close to 170,000 by 1977. At the same time, new agencies and public corporations proliferated rapidly. By 1978, there were approximately 120 central government agencies and 50 public enterprises.[7] The state came to dwarf all other sectors and activities combined.

The conflict between the state and the private sector was manifested first in the mining industry. A number of important medium-sized mine companies complained of a confiscatory tax system. They charged that mining (a key productive sector) was in effect subsidizing the state and other private-sector enterprises, particularly banking, commerce, and agro-industry in the eastern lowland departments, such as Santa Cruz de la Sierra. The issue raised by the mining companies spoke to even deeper dynamics at work during this period.

Since the early days of the revolution, Bolivian governments have pursued a strategy of "national integration," which meant mainly integrating the eastern lowlands into the nation. One effect of this was to shift economic and political power away from the more highly populated western highlands, characterized by traditional peasant agriculture and mining, to the eastern lowlands, which were increasingly based on modern agro-industry and hydrocarbons. Indeed, one could argue—and many have—that the development policies of state capitalism in Bolivia have involved a shift of capital and resources from the highlands to the lowlands that was tantamount to a predatory decapitalization of the former in favor of the latter.[8]

As a result, in the 1970s, the east, and especially Santa Cruz, emerged as a significant economic and political force. It is not at all coincidental that the uprising of 1971 began in Santa Cruz, Bánzer's own department. Moreover, substantial investment flowed to the region, especially in the form of all but concessionary loans. In addition, Santa Cruz, led by a powerful private sector–based civic committee, was able to directly capture a significant amount of the profits generated by the hydrocarbon production in the department, thereby diminishing the resources going into the national coffers.[9]

With such competition among regions, the rise of Santa Cruz introduced a powerful and discordant strain of regionalism into national politics. Furthermore, the Santa Cruz "civic committee" became a potent example to other departments. Others followed suit by forming similar committees that took the lead in pressing regional demands on the central state. Another strain of particularism was introduced, and the neopatrimonial ruler sought to manipulate and contain the new regionalism through the same prebendal clientelism he had used to deal with the myriad other private demands pulling at the national core.

This is not the place to discuss in detail economic policy under Bánzer. Like much of the rest of Latin America, Bolivia enjoyed an era of prosperity during the 1970s. As was common in extractive export-based economies, a "boom" mentality pervaded the economy, and resources flowed into speculative agro-industrial production, luxury construction, and consumption. Growth was fueled by favorable prices for minerals and oil, which allowed both industries to produce profits even though production was declining. Export earnings were supplemented by government-guaranteed external borrowing, the bulk of which went for state maintenance, loans to speculative agriculture, the import bill, or was lost through capital flight.

Hence, growth and prosperity in Bolivia during the 1970s was extremely superficial. When the international economy turned, the pins were knocked out from under the Bolivian economy. Agro-industry and construction activities faltered, leaving a string of bad debts behind. The decline in commodity prices quickly exposed the structural weaknesses of the mining and oil-producing sectors. By the late 1970s, the Bolivian economy began a downward slide from which it has yet to recover, and there was little left from the boom years other than a massive foreign debt.

In some ways, the political legacy of these years was even more dramatic. Labor and popular organizations were suppressed but not eliminated, and society grew increasingly polarized over who should be winners and losers in alternative models of development. It was not simply a matter of class conflict. Class cleavages were embedded in a context of strong centrifugal forces—such as regional and factional rivalries—that cut across class lines. Formal political groups and institutions were extremely weak and all but obliterated by a complex clash of clientelistic factions pivoting around the executive in a political game of ins and outs. Finally, all classes, segments, regions, and factions had come to look upon the state as an entity set above and against society to be assaulted, captured, and used to the benefit of one's own group.

Authoritarian Decompression and Retreat

In the late 1970s, Bolivia—again moving with the general tide in Latin America—began a transition from a de facto authoritarian regime to a formalized democratic system. The process began with Bánzer's call for elections in July 1978. There were probably a number of reasons for Bánzer's move, including the trend toward redemocratization throughout Latin America, pressure from the Carter administration, and Bolivia's looming economic crisis. Behind these, however, was the fact that the byzantine game of clientelistic politics was becoming more difficult to manage in a problematic economic situation. Moreover, Bánzer's hold on power was increasingly unstable. Any alliance of in-factions immediately provoked a counter-coalition that conspired to penetrate the halls of power by any means, including coups d'état. Evidence abounds that Bánzer's hold on the armed forces was particularly tenuous and that a variety of factions were conspiring to oust him. Hence, Bánzer in effect was looking for a new formula by which to reconstruct his hold on power and perhaps relegitimize his regime both nationally and internationally.

The transition to formal democracy in Bolivia was a tumultuous process. The nation lurched from elections to coups d'état to elections for four years. Along the way, Bolivia's political leaders dreamed up a bevy of fascinating formal legal and constitutional formulas by which to rationalize various momentary solutions to the power question. Aside from any long-term ideological considerations, the issue of democracy in Bolivia was bound up with the more immediate but difficult issue of who was going to hold power and how. Formal democracy represented but one potential answer to the question of how. For most of the key groups and individuals in Bolivia, the key question was not democracy but access to power.

The dynamics of the years between 1978 and 1982 demonstrate some important aspects of the values and behavior of Bolivia's political elite on all sides. Political leaders backed the move to democracy not out of any positive commitment to the system in itself. It was for them a way, perhaps temporary, to gain access to power and state patronage after seven years of authoritarian monopoly by Bánzer and his entourage. For some gaining access meant solidifying class and group gains or lifting imposed burdens. For others, it meant pressing the interests of specific regions or economic sectors. For still others, it was mainly a matter of circulating jobs and patronage by substituting one central patrimonial patron for another.

The point is that, while a democratic electoral procedure opened and theoretically rationalized the distribution of power, it was for most, if not all of the players a second-best option. Over the next four years, just about every key faction and group demonstrated their willingness to back a coup if it seemed a quicker, surer way to power, or if they were likely to lose in a democratic electoral contest. Votes were still only one political currency in Bolivia and far from the most valued; all sides were inclined at a moment's notice to switch to the currency of bullets in the market of power.

The patrimonial nature of the system was in a real sense confirmed when, upon announcing his intention to call elections, Bánzer almost immediately lost control of the situation. Neopatrimonial rulers have power only when they actively monopolize the levers of power; a patrimonial lame duck is extremely lame indeed. In Bolivia, however, the military were not organizationally capable of filling the vacuum and (as in Peru and Brazil) asserting control over the transition process. As the patrimonial center decompressed, all control diminished, and power dissipated into the myriad factions, regions, sectors and classes that were vying to achieve some formal control of the state. In that situation, all groups and fragments sought electoral strategies but also simultaneously looked for possible coup coalitions. The military, while critical because of their control of the instruments of force, faltered and fragmented under the push-and-pull of various civilian groups trying to draw the armed forces in their direction. While military officers remained key players throughout, the military institution as such all but collapsed into a collection of armed quasi-feudal factions formed around would-be patrimonial strong men.

Prior to the first electoral battle in 1978, factions in the military rejected Bánzer's bid to contest the elections and pushed in his place General Pereda Asbun. This was an attempt to legitimate a military-mediated patrimonial system with a new figurehead. However, the etiquette of holding elections forced the military to lift the repression of the labor left. In turn, the left surged forward again and, in that polarized situation, was a most credible electoral threat. Not only did the labor left, led by its long-time leader Juan Lechín, reemerge, but also all of the old political parties, including the fractious MNR and its long-standing caudillos, like Víctor Paz Estenssoro, Hernán Siles, and Wálter Guevara, also came back to the fore. In terms of players, the long period of authoritarian military dominance had had little lasting impact on the political game.

The weakness of central power in Bolivia was made clear in the 1978 elections, which the military openly sought to rig. However, the generals and the incumbent regime were unable to dominate the process completely. Like all else, attempts to subvert the democratic process dissipated outward as all contenders openly engaged in various kinds of electoral fraud. Frustrated by their failed attempt to rig the election so as to make Pereda the winner, the factions behind him announced a coup, dumped Bánzer, and installed Pereda in the presidential palace. Almost immediately, rival factions in the military formed against Pereda. On November 24, 1978, a self-declared "institutionalist" coalition of officers ousted Pereda and installed in his place General David Padilla. Seeking still to extricate the military from formal power without slipping into complete disarray, the institutionalists, acting through Padilla, called for a new round of elections in July 1979.

The campaign preceding the elections of 1979 revealed rather dramatically the state to which Bolivian political life had come. The military had only nominal formal control of the situation. The result was a vacuum at the center, and all the various groups, classes, and factions were thrown back on themselves to seek some kind of a way out. In terms of players in the political game, the previous twenty-two years had seen not the elimination of any major personality, groups or forces but only the addition of some new ones. As a result, there was also no component of civil society capable of forging a base from which to dominate the system.

In addition to the political dilemma of finding a new viable regime, Bolivia and its would-be leaders were confronted by an economic crisis that was growing worse by the day. In many respects, the political crisis fueled the economic crisis because the government did not have sufficient authority to act. At the same time, the obvious consequences of any firm attempts to cope with the economic crisis fed into the political scene and limited the maneuvering room of all contenders. Although the political chaos and economic problems interacted and reinforced each other, the government crisis was fundamental. Some sort of political resolution was becoming indispensable to any resolution of the economic crisis.

Whatever the ideological divisions, the various political forces began to take shape around three major personalities contending for the presidential chair. Hernán Siles formed a broad-based center-left coalition, the Popular Democratic Union (UDP). The UDP was made up of a left faction of the MNR (called MNRI), a newer group of young independent leftists called the Left Revolutionary Movement (MIR), the Bolivian Communist party, and some minor groups. To the left of the UDP stood a welter of other leftist groups. On the right stood Paz Estenssoro, leading a tentative coalition of MNR factions called the historical MNR or MNRH, while Bánzer waded back into the fray at the head of a new party called Nationalist Democratic Action (ADN). In that context, Siles stood for some vague idea of national populism, while Paz and Bánzer stood more clearly for a reinvigoration of the state-capitalist economic model.

The electorate was indecisive in choosing a president, but did reveal its almost complete polarization between right and left. Siles led the pack, but his lack of a clear majority threw the choice into the newly elected Congress. Owing to the proportional representation system, the Congress was divided into myriad groups and factions who were unable to forge a majority behind any of the three leading candidates: Siles (35.9 percent), Paz (35.8 percent), and Bánzer (14 percent). After several ballots, the major political forces struck a compromise in which the other old MNR stalwart, Wálter Guevara, would assume the presidency on an interim basis for one year.

The deal that elevated Guevara to the presidency showed rather clearly that the system could not produce a long-term resolution of any key political issues and, hence, government leaders were reduced to finding short-term ways out of specific problems. Guevara tried to put together a grand coalition of MNR factions to bolster his regime, but the supporters of Siles and Paz, with their eyes on the next election, were loath to enter a government they were not able to dominate. Hence, both stayed in the opposition. The result was that the Congress that chose Guevara all but immediately turned against him. He was, to say the least, a weak figure unable to grapple with the economic situation, which continued to deteriorate. The political *salida* that produced Guevara did not produce a government capable of acting.

The superficiality of Bolivian leaders' allegiance to democracy became evident over the next months. Almost at once, civil groups plotted with military factions to mount a coup. Indeed, in a verbal tour de force that revealed the politicians' willingness to play with formalisms, there was even talk of a "constitutional" coup in which the Congress would back and legitimate a new de facto regime. There is evidence that politicians and leaders across the ideological spectrum were involved in coup plans.[10]

In November, plots turned to action when Colonel Alberto Natusch Busch mounted a coup. Again evidence indicates that Natusch thought he would receive broad backing from civil groups in Congress and the labor movement.[11] Guevara refused to yield, and within days each looked to the Congress to legitimate his respective claim to the presidency.[12] As the Congress pondered, Natusch, failing to receive popular backing, put troops into the streets, and the comic opera turned into a tragedy when hundreds were killed by undisciplined soldiers.

The Natusch coup emerged from the political impasse created by the election of 1979, but there were other factors behind it—most specifically, the clear intention of the left to push for inquiries into the behavior of the military during the Bánzer regime. While the generals could not dominate and govern, they clearly could still seek to quash any threat to their institution and thereby define the outward limits of "democratic" behavior.

In any event, the Congress, which at first denounced Natusch and endorsed Guevara, soon backed off and looked for a compromise that would at least leave Congress intact. The result was another *salida* in which both Natusch and Guevara stepped aside for yet another interim president. Another product of the original MNR, Lydia Gueiler, assumed the presidential sash and thereby became the first female president in Bolivian history.

Although a lame duck, the new president tried to mount a viable government. In late November, Gueiler implemented an International Monetary Fund (IMF) economic package so as to qualify for further international loans. The austerity measures of the plan fell most heavily on labor and the popular sectors. The COB responded with an open protest, even while it claimed to support the government and a civil democratic system.

Again an important contradiction was revealed. The economic realities were such that if Bolivia were to stay within the Western system, it would have to come to terms with the IMF. Any such package would of necessity provoke opposition from labor and the left. Hence, there was a real contrast between the "popular" requirements of any type of democratic system or civil regime, and the clear antipopular imperatives of any stabilization program. The new regime found itself trying to impose on the people, within a democratic frame, economic costs that over the previous twenty years had called forth strong authoritarian regimes.

In addition to mounting an economic program, the Gueiler government sought to preside over a reconstruction of the political system by calling new elections in June 1980. As the weeks wore on, however, Gueiler found herself in open confrontation with the commander of the army, General García Meza. Again, the military were reacting to any attempt to hold them accountable for abuses under Bánzer, particularly to recent accusations in Congress.[13] Despite ominous portents, elections were held as scheduled.

The 1980 elections were essentially a replay of 1979, with the same major candidates and coalitions in contention. As before, no candidate gained a majority, leaving things unresolved. However, there was a marked decline in the draw of center-right candidates toward Siles, who this time gained 39 percent, as compared to only 20 percent for Paz and 17 percent for Bánzer. The vote probably reflected the hope that the "populist" Siles would alleviate the burden of the austerity measures on the people. The elections were again to be decided by Congress, which again was fragmented, with no party or coalition in dominance.

On July 17, before Congress could seek a solution, García Meza seized power. The García Meza regime in many ways attested to the exhaustion of the Bolivian political system. In spite of high-flown rhetoric, the regime had no ideological form or thrust.[14] It moved to crush labor, but it was equally brutal toward all opposition. Indeed, one of the hallmarks of the regime was its systematic brutality, as it sought to make the entire society tremble. The fact is that the García Meza government had no significant support from any sector; thus it was really quite weak and had to cling to power by force.[15]

Owing to its ties to the cocaine trade and its blatant corruption, the García Meza regime quickly became an international outlaw as well. It ended as virtually a purely parasitic government openly looting a cowed and frightened nation. Most ominously, the regime saw the final deterioration of the military into little more than a collection of predatory warlords parceling out pieces of the state and the national patrimony among themselves. But, again, the armed forces as such were extremely weak, as illustrated by the regime's use of paramilitary groups to dominate society. Under García Meza, the economy deteriorated to the point of collapse—the general and his clique spent more time dividing the spoils among themselves than they did attempting to govern.[16]

In the latter part of 1981, institutionalist officers dumped García Meza and sought to negotiate the military out of power. Bolivia turned to democracy because it was the only choice. In those circumstances, there was no capacity to mount an authoritarian government. The military was not even able to dictate the terms of its retreat, and left to the civil politicians the task of finding another salida.

The solution was as ingenious as it was reflective of the basic political standoff in Bolivia. Fearful of new elections that would swell the tide for Siles, the key parties agreed to reconvene the Congress of 1980 which would then elect Siles. While providing a way out, this strategy prevented the country from mounting a government with a mandate to rule. It also guaranteed an antagonistic bifurcation between a weak executive and a Congress more or less controlled by a divided and fractious opposition. It was another temporary way out that assured eventual paralysis of the system.

The process of transition that began in 1977 culminated in October 1982, when Hernán Siles assumed the presidency. It seemed an auspicious moment. The military was discredited, and the bulk of the populace clearly supported a return to democracy. Finally, the Siles government had demonstrated wide popular support, especially among labor and the peasantry.

At the same time, the new government and the new democratic system faced enormous economic difficulties manifested in a huge external debt, declining growth rates, inflation, and a bankrupt treasury. Moreover, it was clear that, unless the government was willing to try a shift to the socialist bloc, any attempt to deal with the economic crisis would have to come to terms with the IMF and its demands for tight austerity measures. But any such plan would be quite unpopular with the government's key support groups, especially organized labor.

Fatefully, the COB followed the same political strategy it had since the early 1950s. It supported the UDP government of Siles in principle, but refused to become a part of it on any terms other than full cogovernment at the national level, and eventually in all major public enterprises. When its demands for cogovernment were rejected, the COB assumed an independent stance to the left, from which it offered the government only acquiescence and then only if its concrete demands were met. Failing that, the COB made it plain that it planned to bargain autonomously with the regime by means of direct actions meant to coerce the government to its will.

To the right of the government stood the Confederation of Private Entrepreneurs which for the first time was able to assume the role of class spokesman for the private sector. The confederation, which had never supported Siles, sought to push a more market-oriented approach to policy and at the same time "defend" themselves against leftist and populist policies pushed by the COB and by some of Siles's coalition partners.

At this level, the prime political issues involved, as in most Latin American countries, the politics of economic packages (*paquetes*) designed with the IMF in mind. Siles tried to launch eight *paquetes*, all of which failed. The fact is that the plans designed by technocrats were usually watered down through bargaining in the government's coalition. Then the COB would lead the fight against the watered-down package. After a round of strikes, the government usually gave in. Whereupon the confederation of entrepreneurs mounted its countercampaigns—threatening its own strikes and other actions—unless something was done. In some sense, it was a battle between the COB and the confederation of entrepreneurs in which the government became a foil pushed and hauled by both, but receiving no ongoing political support from either. The tactic became to see who could more effectively coerce the government, and for how long.[17]

Indeed, that has become the dominant way of doing politics at all levels in Bolivia since 1982. The prime political legacy of the military period was a complete deterioration of the political capacity to channel, structure, and contain the relations between state and society and relations among parts of society with each other. In the absence of such infrastructure, a great surge of demands long bottled up by military repression surged forward.

Not only the COB and business groups, but also regional groups, peasants, public employees, and others, all weighed in with their demands that ran counter to the imperatives of any of the economic programs the government came up with. All groups, fragments, and sectors backed their demands with concrete coercive actions such as strikes, blocking of roads, and shutting off of entire regions. Within a short time, the government was again lurching from one mini-crisis to another, and along the way simply giving in to demands.

The most immediate social manifestation of the government's declining capacity to govern was inflation. (At the time, Bolivia's inflation rate was among the worst in the world.) It ran into the thousands of percent while the currency collapsed: in 1983, the official rate of exchange was 200 pesos to the dollar, while the parallel market rate was 800; by July 1985, the official rate was 75,000, while the parallel rate was at 800,000 and climbing. Behind such inflation, a powerless government was held at ransom by segments of civil society and simply meeting demands by printing money in a complex game of robbing Peter to pay Paul.[18]

Aside from the quasi-sovereign behavior of organizations like the COB and regional civic committees, the weakness of the government reflected the fragility of key political institutions. One critical problem was the plethora of fragmented political parties, which in the end were capable only of channeling demands, but not support, to a government. Today, parties in Bolivia are at best vehicles to mount electoral coalitions and assault the patronage resources of the state. They are not capable of underwriting support for an ongoing process of governing, either by linking a government to a stable base of support in the legislature or by channeling and controlling support from key classes, groups, or regions. In short, parties do not mediate between the state and civil society, nor do they anchor both popular demands and support to the state.

In Bolivia there was and is a disjunction between democracy as elections and democracy as governing. Coalitions formed to contest elections cannot be sustained into coalitions to govern and control. The UDP coalition, for example, has fallen apart, fragmented, and been reconstituted almost constantly since 1982. Thus, the very structure of executive power has been in question, and Siles has spent considerable time and energy manipulating the parties and factions around him.

At the same time, the executive and the legislature have been at loggerheads throughout. The problem has not been so much that a unified opposition dominates the legislature but that the government has been unable to maintain a disciplined bloc of supporters. The result is a legislature effectively dominated in a negative way by a fragmented opposition. The legislature does not oppose by means of counterprograms but simply by obstructing any moves the executive tries to make. As a result, the executive has sought to govern without the legislature and, therefore, has in a technical sense been forced to act illegally over its tenure. But the reality is that, given the fact that institutions do not work as prescribed, then all sides resort to illegal or extralegal action simply to get things done.

A deep structural weakness of the present system is that the formal legal rules and institutions are seen not as ways of doing things but as obstructions to any action. Hence, willingness to respect and follow the formal rules is declining apace not only among groups in civil society who routinely "break the law" to achieve their particular goals, but also in all the key branches of the government. Thus, the legislature throughout the period accused Siles of acting illegally even as it debated "constitutional" coups and other modes of confrontation with the executive. Given the incapacity of the legislature and the parties in it, social groups basically ignored the legislature and sought to influence the executive directly. Finally, Siles governed largely by decree and often acted in ways that, while substantively correct, were formally illegal. One example was the recent nationalization of a mining company that all agreed was in violation of myriad laws. The government, aware that the courts would have tied the case up interminably, short-circuited correct legal procedure and simply seized the mines—whereupon private-sector associations attacked the government not for the nationalization as such but for the "illegal" manner in which it was carried out.

Throughout its tenure, the Siles government has expended most of its energy simply attempting to hold onto formal power. It has not been able to govern in any positive sense and has acted mainly in response to the push and haul of social forces. Under Siles, the executive, and by extension the state, have "floated above" civil society, where they appear as mechanisms to be bent to or to be protected from the will of certain groups. Groups and segments of society clearly perceive politics as a zero-sum game in which one must block opponents before pressing one's own interests. Bolivia today exhibits an extreme conflict between the pursuit of the long-term interests of the nation and the short-term specific interests of particular groups, classes, and regions.

In the type of situation Bolivia is in, circumstances reinforce the particularistic pressures and thereby create a vicious circle. The potential short-term losses are so great that no group or segment dares risk acting in any manner other than defending its own interests. The state, in turn, while large in size and significance, is in practical terms very weak. The result is a standoff. The major achievement of the Siles government will be in its ability to turn over power in August 1985 to an elected civil regime—that is, to simply preserve the form of democracy. If he is able to do that, it will have been a first and under the circumstances a great achievement.

The prognosis for democracy in Bolivia is rather shaky, to say the least. Democracy has persisted thus far mainly because the military is weakened, as are authoritarian modes of governance. As disorder mounts and memories fade, the salience of these factors will diminish. The critical factor is how various leaders in both civil society and the military perceive the situation. At the moment, we would argue that Bolivia's leaders back democratic procedures not out of any positive commitment to them but because under democracy they stand to lose less and, more importantly, they can stay in the game. The moment some groups see a more direct road to power or perceive themselves to be marginal in a democratic game, such groups will be more than predisposed to seek a de facto government. In the recent electoral campaign, for example, the COB, contemplating a big electoral victory for the "right," rather openly sought to provoke a coup to negate what it called an electoral coup by the right. The point is that in Bolivia the elite's commitment to formal democracy is tentative at best.

Notes

1. For an expansion of the analysis presented here, see James M. Malloy, *Bolivia: The Uncompleted Revolution* (Pittsburgh, Pa: University of Pittsburgh Press, 1970).

2. For an expanded comparison of the Bolivian and Mexican Revolutions, see Susan Eckstein, *The Impact of Revolution: A Comparative Analysis of Mexico and Bolivia* (London: Sage Publications, 1976), pp. 24–39.

3. For a brief analysis of the period, see James M. Malloy, "Revolutionary

Politics," in *Beyond the Revolution: Bolivia Since 1952*, ed. Malloy and Richard Thorn (Pittsburgh, Pa: University of Pittsburgh Press, 1971), pp. 145–53.

4. For an in-depth analysis on the Torres period and the Asamblea Popular, see Jerry Knudson, *Bolivia's Popular Assembly and the Overthrow of General Juan José Torres* (Buffalo: State University of New York Council of International Studies, Special Studies Series, 1974).

5. For a development of this concept, see Guillermo O'Donnell, *Modernization and Bureaucratic-Authoritarianism: Studies in South American Politics* (Berkeley, Calif.: Institute of International Studies, 1973).

6. For a recent first-hand account of the internal divisions and confrontations within the military, see Gary Prado Salmon, *Poder y Fuerzas Armadas 1949–1982* (La Paz: Editorial Los Amigos del Libro, 1984), pp. 153–421.

7. See Ministerio de Trabajo y Desarrollo Laboral, *Anuario de Estadísticas de Trabajo* (La Paz: Instituto Nacional de Estadísticass, 1980, 1981); and *Estadística Laboral Período 1970–75* (La Paz: Instituto Nacional de Estadísticas, 1976).

8. For a similar analysis, see Pablo Ramos, *Siete años de economía Boliviana* (La Paz: Ediciones Puerta del Sol, 1982).

9. For a detailed analysis of Bolivia's regional problems and the growth in power by civic committees, see José Luis Roca, *Fisionomía del regionalismo Boliviano* (La Paz: Editorial Los Amigos del Libro, 1980).

10. One of the principal plotters in the November 1979 coup has written extensively about the period. See Guillermo Bedregal's account published in *El Diario* (La Paz), February 9, 1980, p. 3.

11. The most widely accepted version was developed in a recent controversial book; see Irving Alcáraz, *Prisionero del palacio* (La Paz: Editorial e Imprenta Amerindia, 1983).

12. Interview with Wálter Guevara Arze, June 1985, La Paz. Guevara's first-hand account is also in an unpublished manuscript, "Los Militares en Bolivia" (1980).

13. The November 1979 coup as well as prior attempts were reactions by sectors of the military who felt threatened by an impeachment trial (Juicio de Responsabilidades) launched by Marcelo Quiroga Santa Cruz against General Hugo Bánzer and his collaborators.

14. Many have argued that García Meza followed an ideological program and position; see Pablo Ramos, *Radiografía de un golpe de estado* (La Paz: Editorial Puerta del Sol, 1983).

15. For an expanded analysis of the García Meza regime, see James M. Malloy, "Bolivia: The Sad and Corrupt End of the Revolution" (USFI Reports, 1982).

16. Ibid., p. 9.

17. For an analysis of the pattern of strikes and stoppages that emerged between October 1982 and June 1983, see Raul Rivadeneira Prada, *Bolivia: Un País en permanente estado de emergencia* (La Paz: CINCO, 1984). During the time period covered by this study, there were 544 strikes and/or stoppages; 84 were at the national level. This pattern became even more pronounced between 1983 and July 1985.

18. For an in-depth analysis of the Bolivian economy in the last three years, see Diego Estévez, "Hiperinflación, drama actual de Bolivia," *Ambito Financiero* (Buenos Aires), May 1985. Reprinted in *Ultima Hora* (La Paz), May 16, 17 and 21, 1985. According to Estévez, the cost-of-living increase for 1985 could reach 139,109 percent.

Luis A. Abugattas

6 Populism and After: The Peruvian Experience

This chapter analyzes the redemocratization of Peruvian politics after twelve years of military-authoritarian rule. Even though the analysis emphasizes the dynamics of regime change in the 1975–1980 period, I attempt to present it within the broader perspective of the alternation of different modes of rule in Peruvian politics since 1963. Since that year, Peru has witnessed two transitions from military to civilian rule, once in 1963 and another in 1980—first the breakdown of a democratic regime, then the demise of an authoritarian one.

Late Populism and Authoritarian Decompression

The rise of the populist state, the establishment of a new method of accumulating capital based on import-substitution industrialization, and the enhancement of the state's role in the economy have been typical responses to the crisis of the oligarchic state in twentieth-century Latin America. In the Peruvian case, populism as a political alternative took a long time to crystallize, and the post-Depression period was characterized by unsuccessful attempts to consolidate a populist coalition and to establish a *desarrollista* model of development. The only successful attempt was the ephemeral regime of the Frente Democrático Nacional (1945–1948).

In Peru, the longevity of the oligarchic state is explained by a combination of factors. In first place, owing to the succession of export booms and to the diversified nature of Peru's exports, the viability of the export model of development was maintained and, with it, the power of the oligarchy. Second, because of inherent weaknesses, the bourgeoisie was slow to emerge as a political force,

121

which inhibited its possibilities for leading a populist coalition. Finally, the political failure of APRA was a fundamental factor in the failure of populism in Peru.

Since the 1930s, the central issue in Peruvian politics has been the confrontation of populist forces, expressed through APRA, and the oligarchic regime, which has relied on the armed forces to keep populist pressures under control. The political scene has been dominated by the military, with the exception of two democratic interregnums: one from 1939 to 1948, and the other from 1956 to 1962, during the second administration of Manuel Prado. These democratic interludes, albeit under oligarchic rule, were made possible because of the international environment. Between 1939 and 1948, the world's struggle against fascist totalitarianism discredited military dictatorships, and all political forces rallied behind the banner of democracy. Another period of liberalization also emerged as a result of temporary agreements reached between APRA and the oligarchy in the so-called *convivencia*. In such arrangements, the party granted its support to the Prado administration in exchange for its return to legality and the chance to run in forthcoming elections.[1] But, between the collapse of the República Aristocrática in 1919 and Belaúnde's election in 1980, Peru witnessed only one constitutional transfer of political power, that of 1945.

The collapse of the export model of development, which had failed to satisfy the growing demands placed on the economy, the emergence of new social groups resulting from the progressive diversification of the economic structure, and the military's changing political role during the 1962–1963 period of military rule, opened the way for the first prolonged populist experience in Peruvian history.

With the election of Fernando Belaúnde Terry in 1963, attempts were made to establish the populist program that large sectors of Peruvian society had been awaiting for so long. However, civilian populism soon came to a standstill because of the political struggle between populist forces and those factions of private capital opposed to the structural reforms proposed by the new government.[2]

The coup d'état of 1968 was spurred by a condition that is characteristic of military involvement in Latin American politics. As O'Donnell points out with regard to the Brazilian and Argentinian coups of the sixties, the pre-coup government "was victimized by, and collaborated in praetorianism."[3] The situation could be characterized as a stalemate: much conflict, sharp differences in demands, and the weakness of the government prevented the implementation of any policy. The government's incapacity, in turn, aggravated social instability and bred more praetorianism. In the Peruvian case, in contrast to the experience of Brazil and Argentina, the military acted not to quash the populist movement as such, but to manage a populist uprising that they believed beyond the control of incompetent and corrupt civilian regimes. The 1968 coup has to be understood as a removal of populist leadership because of the inability of civilian populism to overcome the opposition of the traditional capitalist factions. After 1968, the Gobierno Revolucionario de las Fuerzas Armadas (GRFA) undertook the major reforms that had been the political platform of the Peruvian populist forces since 1930. Even though a democratic mode of rule changed to an authoritarian one, there was a continuity in the populist movement between 1963 and 1976. However, in 1976 military (or authoritarian) populism reached a crisis that called for an antipopulist reaction and the military's withdrawal from government.

What forces produced the collapse of authoritarian populism in Peru, forced the military to withdraw from politics, and generated an antipopulist reaction? In addressing these questions, we confront two basic theoretical challenges. On one hand, events in Peru illustrate the cycle of populism and antipopulist reaction that can be observed in many Latin American countries. On the other hand, they exhibit an alternation between democratic and authoritarian modes of rule. The literature on Latin American political development has sometimes assumed a mechanical correspondence between antipopulist reaction and authoritarianism and between populism and democratic modes of rule.[4] My contention is that these two cycles, even though interrelated, constitute different phenomena. The Peruvian case shows, I believe, that the question of democracy versus authoritarianism is a question of political regimes, whereas the alternation between democratic and authoritarian modes of rule is possible both during a populist as well as an antipopulist phase. In the Peruvian case, we have, within populism, democratic (1963–1968) and authoritarian (1968–1976) variants. Also, the last decade included a classic authoritarian regime (1976–1980) and, most intriguing of all, a democratic antipopulist regime (1980–1985). The main thrust of this essay will be to analyze the alternation of political regimes in Peru, from military populism to democratic antipopulism.

Collapse of Authoritarian Populism

On October 3, 1968, the Gobierno Revolucionario de las Fuerzas Armadas (GRFA) began the Peruvian revolution—one of the most remarkable social experiments in twentieth-century Latin America—by enacting a series of reforms designed to radically transform Peruvian society. Since these events have received wide scholarly attention and the literature on the subject is vast, I will only highlight some of the basic characteristics fundamental to understanding the dynamics that led to the collapse of that regime.[5]

Analysts of the Peruvian revolution agree that in Peru the state emerged as relatively autonomous and separate from the social class structure.[6] In explaining the role of the state in Peruvian politics after 1968, most observers have basically relied upon the classical interpretation of bonapartism, even though certain differences can be seen. That is, the state must rise above social classes because of the acute fragmentation of the ruling class, widespread popular discontent, and the political mobilization of the masses that challenge the social order. According to Cleaves and Pease, in Peru the autonomy of the government from various social interests was encouraged by "the prevalence of authoritarianism in the society, the past frequency of dictatorships, and the exclusion of vast sectors of the population from the political system."[7] Furthermore, the inherent weakness of the institutions of civil society, political parties in particular, coupled with a generalized tacit sympathy with the coup of 1968 and the initial reforms it brought about, inhibited an immediate civilian reaction to the GRFA. The regime headed by General Velasco used the state's autonomy, and the unity of the armed forces that supported it, to advance social reforms that weakened the dominant class and increased the power of the state apparatus.

In the economic sphere, the GRFA followed a classic populist economic policy. It intensified import-substitution industrialization through unlimited protectionism, established price controls and a fixed exchange rate, increased public expenditures, and attempted certain income redistribution policies. These policies, going beyond classic populism, affected the basic structure of ownership in the private sector. Furthermore, the GRFA established state capitalism as the mode of accumulation in the Peruvian economy. The state took the responsibility for organizing production in key economic sectors. It became the link with the international market, regulating foreign

investments and monopolizing most of Peru's foreign economic relations. By 1975, the state controlled 30 percent of the corporate sector, 75 percent of total exports, half the imports, more than half of
fixed investments, two-thirds of bank credit, and a third of all
employment.[8] The spectacular growth of the state was not a result of
new investment, but took place largely at the expense of the private
sector through the nationalization of foreign enterprises and expro-
priation of local capital. As a basic element in the economic model,
the GRFA enacted radical agrarian reforms that broke the backbone of
the landowning faction of the ruling class, and started a cooperative
experiment in the Peruvian countryside.

On the political front, the military demanded a "monopoly on
politics," and the government was reduced to the status of an administrative arm of the armed forces. The GRFA aimed to depoliticize
civil society by repressing any autonomous political participation, and
attempted to enforce through a state-promoted vertical institutional
structure a corporatist relationship between the state and civil
society.[9] Political parties, without being openly repressed, went into
oblivion, and the main institutions of the property-owning classes lost
their official recognition and became principal targets of attack. The
GRFA sought the support of the labor movement but established strict
limits for its participation in politics.

The populist phase in Peru came to an end with the collapse of the
military regime in 1976. The forces that brought it down sprang from
the very nature of authoritarianism and the economic model pursued
by the GRFA. Long-standing tensions were heightened by immediate
events that precipitated the final crisis. By suppressing politics in civil
society, the generals had effectively transferred the struggle over issues
and power to the military institution itself. This generated a process
of politicization and fragmentation that in turn reduced the state's
autonomy. The result was political rigidity and the state's inability to
implement a coherent public policy. This situation led to social
protests and political activism that challenged the institutional legitimacy of the armed forces and aggravated their isolation, setting them
against the society at large. In this situation, as Cótler explains, "only
through withdrawal could it [the GRFA] avoid compromising military
integrity and authority and destroying any legitimacy for future involvement in politics."[10]

Until 1974, the GRFA was able to maintain a high degree of coherence and unity in the armed forces. Even though some friction had

been noticed earlier, it was the result of clashes of personalities within the regime. Velasco's strong leadership, the navy's acceptance of the 1968 coup as a fait accompli, the initial success of the reforms, and the absence of any organized opposition to the GRFA maintained unity within the armed forces. This unity, however, was eroded by the radicalization of the revolutionary process and the intensification of class and sectoral conflicts in civil society. These conflicts had strong repercussions in the officer corps, generating, in turn, ideological differences.[11] By 1974, obvious factions within the army had developed: the *radical* faction, organized around the group of colonels who were the initiators of the coup; the Misión, an anticommunist faction that attempted a fascistic experiment; and an *institutional* faction that gradually emerged, made up of those officers who rejected both extremes and who were concerned with the very survival of the armed forces.[12] Fragmentation of the GRFA was aggravated by the deepening of these cleavages within the military. The navy and the police became alienated from the GRFA because of the intrusion of the revolutionary leadership into their affairs. Furthermore, there were "internal conflicts among ministries, agencies, and the newspapers."[13]

As a result of the fragmentation of the armed forces and intensifying levels of contradiction, a bitter struggle for the control of state power erupted within the GRFA. Representatives of social groups exploited this internal strife to their own advantage, and members of the military factions looked for alliances with groups in civil society to strengthen their position. Political struggle went beyond state limits, mobilizing popular protest and eroding the regime's control over the political process. The events of February 1975, spurred by a police strike, resulted in rioting and the sacking of the capital for three days without a decisive response from the government. This showed the precariousness of military rule under conditions of acute political fragmentation.

Concurrently, the economy reached the limits of possible expansion. Until 1974, the Peruvian economy grew at an annual rate of 6 percent, real wages and salaries constantly increased, and the principal economic indicators showed healthy development. However, by 1975 symptoms of an impending crisis began to be manifested in the decline of the growth rate, a rising government deficit, a serious imbalance in the external sector, and inflationary pressures. In addition to the impact of external factors and inept management, problems sprang from the very nature of the economic model and the populist policy package—as has happened in other populist experiments. The economy was eroded by two fundamental contradictions. First, the consumption demands of the population clashed with the state's need to accumulate capital. Second, the state had to achieve an economic surplus so as to assume the burden of capital accumulation. As Fitzgerald points out, "The inability to achieve this is the inherent contradiction of state capitalism."[14] Local capital maintained control over an important share of the surplus; therefore, the military regime sustained levels of consumption and public investment by relying increasingly on external financing. By 1975, because of the collapse of the export sector and an unmanageable debt service ratio, economic growth was stifled. The government was forced to adopt increasingly antipopular measures that exacerbated the political dissension among the armed forces and generated political instability as the cost of stabilization was imposed on the masses. The GRFA delayed decisive corrective measures during 1975, owing to the tense political crisis, and thereby only aggravated the economic crisis.

The shift to an antipopulist stand has been interpreted by some analysts as a consequence of the ideological orientation of military leadership during the second phase of the revolution. Considering that a policy shift, though tenuous, could be observed in Peru as early as January 1975, and given the recent experiences of other Latin American countries, we must conclude that, irrespective of a regime's ideological orientation or social base, an acute economic crisis in dependent capitalism necessarily generates, in the short term, an antipopulist reaction. This is especially true when the regime is forced into negotiations with international lenders and the International Monetary Fund. The economic crisis placed the regime in a difficult position: it had to maintain a precarious balance between external legitimacy, indispensable for sustaining the inflow of required capital, and the internal popular support needed for its own stability. The political process in Peru was thereafter conditioned by the economic crisis and the regime's attempts to maintain a balance between internal and external demands.

The political crisis at the summit of power led to political paralysis and hampered the government's ability to formulate coherent policy. Moreover, the political scenario was complicated by the international isolation of the regime, by military threats from bordering countries, and by the social dislocations symptomatic of the impending economic crisis.[15] This situation prompted General Velasco's replacement in August 1975.

The 1975 internal coup has been seen by most analysts as a turning point separating the first from the second phase of the revolution. Even though the beginning of the second phase was officially announced after the 1975 coup, a closer look at events shows that the replacement of the military leadership was another step in the struggle among factions within the armed forces. The coup did not produce a clear victory for any faction. All agreed that Velasco had to go and the Misión had to be controlled, but the basic political conflict within the armed forces was not resolved. Moreover, the conflict was intensified by the need to impose drastic economic stabilization measures with all their difficult social and political consequences. The ambiguous policy followed after the coup, and subsequent events, led to another crisis in July 1976. Internal dissent within the armed forces reached its apogee in July. In that month, a rightist military uprising headed by General Bobbio Centurión provoked a sequence of events that led to the resignation of the remaining progressive high-ranking officers in the GRFA. In August, a leftist putsch led by junior officers was suppressed; this movement signaled the fact that all levels of the military had been politicized.

With the solution of the July crisis, the military was strengthened by the restoration of the military junta's ascendancy over the cabinet. With high-ranking officers participating in decision making, and the institutional grievances of the navy and the police resolved, General Morales Bermúdez was able to reestablish a relative internal homogeneity within the GRFA, to make more coherent decisions, and to regain control over the political process.

With the ouster of Velasco, the regime faced two alternatives. The political struggle, both within the GRFA and in society at large, evolved around the future direction of the revolution. The labor movement and those civilian sectors that had supported the GRFA since its inauguration demanded a continuation of the reforms and a frontal attack on the power of capital through a socialist reconstruction of the economy. The labor movement openly supported the GRFA during the period of policy definition (August 1975–July 1976) in an attempt to influence the direction of that process. After the elimination of the radical faction from the GRFA and from the military hierarchy, deepening the revolutionary process ceased to be a viable alternative. The labor movement and the political left then openly confronted the GRFA. This confrontation was intensified by the austerity measures that the regime had to enact beginning in 1976 to deal with the economic crisis. This situation would become a constant during the long period of redemocratization.

A second alternative demanded by certain military officers and the extreme right was a strong repressive regime that would cancel the reforms and impose harsh stabilization measures, forcing the masses to bear the cost of the economic program. This had been the typical path of the military regimes in the Southern Cone. In Peru it would have required a governing alliance between the military and capital interests, with the acquiescence of the major political parties. This alternative, even though it was attempted at times, did not crystallize. Local capital, through its representative institutions, demanded the abolition of the major reforms enacted by the GRFA in an uncompromising position that left no space for a negotiated solution with the military. A drastic reversal of the accomplishments of the GRFA would have denied the legitimacy of the regime as the sponsor of the revolutionary process, intensifying dissension in the military and deepening the contradictions in civil society. It would have required levels of repression that the armed forces were reluctant to apply to safeguard their legitimacy and integrity. Moreover, traditional political parties rallied behind the banner of redemocratization in their tenuous opposition to the GRFA. There was no consensus among the factions that would have permitted a civilian front and an agreement with the GRFA.

After the Morales Bermúdez faction consolidated its control over the GRFA, the military chose to withdraw from government. Even though a temporary solution to the political crisis at the summit of power was achieved, the price had been extremely high. About ten army generals had gone into retirement in violation of military regulations between August 1975 and June 1976, and the military institutions as such had been seriously affected by internal conflict. General Morales Bermúdez declared in October 1976, "We all directly or indirectly, had been witnesses to what was happening to this institution fundamental to our fatherland, and in the same vein, to the other institutions. And we don't want that."[16] Furthermore, constant accusations of widespread corruption were testing whatever legitimacy was left of the military institutions. Moreover, management of the economic crisis called for drastic stabilization measures that would set the GRFA against the masses and threatened to generate new factionalism among the officer corps. After July 1976, the GRFA sought to overcome the growing internal and external isolation of the regime, to confront the economic crisis, and to make an honorable and orderly withdrawal from government.

The Politics of Transition

The circumstances under which an authoritarian regime begins redemocratization will determine the transition process and the prospects of the future regime. Current analyses of redemocratization have centered on the decompression of bureaucratic-authoritarian regimes and on the politics of transition to democratic rule. Although some authors have tried to interpret the second phase of the Peruvian military regime in this light, Peru never experienced a bureaucratic-authoritarian regime.[17] In Peru, redemocratization evolved from the political and economic collapse of authoritarian populism. Military withdrawal was organized after a period of high political mobilization during which the labor movement had been strengthened by the regime's populist policies and the dominant classes had been excluded from rule. On the contrary, redemocratization following a bureaucratic-authoritarian regime comes after a long period of political repression of labor, without widespread political mobilization. The impetus for the transition comes from within the regime's social base, and the pattern of change is determined by the regime's shifting social base among factions of capital.[18] This transformation is usually gradual, with different durations of *apertura* in all aspects of political life ending in the actual transference of government to a civilian regime.

When the regime is detached from and set against civil society, and when the impetus for redemocratization comes from outside the regime's social base, we face a replacement of regime.[19] In the Peruvian case, replacing an authoritarian regime in a highly politicized situation acquired a dual and contradictory nature. On the one hand, the political parties were reactivated to negotiate the conditions of the transference. On the other hand, an orderly transfer of power demanded the reinforcement of state autonomy and the tightening of authoritarian control on civil society. Therefore after July 1976 a dual political process was generated: on one hand, the military had to negotiate with the political parties; on the other hand, the regime had to struggle with capital and labor over the allocation of the stabilization costs and the overall direction of social and economic policy. This duality points to a fundamental factor in Peruvian society: namely, the corporatist nature of interest representation. Local capital is represented through its trade associations without strong organic linkages with major political parties, even though certain ideological affinities can be observed. For its part, labor is represented primarily by union confederations with stronger ties to parties on the left, but which do not directly represent labor interests. Because by and large democratic procedures have not operated in Peru, political parties have not fulfilled this fundamental role. The suppression of parties during military rule has reinforced the roles played by trade associations as representative of various interests. This divorce between political parties and basic interest groups would be maintained during the long march to civilian rule. The transition was made viable by the depoliticization of the transference process.

The GRFA sought the consensus of the officer corps on a political program for the transfer of government. A document was prepared by a military commission, which in turn submitted it for the consideration of the ranking officers. The actual mechanisms for such a transfer, however, were not specified. On February 6, 1977, the Plan Túpac Amaru was published, which made public the military's intention to withdraw from power. With the enunciation of the plan, the GRFA recaptured the political initiative and control of the political scene. The GRFA called for a public discussion of the plan and asked for suggestions from representative institutions in society. In April and May meetings were held with the major political parties to revitalize their structure after eight years of inactivity. Traditional political parties reorganized and returned to the political scene, and new parties sprang up and demanded to be included in the dialogue.

Different opinions were advanced with regard to the transfer mechanisms. Acción Popular (AP) demanded an immediate return to constitutionality. The Partido Popular Cristiano (PPC) proposed a brief transition, with a legislative branch to be elected in 1978 and the executive to be controlled by the military until 1980. At that time, general elections were to be held to replace one-third of the legislature and elect a civilian president. APRA called for immediate local elections, elections for a Constituent Assembly in 1978, and general elections for 1980. Leftist parties, labor, and those groups who had supported the GRFA, such as Democracia Cristiana (DC), denounced the transfer of power as reactionary. They called instead for a continuation of military rule and the deepening of the reforms.[20] Political discourse focused on when the military would leave power.

While negotiating with the political parties, the GRFA sought to control the rising civil unrest, which had reached critical levels. After the general strike produced by the June 1976 economic stabilization measures, and in the face of widespread opposition to the regime, the GRFA tightened its control on society. Freedom of the press was completely curtailed by the closing down of independent magazines, a curfew was imposed on the capital city that lasted for more than nine months, and a fourteen-month state of emergency was decreed that suppressed civil rights. The military regime authorized the firing of the union leadership involved in the strike. Some two thousand labor activists lost their jobs, which seriously affected the strength of the labor movement. These extreme measures aggravated the regime's isolation and set it against society at large.

The nationwide general strike of July 19, 1977, which was the culmination of a series of protests against the regime and which had the massive support of all segments of society, finally defined the issue of military withdrawal. On July 28, 1977, forced by its extreme isolation and its inability to control civil society, even using extreme measures, the regime proposed a concrete transfer program by announcing elections for a Constitutional Assembly for 1978 and general elections for 1980. The redemocratization thrust was reinforced by the human rights policies of the Carter administration and the need to develop external legitimacy in view of the foreign debt negotiations. Negotiations with the IMF had been suspended since mid-1976, and the military government was unable to resume them because of its unwillingness to adopt the "shock policies" demanded by the Fund. The democratic opening caught the attention of the U.S. State Department, and every step in that direction received a positive response, such as an increase in foreign aid to the regime. Moreover, the U.S. embassy received orders to oppose rightist military officers and factions of local capital who sought military *continuismo* along the lines of Southern Cone countries, and it let it be known that this option would not be accepted by the Carter administration.[21] If redemocratization was a possibility after July 1976, after July 1977 it was a fact.

The call for elections for a Constitutional Assembly on the fourth of October, 1977, and the enactment of the electoral law the following month began a new stage in the political process—the actual transition to civilian rule. The GRFA widened the political arena, allowing for a controlled political reactivation of society. The state of emergency was lifted, relative freedom of the press was allowed (after a "gentlemen's agreement" with independent mass media), and political and labor figures were allowed to return from exile.

The key issues of the transition process were the attempts by the military to define the terms of their retreat, to influence and control the political process, and to some degree to shape the new civilian regime. Therefore, the military sought to control the transition, both by imposing the rules and by attempting to influence the outcome of the elections. Although the transfer was depoliticized, the struggle between the military regime and local capital and labor continued. The dispute revolved around economic stabilization policies and the future of the military-decreed reforms. This period was marked by increasing labor unrest, with two national strikes and the regime's subsequent reaction.

The GRFA decided on the timetable for the transfer of power, calling for a Constitutional Assembly as the first step. This decision was motivated by the military's desire to institutionalize Velasco's reforms. At the same time, the election would serve as a trial run, giving the political parties time to reorganize. Finally, a prolonged transition process would buy time for a graceful and negotiated departure from power.[22]

The military (making it clear that the transfer was of the government, not of power) laid down three basic conditions: First, the transfer would proceed only if order in society were preserved. Second, the armed forces would not accept only one political group as the locus of power. Finally, the Constitutional Assembly had to ratify the structural reforms enacted by the GRFA. Morales Bermúdez declared, "If reforms are not ratified, then the de facto government, that is, this government, annuls the Assembly and the story is over; . . . the military government, with me or with another person, will continue."[23]

For the replacement of an authoritarian regime to proceed, short of forced eviction from office, the military must be offered a political alternative that is *viable* (i.e., guarantees minimal stability for the incumbent regime), and *acceptable* to the military (i.e., guarantees the military institutional and personal immunity from legal or political reprisals). Such an alternative depends upon whether social institutions have been preserved during the authoritarian period—in particular, the party structure—and on the behavior of the democratic forces during the transition. If civil institutions have been seriously affected and the party structure weakened, the prospects for transfer are remote, the future of the incumbent regime is bleak. On the other hand, if political parties have been able to maintain their organization, political capabilities, and a strong leadership, and if civil institutions have not been seriously weakened, a transfer is more feasible. At the same time, during the transition process, the democratic forces have to maintain a difficult balance between their attempts to placate the military, therefore making transition a possibility, and the need to gain popular support to become a viable alternative to military rule. An imbalance on either side could jeopardize the transition.

The alternatives to military rule can adopt two basic forms. One is what Hartlyn calls, when analyzing the Colombian redemocratization process, a *transition coalition*.[24] In this case, the relevant political forces agree on the desirability of replacing the military regime and returning to democratic government. A consensus results from the negotiations among the major political parties on the conditions for democratic rule, safeguards for particular interests, and the overall direction of future public policy. This coalition then negotiates the transfer with the military regime. If this does not work, it seeks to overthrow the authoritarian regime. This coalition does not necessarily have to be fixed; the fundamental element is that a "critical coalition" in terms of popular support and programmatic content be maintained.

A second option is for a particular social group to be perceived by the military as *heir* to their rule. This could occur in the absence of a coalition, or when there is an ideological affinity between the outgoing regime and a particular party. This alternative does not preclude the evolution of a transition coalition. Indeed, this was the case in Peru.

As in 1963, when Acción Popular inherited power, and the transition was organized in such a way as to leave that political party in control, in 1977 APRA became the civilian alternative to the GRFA. A series of factors accounted for this. In the first place, the traditional antagonism between the armed forces and APRA was overcome by Morales Bermúdez when he exempted that party from any responsibility for his father's assassination. Furthermore, Haya de la Torre and other *aprista* leaders had presented the party to the masses as a civil alternative to military rule, yet one that had a long-standing affinity for the type of reformist programs followed by the military. Also, APRA was the only political party with proven popular support at that time, and occupied the center of the political spectrum. Acción Popular was not a possibility, since the military could hardly return to power the same party they had ousted. Moreover, Fernando Belaúnde Terry was calling for a Frente Democrático to oppose the GRFA and accelerate the transfer program. Finally, APRA had strong leadership and party discipline that would guarantee that agreements reached with the leadership would be honored. APRA began a long period of close relations with the GRFA. This alliance was not immune to contradictions, but it became the civilian interlocutor with the military. Any explicit pact would have been negated by the *aprista* leadership, but, as Handelman points out, "Even if no formal accord was established, almost all impartial observers agreed that an informal accommodation was reached."[25]

After an initial agreement with the Assembly election process, the AP retired from the electoral process, demanding an immediate return to civilian rule. The other political parties, including the left, accepted the conditions imposed by the GRFA and participated in the electoral contest. The campaign was marked by the ongoing struggle around the economic stabilization measures and the attempts of the military to influence the outcome of the election. Through devices in the electoral law, the GRFA favored APRA. Also, in granting free media space for the political campaign, the government clearly favored that party. Furthermore, during the campaign, the left was repressed; its candidates were deported and its magazines were closed.[26] Therefore, the duality in the political process continued. The transition to civilian rule proceeded, while at the same time the military strengthened its grip on society.

On June 18, 1978, Peruvians went to the polls for the first time in years. APRA won at the national level with 35.3 percent of the vote, gaining thirty-seven seats in the Assembly; the PPC, strengthened by the AP's abstention, won 23.8 percent and twenty-five seats. The surprise was the strong showing of the left. After initial attempts for a united electoral coalition, the unity of the left had been broken, and five leftist parties had presented candidates, obtaining 33 percent of the vote, and thirty-two seats. Political parties representing Velasco's legacy had a poor showing, demonstrating once again the incapacity of military regimes, even radical ones, to develop broad popular support.[27]

On July 28, 1978, the Assembly opened its sessions. The left bloc insisted that the Assembly should go beyond the limited role of writing a constitution and debate fundamental socioeconomic and political issues of the day. The FOCEP, of Trotskyite orientation, insisted that the Assembly was the only legitimate institution and therefore should replace the military government. Enacting one of these leftist positions would have set the Assembly against the military regime and jeopardized the transference. The coalition between APRA and PPC in the Assembly, representing a wide majority, solved the issue by depoliticizing it. A "peaceful coexistence," as Haya de la Torre called it, was arranged with the GRFA. The Assembly limited its task to writing a new constitution.

Coinciding with the Assembly's inauguration were other fundamental developments. In May 1978, an agreement with the IMF was finally reached, alleviating external pressures. Military management of the economy was ended with the calling in of Javier Silva Ruete and Manuel Moreyra, a technocratic team who attempted to close the political distance between the state and local capital by articulating an economic model based on manufacturers' exports. With a depoliticized Assembly, and the regime's tenuous accommodation with local capital, the labor movement was isolated in its confrontation with the GRFA. Weakened by internal dissent, it faced major defeats, such as the abortive general strike of January 1979. These events lead some analysts to point to 1978 as the beginning of a counterreform in Peruvian politics. Furthermore, the economy began an upward swing that would last until 1980, therefore allowing the military to make a graceful departure.

The Assembly took a year to formulate the new constitution. Although dominated by APRA, it needed broader support for its initiatives. The final document reflected the shifting alliances among the political forces represented in the Assembly. The PPC played a vital role in drafting the constitution by negotiating its support to APRA. The left gained influence on those issues where the *aprista* delegates dared not take an openly unpopular stand by opposing them. During the drafting of the constitution and particularly after Haya became ill, the internal divisions in APRA surfaced.[28]

Haya de la Torre, as president of the Assembly, signed the constitution on July 12, 1979, and it was sent to the GRFA for its promulgation. Morales Bermúdez rejected the document because he objected to the transitory dispositions, claiming that they exceeded the prerogatives of the Assembly. A tense situation between the GRFA and the Assembly was produced—a situation that could have frustrated the transition. The Assembly rejected the proposed modifications and dissolved. The military announced that they would continue to rule under their revolutionary statute and under the 1933 constitution. Political parties did not take any action, however, but accepted military domination in order not to antagonize the regime and jeopardize the transfer of power. The new constitution had to wait for the new civilian regime to be promulgated. A fundamental point for the transition was the assurances demanded and received by the GRFA about their future role under democratic rule. The military introduced into the constitution the articles related to military affairs, elaborated by the Consejo de Asesores de la Presidencia and adopted by the Assembly without major discussion. Furthermore, before the transfer of office, the GRFA enacted legislation whereby former military officers could only be accused of offenses before the Supreme Court. Finally, a mobilization law was enacted, providing the legal basis for future military involvement in politics.[29]

The electoral law issued on August 27, 1979, officially announced the beginning of the electoral contest. The election was marked by extreme political factionalization, with fifteen political parties participating. The left made frustrating attempts to build a common electoral front, and APRA was plagued by internal problems. Haya de la Torre's death in 1979 produced a succession crisis that fragmented the party. The crisis weakened APRA's role as heir to military rule, even though the GRFA had clearly supported APRA through the electoral law that granted stronger representation to aprista-traditional strongholds.[30]

General elections were held on May 15, 1980, with surprising results. Acción Popular obtained an astonishing victory, polling 45.4 percent of the national vote in the presidential contest, a majority in the deputy elections, and a strong plurality for the Senate. The party's consistent opposition to the military regime and its refusal to accept military mandates during the transition seem to have acted in its favor. APRA suffered an electoral collapse, obtaining 27 percent of the vote. The left was able to obtain only 16.7 percent of the vote, and the PPC ended in fourth place, with 9.6 percent. The transfer of power occurred on July 28, 1980, ending twelve years of military rule, and signaling the beginning of a new democratic moment in Peruvian history.

In the Peruvian case, the military decided to leave government and return to the barracks despite the absence of strong pressures from civilians to redemocratize. The drive for redemocratization, as in Brazil, began within the military institution itself. It came as a result of the military's acute internal politicization and progressive isolation from society. Civilian pressures for the return to constitutionality grew during the transition process and gained momentum. The relative reinforcement of military unity and state autonomy allowed for the transfer to proceed, inhibiting antidemocratic alliances between military factions and groups in civil society. The will of the military to retire is a necessary but not sufficient condition for redemocratization. A civilian alternative that is both viable and acceptable for the military also has to exist. The accommodation reached first between the GRFA and APRA, and the later coalition with the PPC, allowed this alternative to crystallize. Furthermore, the generals yielded power only after securing their personal and institutional immunity, and guaranteeing that they would maintain their share of power.

An Authoritarian Democracy? July 1980–1984

Acción Popular achieved power in 1980 with unprecedented electoral support and, in alliance with the PPC, held a majority in both chambers of Congress. Furthermore, the gradual recuperation of the economy during 1979–1980 and the growth of foreign reserves gave the regime a relative freedom of action in economic management. The initial measures of Belaúnde's regime fortified democratic institutions. It carried out the mandates of the constitution, reinstated local elections, returned the mass media to its rightful owners, and reaffirmed freedom of the press. Nevertheless, three years later, in the local elections of 1983, the AP suffered a catastrophic collapse. It was able to pool only 17 percent of the votes at the national level, and it could not win a single district government in Lima. This showed the isolation of the regime from all sectors of society. A detailed analysis of the political process during Belaúnde's regime goes beyond the scope of this chapter, but it is necessary to attempt a general assessment of this brief democratic interlude. It constitutes, in my view, a continuation of the antipopulist phase initiated in 1976.

Two distinctive features characterize Peruvian democracy under Belaúnde's regime: the regime's accommodation with the military leaders, and the progressive isolation of the regime from society. The democratic regime respected the conditions for the transition: it did not undertake any investigation of the military's administrative actions and allowed for the military's absolute autonomy in their internal affairs. Furthermore, the democratic regime maintained the legislation enacted by the GRFA in areas of fundamental military concern, and allowed the generals to keep their share of power as a deliberative force in crucial national affairs. Moreover, the regime progressively introduced military officers into governing functions, by including them in the cabinet. Therefore, a balance was achieved between the democratic regime and the armed forces, a balance that has led Pease to characterize Peruvian democracy as a "tutelary democracy."[31]

The peculiarity of Belaúnde's democracy lies in the fact that the state remained isolated and insensitive to pressures arising from civil society in a situation that closely resembles military authoritarianism after 1976. Social forces hoped that the democratic opening would narrow the gap between the state and civil society that had developed under authoritarian rule. Civilian groups demanded a role in formulating public policy to satisfy long-suppressed popular demands. Expectations placed on democracy both by local capital and the labor movement were soon frustrated, however. The opening of the state did not occur. Public policy continued to be formulated by closed technocratic circles, especially as regards economic policy, the center of political debate. The progressive frustration of social groups, owing to their incapacity to participate in government and to impose solutions to their demands, deepened the conflict between the regime and institutions representing labor and local capital.

The relative autonomy of the regime was made possible by AP's control over both the executive and legislative powers and the particular configuration of AP's membership, internal power structure, and the absence of organic links with capital and labor.[32] Using its majority in the Chamber of Deputies and its strength in the Senate in alliance with PPC, the Belaúnde regime minimized the constitutional role of Congress to the point of annulling it. The Congress became merely a sounding box for APRA and for the leftist opposition. Because legislative powers were given to the executive, all major laws were decided and decreed by the executive branch in a closed decision-making process not unlike that which took place during authoritarian rule. Furthermore, interest groups were not able to influence the direction of public policy.

The Peruvian regime's relative isolation was reinforced by a series of factors. First, the regime had to confront an overload of demands at its inauguration. Since 1976, all groups in society had been trying to find solutions to their grievances and the return to democracy generated inflated expectations. This demand overload frustrated the regime's attempts to institutionalize links with representatives of capital and labor through the Consejo Nacional del Trabajo and to negotiate the distribution of the costs of economic stabilization. After the failure of this *concertación social*, the regime lost its institutionalized links with fundamental social forces. Moreover, the Finance Ministry (Ministerio de Economía, Finanzas y Comercio), and the Central Bank emerged as a state within the state, with economic policy being formulated by a group of young technocrats. Some frictions were produced between the economic team and the more politically sensitive members of the government party, but internal autonomy in economic management was reinforced by the agreements with the IMF that more than once were used to control pressures from the government. Finally, the regime was unable to set up channels of participation through which interest groups could present their demands. The weakness of the traditional parties hampered the government's attempts to legitimize the dominant order and institutionalize popular participation. This has been a more or less permanent feature of the Peruvian political system.

A confounding issue is how the regime used its wide discretionary authority to formulate public policy. Social groups and academic observers supported two economic alternatives for the new democracy: growth via the export of manufactured goods, or the deepening of import-substitution industrialization. Both of these options, in the context of the government's consolidation of its accommodation with local capital, were already being implemented, and had been since 1978.[33] Nevertheless, the regime opted for an orthodox neoliberal economic policy that alienated local capital and put the burden of stabilization on the masses, generating acute social and political instability. The reaction to this economic policy generated open confrontation between capital and labor against the regime. At the same time, the antipopulist economic policy eroded the regime's popularity and was responsible for the AP's political collapse in the local elections of 1983 and the general elections in 1985. However, even though there might have been a relative discretionary margin during the first year for a different economic policy, the economic crisis would have demanded sooner or later the imposition of an antipopulist economic policy. Belaúnde's regime had to face the same dilemma that its military predecessor had faced—that is, external legitimacy versus internal popularity. As all Latin American countries are realizing now, the IMF and the international financial community leave little choice. The most serious challenge for Latin America today is to learn how to maintain democratic freedoms in a context of IMF-sponsored stabilization measures.

Notes

1. The period of the *convivencia* is analyzed in François Bourricaud, *Power and Society in Contemporary Peru* (New York: Praeger, 1970).

2. Pedro Pablo Kuczynski, in *Democracia bajo presión económica*, ed. Mosco Azul (Lima 1980), offers an insider's account of the struggle for structural reforms.

3. Guillermo O'Donnell, *Modernization and Bureaucratic-Authoritarianism* (Institute of International Studies, University of California, Berkeley, 1973), p. 77.

4. For example, Lawrence S. Graham, "Democracy and the Bureaucratic State in Latin America," in *The Continuing Struggle for Democracy in Latin America*, ed. H. J. Wiarda (Boulder, Colo: Westview, 1980).

5. Detailed analysis of revolutionary process can be found in *The Peruvian Experiment: Continuity and Change Under Military Rule*, ed. A. Lowenthal (Princeton, N.J.: Princeton University Press, 1975); A. Lowenthal and C. McClintock, eds., *The Peruvian Experiment Reconsidered* (Princeton, N.J.: Princeton University Press, 1983). The best primary source for the period is the *Cronología Política*, published by DESCO, which covers the 1968–1980 period.

6. Peter S. Cleaves and Henry Pease García, "State Autonomy and Military Policymaking" in *The Peruvian Experiment Reconsidered*, ed. Lowenthal and McClintock; A. Stepan, *State and Society: Peru in Comparative Perspective* (Princeton, N.J.: Princeton University Press 1978); A. Quijano, "Imperialismo y capitalismo de estado," *Sociedad y política* (Lima, 1972), among other authors, stresses the extreme autonomy attained by the state from social classes.

7. Cleaves and Pease, "State Autonomy and Military Policymaking," p. 214.

8. E.V.K. Fitzgerald, "State Capitalism in Peru: A Model of Economic Development and its Limitations," in *The Peruvian Experiment Reconsidered*, ed. Lowenthal and McClintock.

9. See J. Malloy, "Authoritarianism, Corporatism and Mobilization in Peru," in *The New Corporativism*, ed. F. Pike and T. Stritch (South Bend, Ind.: Notre Dame University Press, 1974); and Julio Cótler, "Bases del corporativismo en el Perú," in *Sociedad y política* 2 (Lima 1972).

10. Julio Cótler, "Democracy and National Integration in Peru," in *The Peruvian Experiment Reconsidered*, ed. Lowenthal and McClintock, p. 35.

11. This process of ideological differentiation is discussed by Lisa North in "Ideological Orientation of Peru's Military Rulers," in ibid.

12. The political struggle within the state is analyzed by Henry Pease García in *El ocaso del poder oligárquico*, DESCO, 1977; and in *Caminos al poder*, DESCO 1979. Also an interesting discussion can be found in Hernán Rosenkranz, *La Faccionaliación de las fuerzas armadas, dentro de un contexto de movilización política: el caso del Perú*, unpublished, University of Pittsburgh, 1978.

13. Cleaves and Pease, "State Autonomy and Military Policymaking," p. 229.

14. Fitzgerald, "State Capitalism in Peru," p. 93.

15. For a discussion of the international environment in this period, see Efrain Cobas, *Fuerzas armadas, misiones militares y dependencia en el Peru* (Lima: Editorial Horizonte, 1982).

16. Speech by Morales Bermúdez on the Day of the Navy, October 1976.

17. For example, Graham, "Democracy and the Bureaucratic State."

18. This issue is discussed by Guillermo O'Donnell in "Reflections on the Pattern of Change in the Bureaucratic-Authoritarian State," *Latin American Research Review* 13, no. 1 (1978).

19. I am using the term as advanced by Samuel P. Huntington, in "Will more Countries Become Democratic?" *Political Science Quarterly* 99, no. 2 (1984).

20. J. Nieto in *Izquierda y democracia en el Perú* (Lima: DESCO, 1983), presents an account of the positions of the Peruvian left with regard to redemocratization.

21. See Julio Cótler, *Intervenciones militares y transferencia del poder a la civilidad en el Perú* (Wilson Center, 1980).

22. Most analysts of the Peruvian process coincide on the reasons for redemocratization through stages. See Howard Handelman, "The March to Civilian Rule," AUFS, Report 1980/2; also, Cótler, *Intervenciones*; and Pease, *Caminos al poder*.

23. Morales Bermúdez, interview, *El Comercio*, October 16, 1977.

24. Jonathan Hartlyn, "Military Governments and Transition to Civilian Rule, the Colombian Experience of 1957–58," *Journal of Inter-American Studies and World Affairs* 20 (May 1984).

25. Handelman, "The March to Civilian Rule."

26. Fernando Tuesta presents a detailed account of military involvement in the electoral process. See his *Análisis del proceso electoral a la Asamblea Constituyente* (Lima: Universidad Católica, 1979).

27. An analysis of election results can be found in Enrique Bernales, *Crisis política solución electoral* (DESCO, 1980); also in Rafael Roncagliolo, *¿Quién Ganó? Elecciones 1931–1980* (DESCO 1980).

28. For a discussion of Assembly's politics, see Sandra L. Woy-Hazleton, "The Return of Partisan Politics in Peru," in *Post-Revolutionary Peru: The Politics of Transformation*, ed. Stephen M. Gorman (Boulder, Colo.: Westview, 1982).

29. The protection of military interests and the mobilization law are discussed in Victor Villanueva, "Peru's New Professionalism: The Failure of the Technocratic Approach," in *Post-Revolutionary Peru: The Politics of Transformation*, ed. Gorman.

30. According to Villanueva, the GRFA in the last moment turned its support to Acción Popular in view of APRA's internal fragmentation (ibid.).

31. Henry Pease García, "De la dictadura a la democracia Tutelada," in *Democracia y movimientos populares* (DESCO, 1979).

32. This is an aspect of the issue that demands further study. Interesting observations are advanced by A. Filomeno in "Tras las huellas de Acción Popular, trama de poder partidario y casos de corrupción," *Que hacer* 13 (Nov. 1981).

33. See Javier Iguíñiz, *"Reflecciones polémicas sobre dos alternativas a la situación económica actual,"* Fundación F. Ebert/ILDIS, Serie Materiales de Trabajo No. 5 (Lima, 1978); and Jurgen Schuldt, *De la promesa al fracaso: Perú 1980–1984* (CIUP, Lima, 1980).

Catherine M. Conaghan

---

7 Party Politics and Democratization in Ecuador

If any consensus emerges from current debates on the fate of political parties, it is that party systems everywhere are in crisis. Scholars of U.S. politics are fixated on the notion of dealignment and ponder the causes of fading party loyalties. Analysts of Western Europe point to the displacement of parties in the policymaking process and the increasing importance of corporatist-style arrangements. On both sides of the Atlantic, parties appear to be failing in multiple ways—in their roles as interest aggregators, policymakers, and legitimators.[1]

The situation of Latin American parties is equally dire, but for vastly different reasons. While parties in the developed liberal democracies struggle to avoid further erosion in their social bases of support, the recently formed and revived parties in the redemocratizing countries of Latin America are still searching for a constituency. North American and European parties face the problem of how to maintain the integrity and power of their legislatures, while Latin American parties strive to breathe life into representative bodies in situations where corporatism and *golpismo* have long-standing traditions. If the puzzle for parties of the North is how to hold onto past glories, the essential problem for Latin American parties is how to carve out a place for themselves in a fundamentally hostile environment, one in which social forces and the state are able to overshadow actors in the party system and render them irrelevant.

The purpose of this discussion is to analyze the origins and the consequences of the multiple crises that have occurred in the Ecuadorean party system from 1979 to 1984. The principal argument is that the crises of representation, mediation, and rationality that reverberate within parties and between parties and civil society have

145

threatened the consolidation of the reinstalled democratic regime. The ephemeral ties between parties and the masses, between parties and party leaders, and the inability of the party elite to resolve conflicts among themselves have created chronic and destructive struggles that have undermined their legitimacy. Moreover, these crises have contributed to problems of internal organization and coalition building that seriously inhibit the development of parties on the center-left of the political spectrum. In their weakened state, these parties have been unable to stop the recurrence of antidemocratic behavior by parties and institutions on the right. In short, the absence of a cohesive and institutionally developed center-left in Ecuador is also retarding the development of a democratic right.

Before examining the sources of the three crises and their interactive character, I should briefly review the key events in Ecuador's redemocratization process.

El Retorno, El Cambio, Decisión Nacional

To understand the recent development of the party system in Ecuador, one must consider the impact of the transition process (*el retorno constitucional*) and the motivations and maneuverings of the key protagonists from 1976 to 1979. The structure of the party system and the dynamics of the transition determined party behavior during the consolidation phase, from 1979 to 1984.[2]

Two important characteristics marked the process of *el retorno*. First, the transition from a military to an elected civilian regime was not the product of a sustained mass uprising against the military regime. Rather, the generals' decision to return to the barracks was largely the result of persistent pressures exerted by upper-class organizations, especially the Quito and Guayaquil Chambers of Commerce, Industry, and Agriculture. The opposition of the bourgeoisie was aimed at derailing the reformist political project proposed by General Rodríguez Lara, who headed the government from 1972 to 1975. The Rodríguez Lara regime had attempted a watered-down version of Peruvian-style military reformism. Economic reforms that included tighter controls over foreign capital, increased regulation of domestic capital, and agrarian reform were part of his original program. The intransigence of the Ecuadorean bourgeoisie vis-à-vis these reforms was based on both structural considerations and ideological calculations.[3] But in addition to the substantive disagreements on policy between the military and domestic capitalists, a major complaint voiced by all business interest groups was the absence of regularized consultation with relevant economic decision makers. The military regime, originally supported by the bourgeoisie as a way to prevent the election of populist Assad Bucaram to the presidency in 1972, had denied them access to state power. It was within this context that organizations of the bourgeoisie and right-wing parties banded together to spearhead the demands for redemocratization. The military triumvirate that replaced Rodríguez Lara in 1976 immediately announced plans for a return to democratic rule.

The second key characteristic of *el retorno* is closely related to the first. While the economic elite was at the forefront in the movement for redemocratization, the military triumvirate presiding over the transfer of power was able to retain a high degree of control over the restructuring process and did not permit a unilateral takeover of the process by forces on the right. So even during the transition itself, the relative lack of access to the regime remained problematic for the bourgeoisie, particularly as they pondered how the transition would influence their prospects for control in the upcoming democratic government. As a result, right-wing parties and business associations equivocated during the transition process, participating in it while calling its legitimacy into question. Thus, the decision by Minister of Government General Richelieu Levoyer to pursue the transition through a constitutional referendum rather than a constituent assembly provoked a wave of opposition. Business associations sponsored a "null vote" campaign in the 1978 referendum. The strategy was unsuccessful: a new constitution that gave the vote to illiterates and created a unicameral Congress was endorsed by 43 percent of the voters.

The military's resistance to such rightist machinations was matched by its policies to weaken the electoral appeal of parties on the center-left and left. The most serious blow to the progressive parties was the proscription of Assad Bucaram, candidate of the mass-based populist party of Guayaquil, the Concentración de Fuerzas Populares (CFP). In Bucaram's place, the CFP was forced to field an unknown figure, Jaime Roldós, as its presidential candidate. This forced by-passing of a Bucaram candidacy and the CFP's later victory in the presidential contest by Roldós created enormous tensions that eventually rent the party apart in the 1979–1984 period. Along with the restriction on the CFP, the Christian Democratic Democracia Popular (DP) and the left-wing Movimiento Popular Democrático (MPD) were disqualified from the ballot.

The top vote-getters from the field of six candidates in the first-round presidential election of July 1978 were Jaime Roldós of the CFP and Sixto Durán Ballen. Durán Ballen was the candidate of the Social Christian and Conservative parties. The military government undertook an extensive recount of the results, largely to narrow the margin between Roldós and Durán Ballen and to allow the right to regroup for the second round. Despite these efforts, the runoff conducted in April 1979 turned into a massive repudiation of the right by the newly enlarged electorate. Roldós and his DP running mate, Osvaldo Hurtado, took 68 percent of the vote nationally, winning in all but one province.[4] The magnitude of Durán Ballen's defeat, particularly in the traditional sites of support for right-wing parties in the sierra provinces, was a clear indication of the organizational and strategic exhaustion of right-wing parties. Their very future was in question. Along with the impressive Roldós victory, the center and center-left scored a decisive win in the congressional elections. Of the sixty-nine seats in the new unicameral Congress, the CFP took twenty-nine, while fifteen seats went to the social-democratic Izquierda Democrática (ID).

The euphoria of the center-left provoked by the Roldós victory quickly dissipated, however. The progressive parties suffered further fragmentation and difficulties in building legislative coalitions. The most devastating fissure occurred within the ranks of the governing party, the CFP. With Roldós in the presidential palace, Assad Bucaram continued to assert his claim to unilateral leadership over the party from his position as president of Congress. Bucaram bitterly denounced Roldós for passing over CFP militants in his assignment of ministerial posts. The struggle over leadership and patronage within the CFP exploded into a continual conflict between the executive and legislative branches dubbed the *pugna de poderes*. The conflict tore the CFP congressional delegation into two factions, the Roldocistas and the Bucaramistas, of approximately equal strength. The immediate political beneficiaries of this split in the governing party were the congressional forces on the right. Bucaram sought alliances with deputies from the traditional Conservative and Liberal parties. With this hybrid alliance intact, and with control of the legislative agenda in the hands of Bucaram, the Roldós administration was thrown on the defensive and compelled to veto measures passed by Congress instead of forcefully constructing *el cambio*—the twenty-one-point reform program on which he had campaigned.[5] Roldós eventually broke through the stalemate with Bucaram by threatening to call a plebiscite and announcing the formation of his own political party: Pueblo, Cambio, y Democracia (PCD).

Nonetheless, this early fragmentation of the governing party threw Roldós and his successor into nearly constant efforts to construct and maintain congressional alliances. The transitory character of these alliances was reflected in the turnover of ministerial posts during the period. From 1979 to the summer of 1983, fifty-eight individuals served in thirteen cabinet posts.

The efforts to maintain a government majority in Congress were complicated by the vacillating posture struck by the social democratic party, the Izquierda Democrática. Congressman and party leader Rodrigo Borja firmly believed that any explicit involvement in progovernment legislative coalition would seriously damage the ID's prospects for the 1984 elections.[6] Other ID leaders, such as Raúl Baca, maintained that the chronic paralysis of Congress put the democratic game itself in jeopardy. With these contending perspectives within the party, the ID veered in and out of tacit understandings with these governments. These oscillations echoed the political crisis at hand. At moments when the executive-legislative conflicts created conditions for a breakdown in the democratic regime, the ID struck lines of cooperation with the government. This was the basis of the 1981 Convergencia Democrática agreement which brought together ID, DP, and Roldocista legislators. The Convergencia coalesced in the pervasive crisis atmosphere that followed Roldós's death in a May 1981 plane crash, Vice-President Hurtado's succession, and increasing conflict between the government and the business community. With mounting attacks on the regime by the private sector and the prospects of a coup growing, the ID entered into the Convergencia and pledged their cooperation with other center-left parties to defend democratic government.[7] Once the immediate political crisis receded, however, the pact eroded. The ID was quick to demonstrate its independence by voting along with parties of the right to censure Hurtado's minister of government, Carlos Feraud Blum, just a few weeks after the Convergencia pact. The fragmentation among parties of the center-left enhanced the position and maneuverability of the right. In the Congress, Deputy León Febres-Cordero of the Partido Social Cristiano mounted aggressive attacks on the Hurtado government, forcing the censures of two cabinet ministers. Forces on the right outside the government were equally aggressive; business leaders denounced economic policies and suggested the removal of Hurtado. Alongside this elite opposition, Hurtado's austerity measures weakened support for the regime among trade unions and the electorate at large. Under these conditions, the preservation of democracy itself became the primary policy goal of the Hurtado government.[8]

A lack of consensus on the right and a lack of enthusiasm by the armed forces staved off the development of a coalition capable of mounting a coup. As the 1984 presidential and congressional elections neared, the right turned its attention away from the coup option and turned to the takeover of the state by electoral politics. The poor showing of the right in the 1979 contest necessitated the development of a unified right-wing front. Negotiations between the Partido Social Cristiano (PSC), the Partido Ecuatoriano Conservador (PCE), the Partido Liberal Radical Ecuatoriano (PLRE), the Coalición Institucionalista Demócrata (CID), and the Partido Nacionalista Revolucionario (PNR) gave birth to the right-wing electoral front, the Frente de Reconstrucción Nacional (FRN). The FRN backed as its presidential candidate the outspoken congressman and millionaire businessman León Febres-Cordero of the Social Christian party and Blasco Peñaherrera from the Liberal party as his running mate.

Parties on the center-left, however, were unable to coalesce around a single candidate. The scheduling of the congressional elections to coincide with the first round of the presidential elections encouraged these parties to name their own presidential candidates with the hope that a coattails effect would be at work. Eight candidates vied for the political terrain to the left of Febres-Cordero in the first round of elections in January 1984. Emerging as the winner from this crowded field was Rodrigo Borja of the ID. Borja polled 24 percent of the vote, followed by Febres-Cordero, with 23 percent of the vote.[9]

Given the overall performance of parties to the center-left in the first round and their success in the congressional and local contests, the possibility of a second-round victory by the FRN's Febres-Cordero seemed unlikely. In the months between the first and second runoffs, the forces on the right contemplated the implications of defeat. Determined to regain access to state power, they tried some of the tactics employed during the *retorno*. They called into question the legitimacy of the process itself, charging the Tribunal Supremo Electoral with electoral fraud and calling for the impeachment of its directors.[10] Meanwhile, strategists of the FRN reoriented the Febres-Cordero campaign to make inroads into the lower-class vote. The somewhat ominous and vague first-round campaign slogan, *"León: Decisión Nacional"* was retired in favor of the populist promise of *"Pan, Techo y Empleo"* (bread, housing, and work). A methodical door-to-door campaign ensued. Febres-Cordero played heavily on religious and regional themes: he projected himself as a bold, unquestionably macho businessman who would apply the principles of efficient business management to government.[11]

Tensions and rivalries continued to undermine the cohesiveness of center-left parties in the second round. Projecting victory, Rodrigo Borja steadfastly refused to negotiate on the division of political appointments among parties in his upcoming administration. This contributed to key defections from the Borja candidacy by two important regional parties of the coast, the CFP and the Frente Radical Alfarista (FRA). The CFP and the FRA abstained from endorsing Borja, and party leaders on the coast worked openly for Febres-Cordero. On the extreme left, the MPD and the Partido Socialista (PS) also declined to endorse Borja. Borja, who still adamantly believed that any association with the Hurtado government would be damaging, continued to distance himself both from Hurtado's Democracia Popular and from the Partido Demócrata (PD) headed by Francisco Huerta, who participated in the Hurtado government as minister of health. Only FADI, the leftist coalition that included the Communist party, actively campaigned with the ID on Borja's behalf. This unification of the right and the fractionalization on the left produced a narrow victory for Febres-Cordero in the April runoff. Febres-Cordero won with a margin of a little over 80,000 votes, polling 51.9 percent of the vote, with 48.1 percent going to Borja.

With the presidency in the hands of a right-wing administration espousing a neoliberal economic project and a center-left congressional majority, chronic executive-legislative conflicts reemerged. The unexpected shock of the Borja defeat pushed the progressive parties into the formation of a unified legislative coalition, the Bloque Progresista. The Bloque included the ID, DP, FADI, MPD, PD, PS, and the Partido Roldocista Ecuatoriano (PRE), comprised of former Roldocistas. The FRA gave qualified support to the Bloque, while the CFP deserted altogether and struck informal lines of cooperation with the progovernment FRN parties.

The presence of a clear-cut antigovernment majority bloc in Congress once again posed problems regarding the penetrability of this institution by the rightist minority. Initial attempts were made by the Febres-Cordero government to erode the Bloque by inducing individual congressmen to desert their parties and the Bloque. Three defections from the PD, one from the ID, and one from the DP occurred.[12]

Despite this intense pressure on individual congressmen, the progressive bloc managed to maintain itself as a majority. The FRN parties thus engaged in new tactics to undermine the Bloque's control over bureaucratic appointments in government agencies, the Supreme Court, and congressional committees. The catalyst for the struggle was the Bloque's appointments for a new Supreme Court. The FRN parties in Congress and President Febres-Cordero openly challenged the constitutionality of the new appointments and argued that the sitting Supreme Court justices should remain. Congressional activity came to a standstill as sessions were marred by the throwing of tear-gas bombs and physical confrontations between FRN and Bloque leaders.

The resolution of the dispute came after four months of acrimonious negotiations between Febres-Cordero and Raúl Baca, the president of the Congress and leader of the Bloque Progresista. Rather than arriving at any definitive apportionment of authority between executive and legislative branches, the termination of the crisis revolved around *la troncha*, a parceling out of positions between parties. The final agreement entailed the resignation of the contending Supreme Court appointees and the division of the new appointments between FRN and the Bloque Progresista.[13]

The terms of the resolution of the Supreme Court crisis starkly revealed the continuing weakness and inability of the Bloque Progresista parties to contain the right, inside or outside Congress. The parties of the FRN and the president himself clearly indicated their willingness to step outside of normal institutional channels of conflict resolution (such as through the physical disruption of congressional sessions, the president's use of the police to bar entrance to the Supreme Court) to achieve their ends. The Bloque had no resources at its disposal to force the FRN and the president to stay definitively within the bounds of constitutional procedure to resolve conflict. With the viability of democracy itself at stake in the showdown of the Supreme Court, the only alternative for the Bloque was the one chosen—a deal that assured the right of increased access to the

institutional apparatus of the state. Bloque leaders themselves ac-
knowledged the solution as a short-term fix and a political defeat, but
saw it as the only option that kept formal democracy alive.

Representation, Rationality, and Mediation

The central dilemma in the Ecuadorean party system lies in the
inability of parties to carry out the horizontal and vertical control
functions that are pivotal to democratic stability. Political theorists
have underscored the critical role that parties must play in restraining
and channelling both elite and mass behavior in democratic systems.
In the work of Gramsci and Michels, parties are portrayed as exerting
a conservative effect on followers; they encapsulate social classes,
filter out "excessive" demands, and set the stage for bargaining over
policies.[14] At the same time, parties act as a check on the behavior of
other elites and institutions. According to Marxist theorist Nicos Poulantzas, parties play a key role in creating the "unstable equilibrium
of compromise" that is crucial to the maintenance of parliamentary
democracy.[15] This notion that democracy requires a balance between
political actors is also found in the work of Robert Dahl. For Dahl,
the viability of democratic institutions hinges on a widespread distribution of political resources across "government" and "opposition."
The strength of both sets of actors creates incentives for each to
compromise and use democratic procedures to settle conflicts.[16]

Why have Ecuadorean parties been unable to consistently perform
these control functions? To answer this question, it is essential to
examine how the processes of democratization, economic modernization, and the expansion of state power intersected in Ecuador to
produce a late and limited formation of interest groups and an even
later formation of a modern party system.[17] The *timing* and *sequence*
of these processes led to the interrelated crises of representation,
rationality, and mediation in the party system.

The crisis of representation—the absence of strong ties between
parties and social classes—has its roots in the extremely lagged character of Ecuadorean democratization and the preemption of representation functions by interest groups. Parties have been constricted in
their ability to penetrate civil society while civil society itself remains
highly disorganized and fragmented.[18]

The extension of political rights to the masses in Ecuador was a painfully slow process. It remained incomplete until the 1978 constitution gave the vote to illiterates. Prior to the military intervention of 1972, the party system was an amalgam of traditional oligarchic and populist-style parties. The traditional parties of the elite, which dated from the nineteenth century, the Liberals and the Conservatives, vied for power with personalist electoral organizations such as Otto Arosemena's CID or Carlos Julio Arosemena's PNR. Whatever popular discontent with oligarchic politics could be found within the extremely circumscribed ranks of voters was channelled through Ecuador's variants of populism. From the 1930s through the 1960s, José María Velasco Ibarra successfully played on populist themes to win the presidency five times. The CFP, under the leadership of Assad Bucaram, did the same and developed an important regional following in the coastal provinces.[19]

Oligarchic politics owed their longevity in Ecuador to the peculiarities in the class structure that crystallized under export-led dependent capitalism. Ecuador's entry into the world market as a cocoa exporter at the end of the nineteenth century and its later status as the world's leading banana producer in the 1950s created a social order dominated by agro-exporters, financiers, importers, and large landowners. Both the urban middle and industrial working classes remained small, owing to the minimal demands placed on the rest of the economy by the export trade. The majority of the work force was employed in the countryside. In the interior provinces of the sierra, Indian peasants labored in traditional haciendas, agricultural estates that produced for the domestic market. The hacienda system was notorious for its exploitation of Indian labor. Indian peasants were required to render goods and services to their landlords in exchange for the right to cultivate a small subsistence plot. The relations between peasants and hacendados were precapitalist—that is, Indians were paid no wages. In contrast, the organization of export-oriented agriculture on the coast did involve the use of some wage labor. Thus agricultural laborers worked and lived under diverse conditions—a heterogeneity intensified by ethnic and linguistic divisions.

Within this social structure, the growth of popular class organizations and trade unions remained stunted. The restrictions on the labor force inherent in precapitalist production relations and the low level of industrialization meant that aggressive organizations to represent lower-class interests could not develop. When popular protest did occur, selective repression defused it. As such, there was no concerted pressure from below for democratization. Moreover, the relative unity within the dominant elite ruled out the possibility of their seeking out alliances with the peasantry or working class. Under these conditions, it was not difficult for the dominant classes to keep the electorate small through restrictions on suffrage and registration requirements. It is not surprising that parties functioned largely as transitory electoral vehicles. Even elite interest groups and parties remained relatively underdeveloped, because upper-class access to the state apparatus had always been assured.

Important fissures in the oligarchic political system began to appear in the 1950s as economic changes spurred the process of social differentiation. With the ascendancy of developmentalist ideology, the state designated import-substitution industrialization as a major goal. State power expanded as new government agencies charged with the task of economic modernization were created in the late 1950s and 1960s. Economic expansion and industrialization introduced new components into the traditional class structure. Pockets of a modern working class developed in Quito and Guayaquil, while the ranks of the middle class expanded along with the growth of the public sector. All these trends (expansion of the public sector, industrialization, development of the middle and working classes) accelerated dramatically with the initiation of major oil exports during the 1970s.[20]

In response to this expansion of state power in the 1960s and 1970s, formal interest group organizations grew rapidly. Trade union membership increased, agrarian cooperatives were founded, and specialized lobbying groups representing new industrial interests were born. At the same time, middle-class activism produced new political parties such as the Izquierda Democrática and the Christian Democratic party. But with the 1972 military intervention and the proscription of parties, it was interest groups and not parties that took up the tasks of representation. Interest groups assumed a pivotal role in articulating class interests vis-à-vis the military governments. Some interest associations were able to selectively penetrate the state apparatus and developed clientelistic ties.[21]

The absorption of newly emerging social forces into interest groups, the forging of particularistic ties between these groups and segments of the state apparatus, and the proscription of party activities in the initial phase of the military regime created special problems for political parties, particularly the new parties of the center and the left that challenged the oligarchic operation of the party system.[22] The limitations on parties and their exclusion from direct access to policymaking institutions under the military governments damaged their ability to recruit mass constituencies. Without links to the state, the patronage route to party-building was closed to the new aspiring mass parties such as the ID and the DP. The weak or often nonexistent ties between parties and social groups undermined the development of parties of the center and the left, but also affected the maturation of parties on the right. The business elite directed their attention to the Chambers of Industry and Commerce that evolved as the key lobbyists for their economic interests.[23]

The representational dilemma that plagues Ecuador's parties is profound. It involves not just the question of how to capture the loyalties of already organized interests, but also how to forge mass loyalties in an environment in which vast segments of the population stand outside the ranks of organized society. Even though formal interest-group associations proliferated in the past two decades, Ecuadorean society is still relatively unorganized. While it is difficult to estimate exactly how much of the population is not "organized," fragmentary evidence indicates the scope of popular class disorganization. Though many new unions have been formed, unionization in the labor force hovered around 16 percent in the 1970s. Other survey results confirm the low levels of participation in unions and voluntary associations.[24] Thus even if parties were able to forge tighter links to trade unions and other organizations, vast segments of the population would still remain outside the party-group nexus.

The problem of forging party loyalties has not been confined to the party-mass relationship, but also affects the party elite. This crisis of rationality (that is, the disarticulation between the political elite and the party apparatus) is reflected in party fragmentation.[25] While fragmentation was already under way in the 1950s and 1960s, it continued with the reestablishment of electoral politics in 1979. By 1984, seventeen parties were legally recognized by the Tribunal Supremo Electoral. In addition to the creation of new parties, the low level of commitment to parties by the elite was demonstrated in the phenomenon that came to be known as the *cambio de camisetas*—the desertion of congressmen from their respective parties and their reaffiliation with rival parties. This crisis of rationality among the party elite was the product of the interaction between personalism, patronage, and legal arrangements governing the party system.

One of the key provisions of the Ley de Partidos, the law drafted by a civilian commission in 1978 to regulate the operation of the party system, required that parties be legally recognized to qualify for elections and stipulated that candidates be affiliated with one of these parties. The Tribunal Supremo Electoral was charged with the responsibility for licensing the parties. The underlying goal of the law was to remove small personalist parties from the electoral arena and to act as a check against future proliferation. Nevertheless, one of the side effects of this attempt to rationalize the party system through law was that it essentially forced many of the politically ambitious into parties as a matter of convenience rather than conviction. Ties between parties and the new partisan elite were thus often ephemeral. With partisanship so loosely constructed, party affiliations were effortlessly shed by congressmen, once elected, as they calculated their future electoral fortunes and patronage opportunities.

The reasons for the lack of party loyalty among the elite, however, are not entirely juridical. The prevailing political culture as a whole is hostile to the notion of parties. It is important to note that for nearly forty years, political discourse in Ecuador was dominated by the antiparty invocations of José María Velasco Ibarra. Velasco's often quoted dictum, "Give me a balcony, and the people are mine," reflected his lack of concern with party development. Disdain for the principles of party organization is also coupled with popular scorn for professional politicians. Moreover, the history of Ecuadorean parties has not inspired confidence. Because of their traditional weakness and nonthreatening character, Ecuador's parties and their leaders were never subject to the systematic repression experienced by the Peruvian APRA or Venezuelan Acción Democrática during military dictatorships. As such, Ecuadorean parties did not acquire a heroic image as the democratic resistance nor were members expected to display a high degree of psychological commitment.

Because interest-group formation outpaced and overshadowed party development *and* parties are held in low esteem, party leaders and followers have little party loyalty or feelings of solidarity. Party identification is based more on pragmatic than emotional grounds. In the absence of such solidarity, promoting individual self-interest (via patronage) assumes an even greater centrality. But because clientelistic parties depend on a continuing supply of material rewards for followers, party loyalties can shift rapidly when those resources are no longer available.[26]

The preeminence of clientelist rationality creates great internal tension within parties and has made the processes of coalition-building across parties, both inside and outside of Congress, extremely difficult. The struggle for leadership and control over the distribution of patronage waged between Roldós and Bucaram tore the party apart and led to the creation of two new parties, Roldós's PCD and the Partido Roldocistas Ecuatoriano (PRE) that was founded to group together his followers after his death. The disintegration of a unified CFP created a chronic executive-legislative stalemate in the first year of the Roldós administration. Roldós's successor, Osvaldo Hurtado, continued to be plagued by difficulties in maintaining legislative coalitions; the transitory character of progovernment legislative coalitions was reflected in the high turnover of cabinet positions as parties drifted in and out of accommodations with the Hurtado government.

Outside the realm of executive-legislative relations, patronage considerations also worked to seriously undermine the cohesion of an electoral front to support Rodrigo Borja's candidacy in the second-round presidential elections of 1984. The refusal of the FRA and CFP to explicitly endorse Borja in the second round was based on Borja's reluctance to negotiate on patronage. The centrifugal tendencies generated by patronage considerations affect cohesion on the right as well as the left. Febres-Cordero's cabinet appointments, heavily weighted in favor of nonpoliticians drawn from Guayaquil's private sector instead of right-wing party activists, drew bitter criticism from FRN leaders. Dissatisfaction erupted with the lower echelons of the FRN as job claimants outnumbered available public posts.

The ephemeral character of partisanship and the uneven insertion of parties into Ecuadorean society combine to explain the crisis of mediation in the party system. Because of their detachment from social forces and the unpredictable character of elite behavior and coalition strategies, parties have not evolved as institutions capable of solving conflicts through regularized procedures. Instead, they are "emergency" generators that provoke system-threatening clashes. Partisan struggles leading to impasses between the executive and legislative branches have been resolved through ad hoc means, usually involving the intervention/or threat of intervention by the executive to change the rules of the game. The threats of political restructuring were effective in forcing parties into temporary quiescence. But the net results of this improvised mode of conflict resolution are largely negative for institutional development. Conflicts are postponed, only to reemerge while procedural forms to deal with them remained underdeveloped.

During the Roldós and Hurtado administrations, the executive threatened a plebiscite (entailing the possibility of new congressional elections) at various times to brake the actions of the opposition. While the plebiscite threat did circumvent immediate political problems for the executive, the tactic was never successful in forging stable coalitions for the government. Nor did it establish any clear precedent as to under what conditions the plebiscite option could be legitimately used by the president. Similarly, the termination of the Supreme Court crisis under the Febres-Cordero administration left unresolved basic questions concerning the constitutionality of the Bloque Progresista's original decision, along with the legitimacy of the obstructionist tactics used by the FRN in Congress. The politics of intimidation and short-term deals on patronage, rather than long-term understandings on procedure and appropriate behavior, define the mode of conflict resolution in Ecuadorean democracy. The syndrome of system-threatening partisan conflict followed by a quick fix (*medida coyuntural*) indicates the limitations of the party system. The weakness of parties (specifically, their lack of mass mobilization capacity) and the *generalized* perception of that weakness by other political actors means that partisan conflicts escalate quickly; the political elite knows that there is no price to be paid on the street. Yet, within the context of a new and still fluid set of constitutional arrangements, these conflicts are quickly transformed into full-fledged crises.

Parties and the Future of Democracy

The prospects for sustained democratic development in Ecuador are being seriously eroded by these ongoing crises of representation, rationality, and mediation in the party system. These disjunctions between the elite, the party apparatus, and social classes have especially discouraged the development of an equilibrium of forces across the political spectrum. Without thoroughgoing links to the masses and the ability to mobilize them, parties of the center and the left have not been able to develop as effective counterweights to the nondemocratic forces on the right. The representational problem translates into a weak negotiating position for the center-left parties. This was clearly demonstrated in the terms of the resolution of the 1984 Supreme Court crisis.

Despite their general ideological and programmatic affinities, the parties of the center and the left cannot act as watchdogs on the right because of their lack of cohesion and unity. The coalition-building capacity of the center-left is enfeebled by the rationality problems within the parties. Party leaders often defect to other parties or create entirely new ones. They build transitory alliances based on calculations involving patronage and future electoral fortunes. Under the pressure of patronage politics, the solidity of legislative alliances or electoral fronts is always questionable.

With weak parties at the center and on the left, right-wing parties and interest groups (such as the Chambers of Industry and Commerce) face few restraints on their conduct. Between 1979 and 1984, these groups showed little interest in democracy. At various times of economic crisis, party leaders of the right and representatives of the business community were quick to call for extraconstitutional means for removing President Hurtado and establishing an interim government. During the Supreme Court crisis, party leaders of the FRN in Congress resorted to violent tactics to paralyze the legislature. Moreover, the use of violence was not confined to the Congress; President Febres-Cordero ordered the police to physically bar the entrance of the new appointees to their offices. All this calls into the question the commitment of these forces to resolving conflicts in democratic ways.

Leaders of center and left parties, currently allied in the Bloque Progresista, recognize the threats posed to democracy by their own organizational weakness. They fear that concerted attacks on congressional prerogatives by the right minority in the legislature and the executive branch will result in the creation of a "democratic-authoritarian" regime, that is, a regime that would maintain the facade of constitutionalism but take decision-making power away from the legislature and electoral politics. Bloque party leaders believe such a crippling of democratic institutions must occur before the right can implement the neoliberal economic project that President Febres-Cordero espoused during his elections campaign.[27]

If procedural democracy is to survive in Ecuador, the development of a democratic right is essential. Yet, the maturation of the political right as a democratic force has been retarded by the problems that have weakened the development of parties of the center and left. Because of their lack of resources, extensive fragmentation, and feeble coalition-building capacities, the parties of the center-left have not evolved to the point where they provide effective "checks and balances" on the behavior of the right. This disequilibrium in the party system may prove fatal to democracy, since right-wing interests are willing to resort to extralegal means of resolving conflict when their access to the policy-making process is in jeopardy. As such, the democratic vocations of all parties continue to be stifled by the alienation of party from society and party from itself.

Notes

1. For a review of the important literature on the decline in U.S. party identification, see Paul Abramson, *Political Attitudes in America: Formation and Change* (San Francisco: W. H. Freeman, 1983). The notion of corporatism has dominated recent discussions of Western European politics; see *Organizing Interests in Western Europe*, ed. Suzanne Berger (Cambridge: Cambridge University Press, 1981); and *Trends toward Corporatist Intermediation*, ed. Phillipe Schmitter and Gerald Lembruch (London: Sage Publications, 1979).

2. For treatments of the transition process, see Howard Handelman and Thomas Sanders, *Military Government and the Movement Toward Democracy in South America* (Bloomington: Indiana University Press, 1981), pp. 3–74. Also see John Martz, "The Quest for Popular Democracy in Ecuador," *Current History* 78, no. 454 (February 1980): 66–70; Patricio Moncayo, *¿Reforma o democracia? Alternativas del sistema político ecuatoriano* (Quito: Editorial El Conejo, 1982); Luis Calle Vargas, *La Constitución de 1978 y el proceso de reestructuración jurídica del estado 1976–1978* (Guayaquil: Universidad de Guayaquil, 1978); Marcelo Ortiz Villacís, *El control del poder, 1966–1984* (Quito: Gráficas San Pablo, 1984), pp. 58–175.

3. The relationships between dominant class organizations and the Rodríguez Lara regime are discussed in Catherine Conaghan, "Industrialists and the Reformist Interregnum: Dominant Class Behavior and Ideology in Ecuador, 1972–1979" (Ph.D. diss., Yale University, 1983).

4. For a complete analysis of the election returns, see ACSO, *Elecciones en el Ecuador 1978–1980* (Quito: Editorial Oveja Negra, 1983).

5. The original twenty-one-point program can be found in CORDES, *Democracia y crisis: Osvaldo Hurtado, Vicepresidente, 1979–1981* (Quito: CORDES, 1984), pp. 11–49.

6. Rodrigo Borja, interview with author, Quito, 6 December 1984.

7. For Raúl Baca Carbo's views on the Convergencia, see "Las dudas de la Convergencia," *Nueva*, August 1981, pp. 42–47.

8. In Hurtado's view, the maintenance of the democratic regime in and of itself was important so as to socialize the relevant political actors into democratic norms and styles of behavior (interview with author, Quito, 10 December 1984). Given the recurring threats of a coup, the survival of the regime was a significant achievement. In an interview toward the end of his term, Hurtado observed that "there was not a cocktail party" where members of the armed forces were not approached by civilians interested in a coup. See his interview with Benjamín Ortiz in *Democracia y crisis: Diálogos del Presidente Osvaldo Hurtado con la prensa*, ed. CORDES (Quito: CORDES, 1984), p. 240.

9. For a discussion of the first-round returns of 1984, see Alberto Acosta et al., *1984: Ecuador en las urnas* (Quito: Editorial El Conejo, 1984).

162 Catherine M. Conaghan

10. *El Comercio*, 6 April 1984; *Weekly Analysis of Ecuadorean Issues*, 12 April 1984.

11. For a discussion of the campaign strategies and the second round, see Walter Spurrier, "Febres-Cordero Pulls the Election," in *Weekly Analysis of Ecuadorean Issues*, 11 May 1984.

12. For denunciation of FRN manuevers to induce desertions by ID, see *El Comercio*, 11 August 1984 and 21 September 1984.

13. For a review of the progression of events during the crisis, see "Cronología de la crisis política," in *El Comercio*, 16 December 1984. Also see *Weekly Analysis of Ecuadorean Issues*, 28 December 1984.

14. Robert Michels, *Political Parties*, trans. Eden and Cedar Paul (New York: Free Press, 1962); *The Prison Notebooks of Antonio Gramsci*, ed. and trans. Quinton Hoare and Geoffrey Nowell Smith (New York: International Publishers, 1971).

15. Nicos Poulantzas, *Fascism and Dictatorship*, trans. J. White (London: New Left Books, 1974), pp. 71–75. For a discussion of Poulantzas's idea of "unstable equilibrium of compromise," see Bob Jessop, *The Capitalist State: Marxist Theories and Methods* (New York: New York University Press, 1982), p. 164.

16. Robert Dahl, *Polyarchy: Participation and Opposition* (New Haven, Conn: Yale University Press, 1971), p. 15.

17. In a classic piece, Lipset and Rokkan argued that the saliency of different types of social cleavages during the initial stages of democratization are central to understanding the different evolutions of party systems. See S. M. Lipset and Stein Rokkan, "Cleavage Structures, Party Systems, and Voter Alignments: An Introduction," in *Party Systems and Voter Alignments*, ed. Lipset and Rokkan (New York: Free Press, 1967), pp. 1–64.

18. The notion of a "crisis of representation" is taken from the work of Gramsci. See *The Prison Notebooks*, pp. 210–12.

19. For a discussion of the operation of the traditional party system prior to redemocratization in 1979, see John D. Martz, *Ecuador: Conflicting Political Culture and the Quest for Progress* (Boston: Allyn & Bacon, 1972), pp. 108–45. Also see Ronald H. McDonald, *Party Systems and Elections in Latin America* (Chicago: Markham, 1971), pp. 83–89.

20. For an important review of the political and social history of Ecuador, see Osvaldo Hurtado, *Political Power in Ecuador*, trans. Nick D. Mills, Jr. (Albuquerque: University of New Mexico Press, 1980).

21. On interest group–state relations in agriculture, see Gustavo Cosse, *Estado y agro en el Ecuador* (Quito: Corporación Editora Nacional, 1984).

22. For an excellent discussion of the problematic relations between parties and trade unions, see Nick D. Mills, *Crisis, conflicto y consenso: Ecuador 1979–1984* (Quito: Corporación Editora Nacional, 1984), pp. 127–90.

23. In a survey of industrialists in major firms taken in 1979–1980, only 9 percent of those surveyed reported a party affiliation while 74 percent reported memberships in business interest group organizations (see Conaghan, "Industrialists," pp. 249, 252). For a further discussion of the political role played by these groups, see Jorge Hidrobo, "Acción política de las clases sociales y las políticas agrarias e industriales: Ecuador 1972–1979" (Center for Latin American Studies, University of Pittsburgh, August 1981).

24. The figure on unionization is cited in Mills, *Conflicto*, p. 129. In a survey taken in a *barrio popular* in Quito, 78 percent of the residents reported that they did not belong to trade unions and 90 percent reported that they had never participated in neighborhood associations. When asked about political participation, 89 percent responded that they had never engaged in political activity. The findings are from Malva Espinosa, *Ecuador: El horizonte político popular* (Quito: ACSO, 1984), pp. 112, 123.

25. The notion of a "crisis of rationality" is based on the ideas of Alessandro Pizzorno. See his "Interests and Parties in Pluralism," in *Organizing Interests in Western Europe*, ed. Berger, pp. 250–55.

26. For a discussion of the instability associated with clientelist politics, see Steffen Schmidt, "Patrons, Brokers and Clients: Party Linkages in the Colombian System," in *Political Parties and Linkage: A Comparative Perspective*, ed. Kay Lawson (New Haven, Conn.: Yale University Press, 1980), pp. 266–88.

27. In interviews conducted in December 1984 by the author, all of the party leaders of the Bloque Progresista voiced their fears concerning a possible evolution toward a hybrid authoritarian regime. For a discussion of the prospects of the development of dictatorship under Febres-Cordero, see the political reports in *Respuesta* 1 (October 1984), *Respuesta* 2 (November 1984), *Nueva* 107 (October 1984), *Nueva* 109 (November 1984).

III Central America

Mitchell A. Seligson

8 Development, Democratization, and Decay: Central America at the Crossroads

Economic development compels the modification or abandonment of traditional political institutions; it does not determine what political system will replace them.
—Samuel P. Huntington

Democracy has made few allies in Central America.[1] With the important exception of Costa Rica, the region has suffered an almost unbroken chain of dictatorial rule and military domination in which civil rights, human rights, popular participation, and governmental accountability have been conspicuously absent. Moreover, not only have the citizens of the region's states been largely ignored by their rulers, but also national sovereignty has been attenuated by heavy-handed foreign powers and transnational corporations. When all these factors are taken together, it is not surprising that the chickens have finally come home to roost; for the past six years at least, Central America has been caught up in an unprecedented combination of economic crisis, civil war, and foreign intervention. By any measure, these are certainly the worst of times.

Yet, it is paradoxical that as regards prospects for the development of democratic rule in the region, these are certainly the best of times. It has been lost on many observers that never before in the century and a half since their emergence from formal colonial domination have the nations of the region made greater progress toward the establishment of elected civilian government than they have in the last few years. Progress is evident from north to south. In Guatemala a Constituent Assembly was elected in July 1984, and eighty-eight deputies took their seats and began work on a new constitution. In December 1985, a civilian was elected president of Guatemala in

167

what most observers report was a fair and honest election.[2] In El Salvador, in the midst of a brutal civil war in March 1984, citizens voted in unprecedented numbers for a civilian government in elections that were clearly the freest ever held in that tiny republic.[3] Honduras has enjoyed elected civilian rule since January 1982, when a civilian president was installed after an election in which over 82 percent of the registered voters cast their ballots. In 1985, after another open election, one civilian stepped down and another took his place—a peaceful succession almost unknown in Honduras. Nicaraguans went to the polls in November 1984 in their first elections not dominated by the forty-year reign of the Somoza dynasty. While the U.S. press and State Department have widely condemned those elections as no more than a charade, a Latin American Studies Association delegation comprised of fifteen North American social scientists sent to observe the elections concluded that the process was in fact open and democratic.[4] An article recently published by one member of that delegation stated: "The Nicaraguan elections of November 4th were about as fair, competitive and democratic as anyone of minimal good will and objectivity could have demanded."[5] And in Costa Rica, in spite of the deepest economic crisis of the century, free elections were held in 1986 that peacefully transferred power in that country for the ninth consecutive time since the Civil War of 1948.

Central America seems caught between diametrically opposing forces of violence and terror, on the one hand, and the unmistakable movement toward rule by reason and popular consent on the other. Why has democracy, which for so long has been an orphan in this region, suddenly begun to find a home? And why would it pick this time, a period of economic crisis and civil unrest, to do so? That is the puzzle which needs unraveling, not only so that we can achieve a better understanding of how Central America has arrived at the present crossroads, but also so that we can make an educated guess as to the direction in which these countries are headed.

To be able to explain the past and predict the future—a tall order even for a political scientist—one needs to place the Central American cases in a far broader context than most observers seem willing or able to put them. Discussions in the press and in a spate of recent academic writings treat the region as sui generis, outside the main currents of political history. Moreover, there has been little willingness to think about the region from the perspective of social science theory. Finally, virtually no effort has been made to consider Central American regimes in a comparative perspective—such as comparing them as to the extent to which they have or have not established democratic institutions. This chapter, in contrast to most of the previous research on Central America, seeks to overcome these limitations. Its theoretical background is outlined in the discussion of empirical democratic theory found in chapter 1. This essay begins by examining, in a comparative context, the levels of democratic development that each of the Central American nations has attained in recent decades. It then presents data on economic and sociocultural development since the 1920s and 1930s. Finally, the discussion shows why the impact of economic development on the region has helped to produce the paradoxical interplay of democracy and violence discussed above, and points to critical domestic and foreign policies that must be altered if democratic rule is to survive and prosper.

Democratic Development in Central America

Journalistic accounts highlight the frequent violations of democratic liberties in Central America, and even informed observers have suggested that few areas of the world suffer a worse record. Yet, when one steps back and views the situation from a wider perspective, the picture is rather different. Since 1945, scholars have been rating democratic development in twenty nations of Latin America. An examination of the rankings (referred to as the "Fitzgibbon-Johnson index") produced by these scholars' subjective, but nonetheless well-informed, opinions confirms this rather different assessment. Measured on a scale that includes five key measures of democratic performance (free speech, free elections, free party organizations, independence of the judiciary, and civilian supremacy over the military), Central American nations tend to fall in the intermediate range for Latin America (see figure 8.1). Costa Rica is the exception, ranking among the most democratic countries in all of Latin America, while Nicaragua generally falls below the others, ranking in the bottom quarter of Latin American nations.

One could reasonably argue that since few if any Latin American countries have been noted as paragons of democracy, comparisons within this region are of limited utility. Yet, when Central America is placed in a worldwide perspective, the results are similar to those limited to the regional context. Such a perspective is provided by

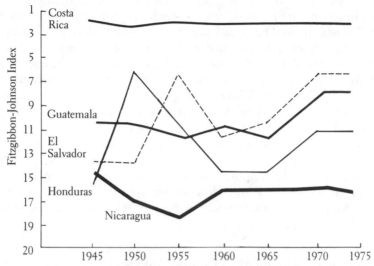

Figure 8.1   Subjective Rankings of Democracy in Central America, 1945–1975

Source: Adapted from Kenneth F. Johnson, "Research Perspectives on the Revised Fitzgibbon-Johnson Index of the Image of Political Democracy in Latin America, 1945–1975," in *Quantitative Latin American Studies: Methods and Findings*, ed. James W. Wilkie and Kenneth Ruddle (Los Angeles: UCLA Latin American Center Publications, 1977), p. 89.

Note: Rankings are based on expert opinion on the following criteria: (1) freedom of speech, (2) free elections, (3) free party organizations, (4) independence of the judiciary, and (5) civilian supremacy over the military.

Kenneth A. Bollen's "Political Democracy Index" of 122 nations, a measure that is generally regarded as the best one yet devised.[6] The basis for the index is less judgmental than the experts' evaluations presented above for the Latin American countries. It includes three measures of political liberty and three of popular sovereignty. Bollen's index avoids the errors of many of its precursors by excluding measures of stability and voter turnout.[7] Unfortunately, Bollen's data cover only 1960 and 1965 and therefore do not provide the longitudinal perspective of the Fitzgibbon-Johnson index.

Even though the Fitzgibbon-Johnson index is based entirely upon the subjective opinions of experts (whereas the Bollen index is based upon somewhat more objectively derived data), there is a very close association between them.[8] The correlation between the rankings of the Fitzgibbon-Johnson index for twenty Latin American countries for 1965 and the Bollen index ranking of the scores provided for those same countries for the same year is .90 (Spearman's *rho*). As shown in figure 8.2, the two indices produce very similar results for the subset of the Central American nations as well; only in the case of Nicaragua did expert opinion yield a substantially different score, no doubt because the personal antipathy of many scholars toward the Somoza regime colored their judgment and resulted in somewhat more negative scores than the data warranted.

The Bollen index appears to provide a reasonably valid indication of the standing of Central American democracy in worldwide perspective. Figure 8.3, which presents the Bollen index scores for the

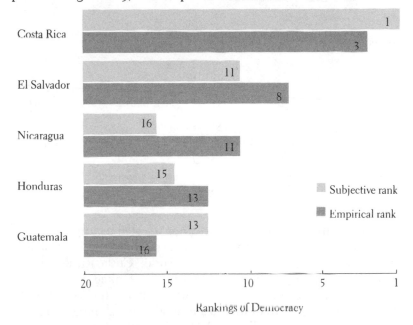

Figure 8.2 Subjective and Empirical Rankings of Democracy in Central America, 1965

Sources: Adapted from Kenneth F. Johnson, "Research Perspectives on the Revised Fitzgibbon-Johnson Index of the Image of Political Democracy in Latin America, 1945–1975," in *Quantitative Latin American Studies: Methods and Findings*, ed. James W. Wilkie and Kenneth Ruddle (Los Angeles: UCLA Latin American Center Publications, 1977), p. 89; Kenneth A. Bollen, "Issues in the Measurement of Political Democracy," *American Sociological Review* 45 (June 1980): 387–88.

Note: The empirical ranking (i.e., the Bollen index) is based on the degree of: (1) press freedom, (2) freedom of group opposition, (3) freedom of group political activity, (4) fairness of elections, (5) elections for executive office, and (6) legislative effectiveness. In this figure, the empirical ranking is based on only the twenty nations included in the subjective ranking.

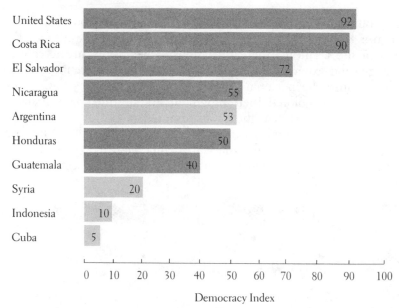

Figure 8.3   Empirical Index of Democracy in Central America, Compared with Selected Other Nations, 1965

Source: Adapted from Kenneth A. Bollen, "Issues in the Measurement of Political Democracy," *American Sociological Review* 45 (June 1980): 387–88.

five nations of the region and a few other selected examples, reveals that in 1965 the Central American nations held an intermediate position compared to other parts of the world. Costa Rica's score of 90.1 nearly approximates that achieved by the United States (92.4). At the other extreme, Guatemala's score, which is the lowest of the five (39.5), is far higher than that of some other developing nations in the Middle East and the Pacific.[9] Within Latin America, for example, only Guatemala scores substantially below Argentina (52.6), and all of the nations of Central America score far higher than Cuba (5.2). This global comparison of democratic achievement seems to show that when one steps back and looks at the wider picture, Central America, at least in 1965, was not as badly off as some would have us believe. These data suggest that many observers of Central America have been myopic—a tendency common to those who focus their attention upon only one small region and exaggerate the deficiencies that they find there.

The Threshold and the Central American Case

I have shown in chapter 1 that minimum levels of wealth and literacy are necessary but not sufficient conditions for the development of democracy. The empirical studies reviewed in the introduction suggest that the threshold of around $250 GNP per capita (in 1957 dollars) and 50 percent literacy must be crossed before democracy has any reasonable chance of survival in a given nation. The data to support this theory may be able to explain the evolution of democracy in Central America. Moreover, if the theory is of any value, it should enable us to explain the exception to the rule in Central America—namely, Costa Rica, which evolved a fairly high level of democratic rule by the 1930s and achieved stable democracy in the early 1950s.[10]

The data from Central America are indeed consistent with the theory. A look at the GNP per capita data shown in figure 8.4 reveals that in 1957, only Costa Rica had crossed the economic threshold. Moreover, only Costa Rica, with a literacy level of 79 percent in 1950, had crossed the sociocultural threshold. In the 1950s, it is clear, the fundamental prerequisites for democracy were simply not present in Central America outside of Costa Rica, and so it is therefore not surprising that democracy had not emerged there.

If the absence of the fundamental prerequisites for democracy can

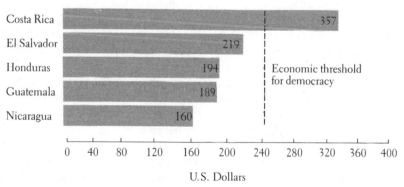

U.S. Dollars

Figure 8.4 GNP Per Capita in Central America, 1957 (in U.S. dollars)

Source: Adapted from Bruce M. Russett, Hayward R. Alker, Jr., Karl W. Deutsch, and Harold D. Lasswell, *World Handbook of Political and Social Indicators* (New Haven, Conn.: Yale University Press, 1964), p. 165.

Note: Nicaragua seems to be underestimated by this source. See figure 8.5 for more recent estimates.

explain why democracy has not flourished in the region over the past century and a half, then how are we to explain the recent positive democratic developments mentioned at the outset of this chapter? A look again at the data gives some clear answers. The turmoil of the past few years, accompanied by economic declines, has tended to obscure the longer-run pattern of growth. A new set of data that traces GNP per capita for each of the five countries for the period 1920–1982 makes this clear. The compiler of the data concludes that there is a pattern of

> steady (but not spectacular) economic growth, with the excep-
> tions provided by the long-run stagnation of Honduras and the
> collapse of the last few years. There is little support here for the
> notion of Central America as an area locked into traditional
> methods of production and isolated from advances in the world
> economy.
> On the contrary, the evidence on growth presented . . . sug-
> gests an economy which over the last sixty years has been sub-
> jected to a considerable degree of transformation.[11]

One would expect, from the theory presented, that the long-term economic growth enjoyed by the region, once it surpassed the $250 per capita threshold, would allow democracy to develop, especially if that growth were accompanied by improvements in literacy. This expectation is confirmed. In 1939 Costa Rica had a GNP per capita of $252 in 1950 dollars (see figure 8.5), and had achieved 70 percent literacy by 1940 (see figure 8.6). By that time, electoral reforms of 1925 and 1927 had instituted a secret ballot, a national voter registration system, and an independent election supervision board. The electorate was being expanded and regular elections were becoming firmly entrenched. By 1939 Guatemala also had broken through the $250 threshold and in 1944 the first open elections in the country's history were held, although many restrictions on voting still remained. Guatemala's literacy level, however, was far below the minimum at 29 percent. By 1949 Guatemala's GNP per capita income had dropped to $220 and in 1954 democracy was extinguished by a U.S.-supported invasion. The other three countries in the region had per capita incomes far below the minimum in 1939, and as figure 8.5 shows, remained below that minimum throughout the 1950s.

In the 1960–1969 period, however, steady economic growth, stimulated by the expansion of the Central American Common Mar-

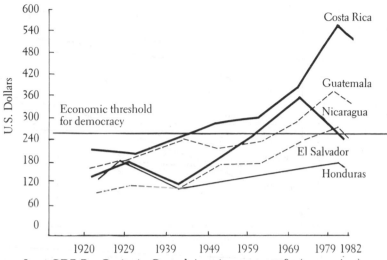

Figure 8.5   GDP Per Capita in Central America, 1920–1982 (1950 prices)

Source: Adapted from V. Bulmer-Thomas, "Economic Development Over the Long Run—Central America Since 1920," *Journal of Latin American Studies* 15 (November 1983): 276.

ket, pushed all of the countries in the region except Honduras above the economic threshold.[12] And an examination of the literacy data (figure 8.6) shows that during the 1960s, literacy levels for all of the countries exceeded 50 percent, with the exception of Guatemala, which remained slightly below the threshold.

The empirical evidence suggests quite clearly that the economic and sociocultural conditions that have been prerequisites for democratic growth elsewhere in the world have been emerging over the past ten to fifteen years throughout Central America. Central American countries, then, have entered what Samuel Huntington has labeled a "zone of transition or choice, in which traditional forms of rule become increasingly difficult to maintain and new types of political institutions are required to aggregate the demands of an increasingly complex society and to implement public policies."[13] Sociocultural and economic development are only necessary conditions, not necessary *and* sufficient conditions for democracy; their achievement does not guarantee its development and stability. Moreover, no teleological perspective in which all political systems are seen as "naturally" tending toward democratic rule is implied. Yet, in recent years there have been unmistakable signs

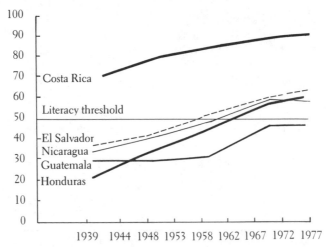

Figure 8.6 Adult Literacy in Central America, 1940–1977 (in percent)

Sources: 1940: James W. Wilkie and Maj-Britt Nilsson, "Projecting the HEC [Health, Education, and Communication] Index for Latin America Back to 1940," in *Quantitative Latin American Studies: Methods and Findings*, ed. James W. Wilkie and Kenneth Ruddle (Los Angeles: UCLA Latin American Center Publications, 1977), p. 81, which is based on Roberto Moreno y García, *Analfabetismo y cultura popular en América* (Mexico City: Editorial Atlantes, 1941), data adjusted to conform with the 15-year-old age standard.

Early United Nations data vary from these figures: El Salvador, 1930: 29.5% of 15–17-year-olds; Guatemala, 1940: 34.6% of those 7 years old and older; Honduras, 1945: 36.9%; Costa Rica and Nicaragua, no data. See *United Nations Statistical Yearbook, 1949–50* (New York: Statistical Office of the United Nations, 1950), p. 487.

El Salvador's figure is adjusted, because the Wilkie and Nilsson figure of 49% is identical with the 1960 figure reported by James W. Wilkie and Peter Reich, *Statistical Abstract of Latin America*, vol. 19 (Los Angeles: UCLA Latin American Center, 1979), p. 118, and nearly 10% above the 1950 figure reported by Bruce M. Russett et al., *World Handbook of Political and Social Indicators* (New Haven, Conn.: Yale University Press, 1964).

1950: Russett et al., *World Handbook*, pp. 222–23. Honduras is estimated.

1960: World Bank, *World Development Report, 1982* (New York: Oxford University Press, 1982), pp. 154–55; Wilkie and Reich, *Statistical Abstract*, p. 118.

1970: Wilkie and Reich, *Statistical Abstract*, p. 118.

1977: World Bank, *World Development Report, 1982*, pp. 154–55; Guatemala, 1981: Robert L. Peterson, "Guatemala," in *Latin America and Caribbean Contemporary Record*, Vol. 2: 1982–83, ed. Jack W. Hopkins (New York: Holmes and Meier, 1984), p. 508; Nicaragua, 1975: World Bank, *World Development Report, 1980.*

that democracy, however fragile, is beginning to emerge in the region. At the same time, it appears paradoxical that just as these conditions have emerged, and the institutional bases of democracy are being established, the region has been caught up in unprecedented social unrest.

One easy explanation for this paradox can be derived from theories predicting that social and economic development will produce social unrest.[14] Hence, according to this perspective, the growth that is responsible for the emergence of democracy is also responsible for the social unrest that destabilizes it. But such theories posit unrest as a function of *rapid* growth, something that is clearly not a feature of Central America's economies (see figure 8.5). Similarly, theories suggesting that rapid declines produce "J-curves" of "revolutionary gaps" between expectations and performance have little applicability to the region. The economic declines of the late 1970s and early 1980s, brought on by rising petroleum prices and slipping coffee prices, occurred *after* the turmoil currently present in the region had already distinctly emerged. Moreover, a recent review of the best empirical evidence linking both economic growth and decline to political violence has led Ekkart Zimmerman to conclude, "In general it seems that rapid socioeconomic change cannot be considered to be an important direct determinant of political violence. Neither the rate of economic growth nor that of economic decline are consistent predictors of the dependent variable [i.e., violence]."[15] Another study of the linkage between economic growth or decline and political stability, conducted by Edward Muller, further undermines the thesis by showing that it does not even apply to the limited subset of developing democracies.[16]

Democratization and Inequality in Central America

The difficulty of applying these disputed explanations to the Central American case is that they ignore the particular nature of the economic growth that has taken place in the region. Simplifying a great deal of theory, it is possible to argue that economic questions can be reduced to only two: the production problem and the distribution problem. The economic growth that has taken place in Central America has begun to solve the production problem—although, it should be stressed, with an average GNP per capita for Central America of only $936 in 1981, compared to an average of $11,200 for the industrialized nations, the production problem is far from solved.[17]

The distribution problem, however, has not only not been solved, but has worsened over the past few decades. And it is the distribution problem that is a principal cause of the current dilemma. Ironically, economic growth is probably partially responsible for the growing distortions in distribution in Central America and the consequently exacerbated inequality. Simon Kuznets won a Nobel Prize for showing that as nations move away from agriculture-based economies and toward industrialization, income distribution worsens. Only in the later stages of industrialization, when high mass consumption and the welfare state have emerged, are these increases in inequality reversed.[18] Much empirical research has tended to confirm Kuznets's thesis.[19] Unfortunately, the data on income distribution vary greatly in quality, and there are no universally accepted standards for their collection.[20] The problems are particularly severe in the developing nations, which have neither the resources nor the political will to conduct studies in areas of such potential political sensitivity. These problems limit greatly the data on income distribution for Central America.

The best data available for the region are summarized in figure 8.7, which presents information for the upper 20 percent of the income earners.[21] (However, see the limitations discussed in the table note.) The mean incomes earned by the upper quintile of the non–oil exporting developing nations and the industrialized nations are indicated by two vertical lines. The figure reveals that income is far more concentrated in all of the Central American nations than it is in the industrialized nations. This comes as no surprise, and is entirely consistent with the Kuznets thesis. What is surprising is that even when Central American nations are compared to other nations that are not oil exporters, a group of nations reasonably similar in level of development to those in Central America, only Costa Rica has a lower concentration of income. Although this is not shown in figure 8.7, Central America also fares worse than the group of oil-exporting nations (mean of top quintile = 57.4 percent) and also has a more concentrated distribution of income than the semi-industrial developing nations (mean of top quintile = 51.8 percent).[22] The country with the highest concentration of income in the world among the upper 20 percent of income earners is Ecuador, with 73.5 percent of the income earned going to that group. However, Ecuador exceeded Guatemala by only less than one percent (72.7 percent). And all of the Central American nations are far worse off in income distribution terms than Sri Lanka, a developing democracy with a GNP per capita of only $300 (in 1981). This was half that of Honduras, the poorest in Central America.

Without underestimating the limitations in the quality of the data,

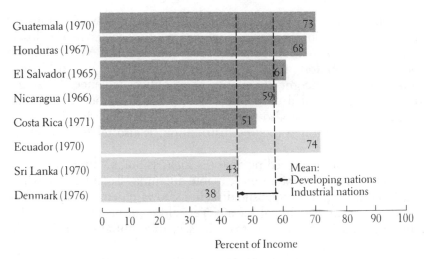

Figure 8.7 Income Share of the Top 20 Percent in Central America and Selected Other Countries, 1965–1970

Sources: Edward N. Muller, "Financial Dependence," in *The Gap Between Rich and Poor*, ed. Mitchell A. Seligson (Boulder, Colo.: Westview Press, 1984), p. 266; Guatemala and Nicaragua: Michael H. Best, "Political Power and Tax Revenues in Central America," *Journal of Development Economics* 3 (March 1976): 77.

Numbers are rounded. Disagreements among various sources abound, but most are reasonably close except for Guatemala. The Guatemala figure reported here is from a 1970 study based on personal income tax returns. Best also reports 63.5% for 1968, based on the income of salary earners. Figures of 50.8% for 1970 and 54.1% for 1980 are reported in the Economic Commission for Latin America, "Notas sobre la evolución del desarrollo social del Istmo Centroamericano hasta 1980," in *Indicadores socioeconómicos para el desarrollo*, ed. Francisco Rojas Arvaena (San José, Costa Rica: Ediciones FLACSO, 1983, p. 113). The figure of 63% for 1968 is reported by Clark Reynolds, "Employment Problems of Export Economies in a Common Market: The Case of Central America," in *Economic Integration in Central America*, ed. William R. Cline and Enrique Delgado (Washington, D.C.: Brookings, 1979), p. 243.

one can see unmistakably that economic development in Central America has not begun to resolve the distribution question. Indeed, a recent study concludes that the major impact of industrialization under the Central American Common Market has been to increase inequality.[23]

Economic growth, then, has simultaneously established the preconditions for democratic change in Central America, while it has exacerbated the region's already formidable inequalities in income distribution. Growth with inequality, therefore, has led to political decay in the form of increasing political violence. Such a pattern has often been observed in other national settings; it is well established empirically that income inequality and political violence are closely linked. In a cross-national study by Lee Sigelman and Miles Simpson of a sample of forty-nine nations, a direct linear relationship was found between income inequality and political violence.[24] Using a refined and expanded data base, Muller and Seligson come to the same conclusion, but also find that inequality in land distribution, as it is mediated through income distribution, is also related to increasing violence.[25]

The logic of the preceding analysis suggests that Central America is caught on the horns of an inescapable dilemma. Economic growth is pushing the region in opposite directions: toward democratic development and toward political decay. Yet, closer inspection reveals that the dilemma is not only far from inescapable, but also largely of the region's own making.

The early stages of economic growth have been responsible for increasing income inequality in many cases around the globe, but not in all. The most dramatic exceptions are the cases of Taiwan, South Korea, and Japan. In Taiwan, for example, the upper 20 percent of the income earners in 1953 garnered 61.4 percent of the income. (Coincidentally, this was identical to the share earned by El Salvador's highest income earners in 1965; see figure 8.7.) By 1964, however, the richest 20 percent in Taiwan saw their share drop dramatically to only 41.0 percent, and by 1979 it had dropped even further to 37.5 percent, tying Taiwan with Denmark as the most equitable of all nonsocialist nations.[26] This major reversal of income inequality occurred during a period of unprecedented economic growth; in the thirty-year period 1950–1980, economic growth in Taiwan averaged 9.2 percent annually, with the GNP increasing more than elevenfold and per capita income rising from about $70 at the close of World War II to $2,280 in 1980. Most analysts agree that the major cause of the decline in income concentration in Taiwan was massive land reform and the establishment of a progressive tax structure.

Cross-national studies of the relationship between growth and equality have demonstrated that nations can escape from the Kuznets dilemma if they enact and enforce redistributive policies. Irma Adelman and Cynthia Taft Morris conclude their comparative study of seventy-four developing countries in this way:

The record of economic intervention in underdeveloped countries, good as it is in terms of economic growth, has been dismal in terms of social justice. Indeed, economic growth, whether planned or unplanned, has only made things worse. Since there is apparently no simple way of changing things for the better, some radical reorientation of both ends and means is apparently in order. [27]

And a more recent cross-national study by Muller finds no support for the theory that attributes increasing income inequality in developing nations to the dependent position of those nations in the world capitalist system. Muller suggests that variations in income distribution can be more directly attributed to the "internal dynamics" of nations. [28]

Empirical support for the internal dynamics thesis has recently come from a study of the impact of government expenditure policies on income distribution. [29] While the study's focus is limited to the developed market economies and therefore may not have more general applicability, the results show that expenditures on education, social security and welfare, housing, and community amenities serve to lessen income inequality. The weight of the combined evidence seems to demonstrate that income inequality is by no means an inevitable consequence of economic growth, but is very much subject to domestic policies.

One need not travel as far as Taiwan to find examples of economic growth yielding improvements in income distribution. In Central America, Costa Rica has achieved neither the spectacular growth nor the massive redistribution that has taken place in Taiwan, but its record has nonetheless been enviable. Over the period 1961 to 1971, the share of the income earned by the top 20 percent of income earners dropped from 60.0 percent to 50.6 percent. [30] This occurred at a time when Costa Rica's GNP was growing at an annual rate of 6.5 percent. Social progress was also marked during this period, with infant mortality dropping from 83.2 per thousand to 43.1 and life expectancy increasing from 63.3 years to 68.3 years. [31] The birth rate dropped from 46.7 per thousand in 1961 to 31.7 in 1971. [32] These achievements came as a direct result of government policies that emphasized social progress. State income was invested heavily in public education rather than in public security. For example, in

1960, 18 percent of the budget of the central government was spent on public education. By 1970, that figure had risen to 22 percent, and by 1976 had reached 30 percent as compared to only 7 percent for the world as a whole. During that same period, spending on public security amounted to only 5 to 6 percent of the budget.[33]

Cross-national comparisons within Central America of public expenditures on education and social security and welfare, two of the key expenditure categories that have been found to be directly linked to reducing income inequality, reveal substantial differences among the five nations.[34] Figures 8.8 and 8.9 show that Costa Rica directs a far greater proportion of its central government budget to these categories. In 1981, for example, over 54 percent of the entire budget of the central government was devoted to the combined categories of education, and social security and welfare. Of considerable concern is the steady decline in spending for education which is apparent for all of these nations in the 1975–1980 period; all of the nations in the region ended the decade spending a far lower proportion of their budgets on education than five years earlier. Scarce public funds were steadily being shifted into defense and debt service, a trend that does not bode well for income distribution.

Costa Rica's success at pursuing growth and social equity at the same time should not be overemphasized, however. The economic reverses of the past few years have been unprecedented. Growth rates

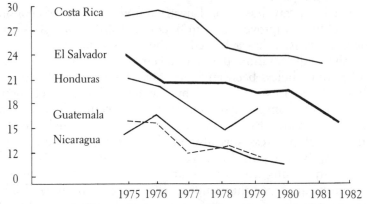

Figure 8.8   Central American Governments' Expenditures on Education (in percent)

Source: Adapted from the International Monetary Fund, *Government Financial Statistics Yearbook, 1983* (Washington, D.C.: IMF, 1983).

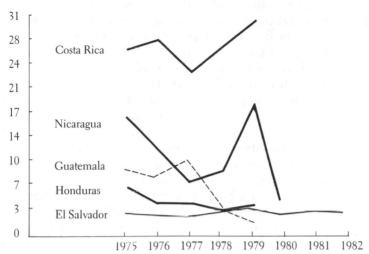

Figure 8.9   Central American Governments' Expenditures on Social Security and Welfare (in percent)

Source: Adapted from the International Monetary Fund, *Government Financial Statistics Year-book,* 1983 (Washington, D.C.: IMF, 1983).

per capita of approximately 4 percent in 1976–1978 dropped to zero in 1979 and fell to approximately −3 percent by 1980 and −6 percent in 1981. The GDP per capita is not projected to return to 1980 levels until 1990.[35] The foreign debt grew to over $3 billion, in a country of only 2.4 million persons—yielding one of the largest, if not the largest, per capita external debts in the world.[36] In 1982 inflation reached nearly 100 percent and the bottom fell out of the local currency, although both inflation and the exchange rate have been brought back under control at least for the moment.

Most observers believe that the Costa Rican economic crisis is having a deleterious effect on income distribution, perhaps reversing all of the gains made in the 1960s.[37] Indeed, one study, based on limited data, has suggested that those gains had already been eroded by the time the crisis began.[38] A more extensive study is now under way and the results should be available shortly, but if it is found that income distribution has considerably worsened, then Costa Rica may have to confront the violent protest of its citizens, a population long accustomed to active political participation as a method of achieving their goals.[39]

Of equal concern is that Costa Rica has made little progress in land redistribution. Land reform has been under way in Costa Rica since the early 1960s, but financial support generally has been limited. As a result, inequality in land distribution has remained extremely high, even for Central America. Only 3.3 percent of the national land area has been redistributed to the landless. This means that only about 8 percent of the potential population of beneficiaries has been given land. Moreover, the rate of growth of the landless and land-poor population exceeds the rate of land redistribution.[40] If the key to lowering income inequality in Taiwan was wealth redistribution through land reform, Costa Rica is not following the same path.

Looking at the region as a whole, one finds little evidence showing that public policies favor income redistribution. Indeed, studies have shown that public policy in the region favors increased inequality. One of the most powerful tools at the disposal of governments that can serve to redistribute income is the tax structure. In Central America, however, that structure is highly regressive. Even when compared to the Latin American region as a whole, a region not noted for progressive tax structures, Central America fares badly. Direct taxes in Central America average only 21 percent of total central government revenues compared to 32 percent for Latin America as a whole. Indirect taxes on consumption and production, generally considered to be among the most regressive of all taxes, averaged 44 percent in Central America. Not only are taxes regressive, but also tax rates are far too low to provide the developmental stimulus so badly needed in the region. Tax rates in Central America average only half the rate for Latin America as a whole, and income taxes exceeded 2 percent of GNP in only two countries—Honduras and Costa Rica. Collections in Guatemala averaged only .9 percent and only .7 percent in Somoza's Nicaragua. Translated into terms more directly related to income distribution, if the tax rate on the top 20 percent of income earners were increased to an overall rate of 20 percent (which would be far lower than it is in nearly all industrialized nations), this single source of tax revenue would be greater than the tax revenues from all other sources in all of the Central American countries except Costa Rica.[41]

These tax structures are not immutable. Improvements achieved in Costa Rica came about as a direct result of government policies in the 1950s and 1960s that resulted in the tripling of income tax revenues. And one need not take seriously the supply-side argument, at least in the Central American case, that to increase taxes would discourage investment, since the extraordinarily low rates that have characterized the past have not stimulated investment. In the most extensive comparative study of taxation policy in Central America yet conducted, Michael Best was led to conclude that the region is characterized by a highly regressive tax structure, and argues that the actual tax structure is ideal for only one economic group: the large landowners.[42]

Large landowners not only enjoy a tax structure created in their own image, but in general have been able to block any major land reforms in the region. Land reform programs have been initiated in all of the countries, but with very limited success. The extensive reforms of the 1952–1954 period in Guatemala were largely reversed, and the annual rate of redistribution since that time has been only one-sixteenth of the 1950–1954 rate. Between 1974 and 1981, for example, only 5.7 percent of the estimated 309,000 beneficiaries had received land.[43] Analysis has shown that even if the existing land reform legislation in Guatemala were fully implemented, less than half of the landless peasants could be accommodated.[44]

Elsewhere in Central America, the prospects for land reform are not particularly encouraging. One study shows that over the period 1962–1979, only less than one-quarter of the Honduran landless and land-poor benefited from the reforms.[45] More distressing is that the rate of land redistribution in Honduras has slowed considerably in recent years, in spite of the fact that the population growth rate (3.4 percent annually in 1970–1981), one of the highest rates in the world, continues to swell the ranks of the landless. Since 1982, the emphasis has shifted from redistribution to title security.[46] Land reform in El Salvador got off to a promising start, but has been so highly politicized, occurring in the midst of civil war, that it is difficult to speculate as to its ultimate impact.[47] Nicaragua has made much progress in land reform, but indications are that there is considerable peasant resistance to at least some components of the reform.[48]

The External Environment

A key external variable in the democratization-development-decay equation is the role of the United States. Samuel Huntington has recently argued that U.S. influence in a region helps stimulate democratic development.[49] In his view, the growth of democracy in "transitional" nations during the immediate post–World War II period can be attributed in part to the growth of U.S. power, but that when that influence waned in the 1970s, democracy declined in both East Asia and Latin America.

Most experts on Central America would stand Huntington's observation on its head. For most of this century, at least, U.S. policy toward Central America has been defined by a national security doctrine that embraces strongmen who oppose the intervention of extraregional foreign powers, especially those allied with the Soviet Union.[50] That policy has almost inevitably led the United States to support a string of unsavory characters who seem to have spent most of their time brutalizing the peasantry and working class. The Somozas were only the best known of the lot, but other dictators in the region probably have surpassed them in cruelty and rabid anticommunism.

Beginning with President Carter's decision to curtail U.S. support for Somoza, one can sense a marked change in U.S. policy.[51] The policy certainly has been subject to many zigs and zags, but overall it appears that the State Department has finally come to recognize that it needs to support Central American leaders who have some chance of winning the hearts and minds of their citizenry. It would seem that, at least in part, U.S. policy has begun to recognize the wisdom of a comment made by Fernando Cardenal, the Sandinista minister of culture: "We only want for ourselves what you want for yourselves. If you don't want dictators in the United States, do not support them in our countries."[52] The strong support shown by the Reagan administration for reformist José Napoleon Duarte in El Salvador is only one sign of this shift in policy. Under the old policy, one would have expected that the Reagan administration might well have been a supporter of Roberto d'Aubuisson.

In order to be fully effective, U.S. policy must go beyond supporting reformist leaders and give full support to reformist programs. At present, U.S. foreign aid is a critical element in the stability of the economies of Honduras, El Salvador, and Costa Rica. Those funds need to be directed toward structural reforms that will yield growth with equity.[53] To emphasize growth alone would be sheer folly, because growth with inequality would merely fertilize the seeds of violence and thereby threaten the health of the roots of democracy. Democratic rule is by no means the inevitable outcome of economic growth, not even under conditions of improved income equality. The case of Taiwan, discussed above, clearly points this out. But economic growth without improved distribution is a sure recipe for instability, government repression, and, eventually, revolution.

Conclusions

Central American nations seem bent on avoiding the major structural changes that are needed to reduce income inequality, while at the same time pursuing economic growth. Exacerbated disparities in income are not necessary concomitants of economic growth—it is public policies that largely determine how the benefits from growth will be distributed. It is a safe bet that unless the existing policies are reversed, one can expect continuing unrest and political violence. It is also a safe bet that if the United States—either out of frustration with the "inefficiency" of the nascent democratic regimes in the region or because of a need to demand guaranteed support for its misguided policies toward Nicaragua—returns to its policy of siding with military strongmen, the prospects for democracy will be greatly dimmed.

Central America today finds itself in the middle of a "transition zone" between its authoritarian past and a potentially democratic future. Domestic and external policies will determine which path the region will take.

Notes

The author would like to thank Mark Rosenberg and John Booth for their several helpful comments. An International Relations Fellowship (1984–1986) from the Rockefeller Foundation made this research possible.

1. This chapter concerns itself only with the five nations traditionally considered to form the Central American region: Guatemala, El Salvador, Honduras, Nicaragua, and Costa Rica. Panama, owing to the exceptional circumstance of its dominance by the the Canal Zone throughout its independent history, has evolved rather differently from the rest of the region and is therefore excluded here. Belize became independent of British rule only in September 1981 and is therefore excluded from this study, which is concerned with long-term changes in democratization in the region.

2. John A. Booth et al., *The 1985 Guatemalan Elections: Will the Military Relinquish Power?* Report of the Delegation sponsored by the International Human Rights Law Group and the Washington Office on Latin America (Washington, D.C., December, 1985).

3. Many observers of El Salvador's elections were critical for a variety of reasons, not the least of which was the failure of the FMLN guerrillas to participate in them. But even critics agree that participation and competition were extensive, and the mechanical aspects were generally well run. See Pratap C. Chitnis, "Observing El Salvador: The 1984 Elections," *Third World Quarterly* 6 (October): 963–80.

4. Latin American Studies Association, "Report of the Latin American Studies Association Delegation to Observe the Nicaraguan General Election of November 4, 1984," *LASA Forum* 15 (Winter 1985): 9–43.

5. James M. Malloy, "The Elections of November 4th and Nicaragua's Uncertain Political Future," *Caribbean Review* 14 (January 1985): 44.

6. Kenneth A. Bollen, "Issues in the Measurement of Political Democracy," *American Sociological Review* 45 (June 1980): 370–90.

7. See Phillips Cutright, "National Political Development: Measurement and Analysis," *American Sociological Review* 28 (April 1963): 253–64; Robert Jackman, *Politics and Social Equality: A Comparative Analysis* (New York: Wiley, 1975); and Philip Coulter, *Social Mobilization and Liberal Democracy* (Lexington, Mass.: Lexington Books, 1975). Studies that include measures of stability end up giving higher scores to both authoritarian and democratic stable regimes. Voter turnout is problematic because in many nations voting is obligatory and in other nations low turnout may be an indication of either satisfaction or alienation.

8. Bollen's index is derived from major compilations of cross-national data such as Charles Taylor and Michael C. Hudson, *World Handbook of Political and Social Indicators*, 2d ed. (New Haven, Conn.: Yale University Press, 1972), which attempt to utilize the best "hard" data available.

9. According to Bollen, in 1960 Guatemala's score was far higher (69.8) than it was in 1965, as was Honduras's (70.1). El Salvador, however, was far lower in 1960 (53.5) than in 1965.

10. Mitchell A. Seligson, "Costa Rica," in *Latin America and Caribbean Contemporary Record*, vol. 2: 1982–1983, ed. Jack W. Hopkins (New York: Holmes and Meier Publishers, 1984); and "Costa Rica and Jamaica," in *Competitive Elections in Developing Countries*, ed. Myron Weiner and Ergun Ozbudun (Durham, N.C.: Duke University Press, forthcoming).

11. V. Bulmer-Thomas, "Economic Development Over the Long Run—Central America Since 1920," *Journal of Latin American Studies* 15 (November 1983): 276.

12. William R. Cline and Enrique Delgado, eds., *Economic Integration in Central America* (Washington, D.C.: Brookings, 1979).

13. Samuel P. Huntington, "Will More Countries Become Democratic?" *Political Science Quarterly* 99 (Summer 1984): 201.

14. Mancur Olson, "Rapid Growth as a Destabilizing Force," *Journal of Economic History* 23 (December 1963): 529–52.

15. Ekkart Zimmerman, "Macro-Comparative Research on Political Protest," in *Handbook of Political Conflict*, ed. Ted Robert Gurr (New York: Free Press, 1980), pp. 182–83.

16. Edward N. Muller, "Economic Development and Democracy Revisited," presented at the Shambaugh Conference, "Political Science at Iowa," University of Iowa, Iowa City, 1982.

17. Data are from the World Bank, *World Development Report*, 1983 (New York: Oxford University Press, 1983), pp. 148–49.

18. The longitudinal trend produces an "inverted U-curve," which has become the hallmark of Kuznets's theory.

19. Many of the major contributions to the debate over Kuznets's thesis are found in *The Gap Between Rich and Poor: Contending Perspectives on the Political Economy of Development*, ed. Mitchell A. Seligson (Boulder, Colo.: Westview Press, 1984). Recent writings on dependency theory hold that income inequality is produced in the periphery because of the contact of the periphery with the center. Although empirical research initially tended to confirm this perspective, much recent evidence has disputed it. See Erich Weede and Horst Tiefenbach, "Some Recent Explanations of Income Inequality," and Edward N. Muller, "Financial Dependence in the Capitalist World Economy and the Distribution of Income Within Nations," in ibid.

20. See World Bank, *World Development Report, 1983*, p. 212; P. T. Bauer, "The Vicious Circle of Poverty," in *The Gap Between Rich and Poor*, ed. Seligson, pp. 330–33; and William Lochr, "Some Questions on the Validity of Income Distribution Data," in ibid.

21. Some analysts prefer to look at other sectors of the distribution. A study by Alain de Janvry, for example, looks at the poorest 20 percent in Latin America for 1960 and 1970 (*The Agrarian Question and Reformism in Latin America* [Baltimore: Johns Hopkins University Press, 1981], p. 36). The range of variation in this quintile is so small, however, as to likely render meaningless the differences found, given the wide confidence intervals present in this type of data. For example, de Janvry's 1970 data for the poorest 20 percent range from a low of 2.0 percent of the income in Peru to a high of 6.7 percent in the United States. The poorest quintile of any nation in Latin America earns no more than 5.0 percent of the income. The conclusion that de Janvry draws from the examination of the changes from 1960 to 1970 is that "the share of income received by the poorest 20 percent of the population declined or remained constant between 1960 and 1970 in all Latin American countries for which data are available except in Colombia, where the change observed is virtually insignificant" (p. 35). Since all of the countries for which de Janvry presents data for the period 1960–1970 experienced per capita economic growth, generally averaging 2 to 4 percent per annum according to the World Bank, the greater inequality in income distribution might reasonably be seen as further support of the Kuznets thesis. One novel approach to the distribution curve is taken by Muller ("Financial Dependence"), who looks at the middle 60 percent.

22. Muller, "Financial Dependence," p. 266.

23. Hector Pérez Brignoli and Yolanda Baires Martínez, "Growth and Crisis in the Central American Economies," *Journal of Latin American Studies* 15 (November 1983): 365–98.

24. Lee Sigelman and Miles Simpson, "A Cross-National Test of the Linkage Between Economic Inequality and Political Violence," *Journal of Conflict Resolution* 21 (March 1977): 105–28.

25. Edward N. Muller and Mitchell A. Seligson, "Inequality and Insurgency," *American Political Science Review*, forthcoming. Studies by Hardy and Weede argue that the relationship between income and land inequality washes out when the effect of economic development is considered. M. A. Hardy, "Economic Growth, Distributional Inequality and Political Conflict in Industrial Societies," *Journal of Political and Military Sociology* 5 (Fall 1979): 209–27; Erich Weede, "Income Inequality,

Average Income and Domestic Violence," *Journal of Conflict Resolution* 25 (December 1981): 639–54.

26. John C. Fei, Gustav Ranis, and Shirely W. Y. Kuo, *Growth with Equity: The Taiwan Case* (New York: Oxford University Press, 1979); Shirley W. Y. Kuo, Gustav Ranis, and John C. H. Fei, *The Taiwan Success Story: Rapid Growth with Improved Distribution in the Republic of China, 1952–1979* (Boulder, Colo.: Westview Press, 1981), and "Rapid Growth with Improved Income Distribution: The Taiwan Success Story," in *The Gap Between Rich and Poor*, ed. Seligson.

27. Adelman and Taft, *Economic Growth*, p. 199.

28. Muller, "Financial Dependence," p. 279.

29. Vincent A. Mahler and Claudio J. Katz, "The Impact of Government Expenditures on Growth and Distribution in Developed Market Economy Countries: A Cross-National Study," presented at the annual meeting of the American Political Science Association, Washington, D.C., 1984.

30. Victor Hugo Céspedes S., *Evolución de la distribución del ingreso en Costa Rica*, Serie Divulgación Económica No. 18 (Ciudad Universitaria Rodrigo Facio: Universidad de Costa Rica, 1979), p. 47.

31. Carlos Denton and Olda Ma. Acuña, *Población, fecundidad y desarrollo en Costa Rica, 1950–1970*, Informe de Trabajo No. 19 (Heredia, Costa Rica: IDESPO, 1984), p. 119. These demographic figures are for the census years 1963 and 1973, and hence do not precisely coincide with the 1961–1971 inequality data. However, the trends are consistent throughout the 1960s and 1970s and therefore there is little distortion in their interpretation.

32. Ibid., p. 97.

33. Ibid., pp. 60–61; International Monetary Fund, *Government Financial Statistics Yearbook, 1983* (Washington, D.C.: IMF, 1983), pp. 41–44.

34. Expenditures on housing and community amenities were also found to be related to income distribution, but this is generally a very small budget item in Central America, generally summing to no more than 3 percent of the total budget and is therefore not discussed here.

35. Seligson, "Costa Rica"; Victor Hugo Céspedes S., Ronulfo Jiménez R. and Eduardo Lizano F., *Costa Rica: Crisis y empobrecimiento* (San José, Costa Rica: Editorial Studium por la Academia de Centroamérica, 1983); Victor Hugo Céspedes S., Ronulfo Jiménez, Caludio González Vega, and Eduardo Lizano, *Costa Rica: Estabilidad sin crecimiento* (San José, Costa Rica: Academia de Centroamérica, 1984).

36. Dirección General de Estadística y Censos (Costa Rica), "Indicadores sociales y económicas" and "Población de la República de Costa Rica por Provincias, Cantones y Distritos, No. 52, Estimación al: 1° de julio 1983," San José, Costa Rica: Ministerio de Economía y Comercio, 1984.

37. Fuat M. Andic, *What Price Equity? A Macroeconomic Evaluation of Government Policies in Costa Rica*, Caribbean Occasional Series No. 4 (Puerto Rico: Institute of Caribbean Studies of the University of Puerto Rico, 1983); Claudio González Vega, *Temor al ajuste: Los costos sociales de las políticas económicas en Costa Rica durante la Década de los 70* (San José, Costa Rica: Academia de Centroamérica, 1984).

38. Juan Manuel Villasuso E., "Evolución de la crisis económica en Costa Rica y su impacto sobre la distribución del ingreso," Documentos de Trabajo No. 40, San

Pedro de Montes de Oca, Costa Rica: Instituto de Investigaciones en Ciencias Económicas, 1982.

39. Mitchell A. Seligson, *Peasants of Costa Rica and the Development of Agrarian Capitalism* (Madison: University of Wisconsin Press, 1980); Seligson, "Trust, Efficacy and Modes of Political Participation: A Study of Costa Rican Peasants," *British Journal of Political Science* 10 (January 1980): 75–98; Seligson, "Costa Rica and Jamaica"; and John A. Booth and Mitchell A. Seligson, "Peasants as Activists: A Reevaluation of Political Participation in the Countryside," *Comparative Political Studies* 12 (April 1979): 29–59.

40. Mitchell A. Seligson, "Implementing Land Reform: The Case of Costa Rica," *Managing International Development* 1 (March/April 1984): 29–46.

41. Michael H. Best, "Political Power and Tax Revenues in Central America," *Journal of Development Economics* 3 (March 1976): 49–82.

42. Ibid.

43. This estimate of the potential beneficiaries excludes the permanently employed plantation workers, a total of some 110,000 in 1981, even though under the 1952 agrarian reform legislation these workers were eligible beneficiaries. If this group were included, only 4.3 percent of the landless would have been benefited during the 1974–1981 period. For calculations, see Richard Hough, John Kelley, Stephen Miller, Russell Derossier, Fred L. Mann, and Mitchell A. Seligson, *Land and Labor in Guatemala: An Assessment* (Guatemala City: Ediciones Papiro, 1982), p. 15.

44. Hough et al., *Land and Labor*. The estimates range from a worst-case scenario of accommodating 23 percent of the landless to a best-case scenario of accommodating 64 percent. The latter scenario, however, excludes all permanently employed workers. Including this landless group lowers the best-case scenario to 48 percent. But even this calculation assumes utilization of most of the karst and swampland in Guatemala, land which could only be considered arable if vast sums of money were spent on draining swamps and upgrading karst soil with expensive cultivation and fertilization methods. Since these assumptions are very unrealistic, it is probably safer to assume that only 23 percent of all landless, or 31 percent of the landless and not permanently employed peasants could be accommodated under existing legislation. For an extended discussion of these calculations, see Hough et al., annex 2.

45. Mark Ruhl, "Agrarian Structure and Political Stability in Honduras," *Journal of Interamerican Studies and World Affairs* 26 (February 1984): 53.

46. Mitchell A. Seligson, Earl Jones, Edgar Nesman, Jack Hood Vaughn, and Michael Wise, *Baseline Survey of the Honduran Small Farmer Titling Program: Design, Field Work and Univariate Distributions* (Arlington, Va.: Development Associates, Inc., 1983); Earl Jones, Edgar Nesman, Mitchell A. Seligson, and Jack Hood Vaughn, *Baseline Survey of the Honduran Small Farmer Titling Project: Descriptive Analysis of the 1983 Sample* (San Francisco, California: Development Associates, Inc., 1984).

47. Checchi and Company, "Agrarian Reform in El Salvador," Report Prepared for the Agency for International Development (Washington, D.C., 1981); Michael Wise, "Agrarian Reform in El Salvador: Process and Progresses," Report Prepared for the United States Agency for International Development (San Salvador, El Salvador, 1983).

48. Forrest D. Colburn, "Rural Labor and the State in Postrevolutionary Nicaragua," *Latin American Research Review* 19, no. 3 (1984): 103–17.

49. Huntington, "Will More Countries Become Democratic?" pp. 205–07.

50. Robert A. Packenham, *Liberal America and the Third World* (Princeton, N.J.: Princeton University Press, 1973).

51. Lars Schoultz, *Human Rights and United States Policy Toward Latin America* (Princeton, N.J.: Princeton University Press, 1981).

52. As quoted by Penny Lernoux, *Fear and Hope: Toward Political Democracy in Central America* (New York: Field Foundation, 1984).

53. This is a point stressed by Huntington in "Will More Countries Become Democratic?" p. 218, but he also emphasizes that the United States should increase its own military and political power so that it can increase its influence among countries in the "transition zone."

Mark B. Rosenberg

9   Political Obstacles to Democracy
in Central America

While much has been written about the return to democracy in South America, little has been said about democracy in Central America. Despite important electoral developments in El Salvador, Honduras, Guatemala, and Nicaragua, the literature on these countries tends to focus on other issues: revolution, agrarian reform, foreign intervention and the role of the church.[1] We know that there are serious problems of democratic governance in most Central American countries, but we have little information as to why. Democracy may be generally desired in the region, but pluralism is not, particularly if it implies the institutionalization of mass interest representation. While much research remains to be done on the region's political culture, inevitably it is the institutional framework, the political process, and the act of governance itself that need serious analysis. This study reviews the obstacles to democracy in Central America. It suggests that the political organization of Central American nations is not yet conducive to the establishment of democratic institutions.

Is Democracy Possible?

The lack of research on democracy in Central America is, no doubt, a reflection of the region's history. There have been few periods in any of the countries' histories when anything approaching fair elections have taken place. Only Costa Rica has held free and fair elections periodically since 1948—after a civil war was fought, in part, over the forms that the succeeding government would take. As table 9.1 illustrates, of the forty-six changes of goverment in the other four

Table 9.1   Access to Power in Central America, 1948–1982

Date	Chief Executive	Means of Achieving Power	Type of Government
GUATEMALA			
1950–1954	J. Arbenz	Election	Military
1954–1957	C. Castillo Armas	Counterrevolution	Military
1957	L. A. González López	Succession (after assassination of Castillo)	Civilian
1957–1958	G. Flores Avendano	Designated by Congress	Military
1958–1963	M. Idigoras Fuentes	Election	Military
1963–1966	E. Peralta Azurdia	Coup d'état	Military
1966–1970	J. Méndez Montenegro	Election	Civilian
1970–1974	C. M. Arana Osorio	Election	Military
1974–1978	K. Laugerud García	Election (fraudulent)	Military
1978–1982	R. Lucas García	Election (fraudulent)	Military
1982–1983	E. Ríos Montt	Coup d'état	Military
1983–	H. Mejía Victores	Coup d'état	Military
EL SALVADOR			
1948–1950	Government junta (O. Bolanos, H. Costa, R. Gallindo, O. Osorio)	Coup d'état	Civil-military
1950–1956	O. Osorio	Election	Military
1956–1960	J. M. Lemus	Election	Military
1960–1961	Government junta (R. Fortín, F. Castillo, three military leaders)	Coup d'état	Civil-military
1961–1962	Civil-military directory	Coup d'état	Civil-military
1962	R. E. Cordón	Executive decree	Civil-military
1963–1967	J. A. Rivera	Election (one-candidate)	Military
1967–1972	F. Sánchez Hernández	Election (fraudulent)	Military
1972–1977	A. Molina	Election (fraudulent)	Military
1977–1979	C. H. Romero	Election (fraudulent)	Military
1979–1980	Government junta (G. M. Ungo, A. Majano, J. A. Gutiérrez, R. Mayorga)	Coup d'état	Civil-military
1980	Government junta (J. N. Duarte, A. Morales Erlich, J. A. Gutiérrez, A. Majano, R. Avalos, H. Dada)	Resignation of civilian members	Civil-military

1980–1982	J. N. Duarte	Designation by junta	Civilian
1982–1984	A. Magana	Designation by Constitutional Assembly	Civilian
1984–	J. N. Duarte	Election	Civilian

HONDURAS

1949–1954	J. Manuel Galvez	Presidential election	Civilian
1954–1956	J. Lozano Díaz	Designation by Congress	Civilian
1956	Government junta	Coup d'état	Military
1957–1963	R. Villeda Morales	Election	Civilian
1963–1965	O. López Arellano	Coup d'état	Military
1965–1971	O. López Arellano	National Assembly elections	Military
1971–1972	R. Cruz	Election	Civilian
1972–1975	O. López Arellano	Coup d'état	Military
1975–1978	J. A. Melgar Castro	Coup d'état	Military
1978–1980	P. Paz García	Coup d'état	Military
1980–1981	P. Paz García	National Assembly elections	Military
1982	R. Suazo Cordova	Election	Civilian

NICARAGUA

1948–1950	V. M. Ramos y Reyes	* * *	* * *
1951–1956	A. Somoza García	Coup d'état	Military
1956–1963	L. Somoza García	Election	Military
1963–1967	R. Schick	Election	Military
1967–1972	A. Somoza Debayle	Election	Military
1972–1974	Triumvirate	Election	Civilian
1974–1979	A. Somoza Debayle	Election	Military
1980–1984	Government Junta of National Reconstruction	Revolution	Civil-military
1984	D. Ortega	Election	Civil-military

COSTA RICA

1949–1953	O. Ulate	Election	Civilian
1953–1958	J. Figueres Ferrer	Election	Civilian
1958–1962	M. Echandi	Election	Civilian
1962–1966	F. Orlich	Election	Civilian
1966–1970	J. J. Trejos	Election	Civilian
1970–1974	J. Figueres Ferrer	Election	Civilian
1974–1978	D. Obuder	Election	Civilian
1978–1982	R. Carazo	Election	Civilian
1982–	L. A. Monge	Election	Civilian

Source: Adapted from Mario Solorzano, "Centroamérica: Democracias de fachada," *Polémica* 12 (November–December 1983).

countries of the region since 1948, only twenty-two were realized through elections and many of these were accompanied by some form of fraud. *Candidato único* elections, *elecciones con fraude*, and elections in which a military leader was elected have dominated the region's political scene since 1948.

How can the lack of meaningful elections in the region be explained? Roland Ebel's essay "Governing the City-State: Notes on the Politics of the Small Latin American Countries"[2] and his subsequent update[3] are useful points of departure for an understanding of Central America's sociopolitical environment. He argues that "national politics" in many Latin American countries are really "city politics." The Central American city-states are very small economies with restricted markets; economic concentration reinforces the tendency to "corporative" sociopolitical organization and that inevitably translates into concentrated political power. Ebel interprets politics in such city-states as a struggle between those in power over the allocation of extremely scarce goods and values. He states:

> While the *Presidente de la República* looks impressive, and from his office and those of his subordinates flow streams of *licencias, diligencias, permisos, avisos, prorrogas and trámites*, he is in reality something of a paper tiger. Much of the time he is performing a delicate balancing act in his attempt to coordinate the activities and harmonize the conflicting demands of such powerful interests as *algonoderos, bananeros, eclesiásticos, militares,* and *Norteamericanos.*[4]

Ebel argues that government in the Central American city-state is overcentralized in administration, decentralized in decision making, and usually oblivious to if not consciously subversive of constitutional arrangements.

Mitchell Seligson's analysis in this volume examines the prospects for the emergence of democracy in Central America. In response to the question, "Why has democracy, which for so long has been an orphan in this region, suddenly begun to find a home?" he notes that the "economic and sociocultural conditions that have been prerequisites for democratic growth . . . have been emerging over the past ten to fifteen years throughout Central America."[5] Seligson notes, however, that the emergence of conditions conducive to democracy have coincided with unprecedented violence, attributed to public policies promoting income and land inequality. He argues that unless "existing policies are reversed, one can expect continuing unrest and political violence."[6]

The analytical implications of Ebel's and Seligson's work suggest areas that should be emphasized in an examination of the prospects for the emergence of democracy in Central America. First, because of the small size and limited economy of the region's city-states, politics ultimately entails inevitable personalistic features. Family, clique, and regional factors may be just as important as ideological and partisan explanations. Sex, business deals (*movidas, chambas, telefonazos*), and other idiosyncratic phenomena may be the only valid explanations of why some things get done and others do not.

Second, formal government institutions often have few manifest functions and many important latent functions. Political parties, government agencies, and interest groups may be only incidental to the real struggles over political allocations. Vertical patronage networks are usally critical to gaining political access in the region. Formally constituted political institutions may serve, at best, as mere artifices to supply political favors, to co-opt uninformed challengers, and to demobilize and deaden public interest among those who might try to gain political access outside the available patronage networks.[7]

Broad notions of political legitimacy have no currency in this context. Government can only serve particularistic interests. There is no tradition of *public interest* that can be defined beyond the narrow interest of the groups in power. The necessity of meeting specific clients' needs, and the intensity of those clients' expectations and demands, means that there are few overall pressures in Central America for responsive government. What matters is keeping the particular clientele interests dependent on one's access to power and largesse. While this clientelistic model is similar to "machine" politics and political "bossism" in other countries, scarcity and political and economic instability impose particularistic imperatives on public officeholders that work against obeying any larger notion of the public good. There are few incentives to perform one's official duties with probity.

Third, the role of the United States in each Central American country distorts the possibility for indigenous political alignments. In Central America, the United States has unrivaled political power and resources and represents one of the largest economic enterprises in each country. The U.S. embassy's budget (through economic and military aid as well as staffing) may be the only budget in the country that is expanding. Thus the United States often sets the country's social agenda. The U.S. ambassador is one of the most studied figures in each country. The embassy itself, its staff, programs, and aid activities, are analyzed, scrutinized, and then hustled by locals who specialize in "working" the U.S. institution. If knowing someone or having access on the local scene is important, one of any Central American *bon-savant*'s essential resources is access to high embassy officials and the ability, at decorous intervals, to be seen at the ambassador's receptions for traveling notables. Such is the importance of the U.S. mission in Central America that Howard Wiarda has said, "The United States is not only the most important external power operating throughout Central America, but the American embassy . . . operating in its proconsular capacity is also a major domestic force if not *the* major domestic force."[8]

The large U.S. presence is magnified by the fact that so many other public and private institutions in Central America are weak. It is also made more complex by the fact that the embassy often serves as an important source of information and disinformation. Moreover, even if the embassy does not want to get involved in certain issues, it may do so because it is dragged in or implicated by another actor. And the embassy is often part of a complex political game which thrusts it, from time to time, into a political equivalent of musical chairs with struggling local political factions. The manipulation of embassy interests, symbols, and messages is as important in Central American politics as is their manipulation by other local and national groups. National politicians and military officials inevitably spend as much time cultivating U.S. embassy clientele and visiting dignitaries as they do with their own nationals.

The important role played by the United States underlines another essential aspect of Central America that bears on democracy: the extreme dependence on, and belief in, the importance of U.S. institutions. While this varies from country to country, there are few political actors who underestimate the United States' power for good or ill in Central America. In part, this belief in the efficacy of U.S. institutions derives from the overwhelming influence of American customs and culture in the region.[9] Perhaps more important, it derives from a strong desire among Central Americans to create in their countries the favorable living conditions that they so desperately lack. Finally, Central Americans tend to be woefully short on understanding how the U.S. policy process really works, particularly regarding policy toward their countries. While diplomatic relations with the United States are the principal element in each country's foreign policy, U.S. policy toward Central America has historically been one of the least important diplomatic items on the foreign policy agenda. Thus there is an incongruent relationship which inevitably makes the United States more important to Central America than Central America is to the United States.

A final political reality relevant to an understanding of democracy in the region is that many of Central America's political questions are not being debated and resolved internally but rather internationally. The region's leaders have traditionally preferred elevating their problems to the international arena because of the abundance of resources found there as well as the reduced threat to personal safety. This tradition is explained in part by the lack of internal structures for promoting and fostering open discussions about political issues. Few of the region's countries have allowed for ongoing debate and discussion among moderates and the nonrevolutionary left.[10] Moreover, the ability to manipulate international organizations, to utilize the prestige mass media, to travel to international gatherings, and to be photographed with important world leaders, all have their local political salience and impact.

Definition and Analysis

Two schools of thought characterize approaches toward democracy in less developed countries. The first is traditional, emphasizing process, procedure, and form and assumes some general consensus regarding the rules of the game. Interest groups, political parties, and pluralism are understood to be essential to the maintenance of a democratic system. The second school looks less at means than at ends, emphasizing the broader socioeconomic gains and political participation engendered by enhanced material well-being and social equity. This school approaches issues with a collectivist bias.

A recent analysis of Central America's crisis by Gabriel Aguilera directly illustrates these conflicting perspectives by examining the two types of democracy currently possible in Central America.[11] While he analyzes the current efforts at democratization in Guatemala, Honduras, and El Salvador as a means by which to keep the traditional political economy functioning without any major upheavals, Aguilera views the revolution in Nicaragua in a more principled sense. Its objective is the creation of a democracy in which popular living conditions are improved as rapidly as possible and where racism and exploitation are minimized. Aguilera further states, "While the first approach guarantees freedom of movement and expression to political interests of diverse classes, the second refers to the building of new societies with the participation of all the population."[12] Interpreted in this fashion, "the democratic and participatory [organizations of government] are not necessarily realized through elections and political parties and they are not measured simply by electoral results, but rather by indices of participation and by changes in living conditions for the majority of people."[13]

The recent experience of redemocratizing South American countries is noteworthy within this context. In each of the countries (Peru, Bolivia, Ecuador, Brazil, Argentina, Uruguay) that have recently returned to democracy, the emphasis has been on the formal and procedural aspects of political organization rather than on the distributional aspects of democracy, as suggested in the second approach. Indeed, it may have been frustration and anger over the inability to make progress in the second area of political economy that has provided the rationale for returning to a less economically but politically more ambitious effort to order themselves.

Seligson uses the definition of democracy provided by Myron Weiner in his comparative study of competitive elections in developing nations to examine the possibilities for democracy in Central America.[14] This definition is oriented toward formalistic and procedural issues and places great emphasis on elections and parties. It does not address some of the larger issues of equity and distribution. However, Weiner's approach to democracy highlights many of the aspects of the return to democracy in South America, particularly the emphasis on procedure and party-oriented politics. Less specified are the ends or goals of that process, except to put civilians back into formal governmental control.

Weiner's study nonetheless provides the general dimensions of a useful definition that can be applied to Central America: (1) government leaders are chosen in competitive elections in which there are opposition political parties; (2) political parties, including opponents of the existing government, have the right to openly seek public support: they have access to the press, the right of assembly and freedom of speech and are protected against unwarranted arrest; (3) governments defeated in an election step down; losers are not punished by the winners nor are defeated leaders punished unless in that act of governance they have broken the law and their punishment is based upon due process; (4) elected governments are not figureheads; they exercise power and make policies and they are accountable to the electors, not to the military, the monarchy, the bureaucracy or some oligarchy. Each element of Weiner's definition can be examined in greater detail as they apply to Central America.

Competitive Elections

With the exception of Costa Rica, where a strong competitive tradition has existed since the mid-1940s, the number of competitive elections in other countries of the region can be counted almost on one hand. Reasons for the lack of competitive elections abound. In the first place, the elite in Central America has always had other means of exploiting power. As Robert Dahl has stated, in any society there must be some "underlying consensus" on policy among a predominant portion of its politically active members.[15] Elections are just one of the many ways to implement public policy. Eldon Kenworthy has written that "actors" cannot agree on one "currency" for measuring power. The dual currency game, alternating between coercion and popularity, can be translated into almost equal amounts of power.[16] And elections often tend to promote rather than resolve conflict. In Glen Dealy's words, "By accenting differences, elections [in Latin America] exacerbate latent conflicts and disrupt the whole both in theory and in practice. Partisan speeches, stuffed ballot boxes, extravagant claims of alternate teleologies and military coups are just a few of the factors that have come to characterize the so-called electoral process."[17] Robert Dahl himself admits that elections and political competition "vastly increase in size, number and variety the minorities whose preferences must be taken into account by leaders making policy choices."[18]

Even if there were faith in elections as an important mechanism for the transfer of power, Central America's electoral institutions have had much difficulty in establishing an electoral process that meets the needs of the diverse interest groups that ultimately vote. Debates abound over the type of ballot, the campaigns, financing, voter registration, selection of candidates, and district representation. While this lack of consensus reflects the larger problems concerning the legitimacy of the process itself, it ultimately further questions that legitimacy, as part of a vicious circle. To be competitive, elections must ultimately pit opposing parties against each other. In the region, there has been no shortage of opposing parties. As one analysis has pointed out for El Salvador, "In the 1960s and 1970s Salvadoran political life swarmed with broad-based political parties, grassroots movements, coalitions, demonstrations . . . and popular organization."[19] However, the ability of parties to aggregate general interests has been an issue.

Central America's dilemma is that the contending parties increasingly represent smaller and smaller sectors of the population. Perhaps, surprisingly, this has occurred because the region has always had distinct ideological differences that translated into "conservative" and "liberal" party formations. These party distinctions were particularly acute before the 1930s, but seemed to collapse as the Depression forced dominant groups together to protect their mutual interests. Since the 1940s, traditional parties have not been able to aggregate emergent new interests. One Latin American constitutional expert has noted that "pluralism has been restricted."[20] The predictable results have been the formation of guerrilla movements, revolutionary groups, and clandestine political organizations on both the left and the right. The failure of the traditional parties to provide meaningful political alternatives is a deficiency that speaks to Weiner's second component of democracy.

Political Parties and their Dilemma

Weiner's definition of democracy states that "political parties, including opponents of the existing government, have the right to openly seek public support: they have access to the press, the right of assembly and freedom of speech and are protected against unwarranted arrest." With few exceptions, these conditions have rarely obtained in the region. Generally, there have been four types of political parties in Central America. They will be discussed in turn.

1. *Traditional parties* are now passing from the Central American political scene, by and large. Even while they often articulated a coherent political and ideological philosophy, they tended to be rent with personalism and *caudillismo*. In practice, they existed for patronage and clientelistic purposes. Examples include the National and Liberal parties of Honduras, the Conservative party of Nicaragua, and the Party of National Conciliation in El Salvador.

2. *Modernizing parties*, characterized by their European-oriented

ideology are now in power in both Costa Rica (the National Liberation party) and El Salvador (the Christian Democratic party). These
parties have rarely captured over 50 percent electoral support and
normally encounter strong opposition because of their statist tendencies. While fostering a programmatic, mobilizational image, in practice they must content themselves with some mix of program and
patronage. In many respects, their programmatic orientation provides
a convenient, if not ideological and thus purer pretext for rewarding
party faithfuls in jobs, status, and security.

3. *Extremist parties* are characterized by militant dogmatism and a
willingness to use violence to achieve their ends. Extremist politics
often leave little room for differentiating between conservative (rightist) and radical (leftist) movements. The means inevitably become
confused with the ends, and a vicious cycle is created whereby violence seems to be the only response to violence. Both extremes often
show little faith in democratic procedures and even less confidence in
"centrist" politicians. Both can undermine political compromise and
both challenge political forces toward the extremes of the spectrum
that are not fully committed to any type of political governance,
thereby making that governance even more tenuous. While these
parties openly espouse their positions, extremist parties of the left
have often gone underground or are in exile. Examples of these
parties include the National Liberation Movement and the Authentic
National Center, both of Guatemala.

4. *Dominant mass parties* are those that tend to dominate government and nonofficial elements of public life. The explicit model that
they follow is Mexico's Institutional Revolutionary party (PRI). The
Sandinista National Liberation Front (FSLN) in Nicaragua is the most
recent example, but the PCN of El Salvador aspired to this type of
political hegemony before it lost its momentum in the 1970s. PLN
ideologues openly spoke of establishing a PRI-type political dominance in Costa Rica during the mid-1970s.

Like political parties in other parts of the world, Central America's
political parties tend to be rent by personalism and factionalism.
Even the region's most successful political party, the PLN of Costa
Rica, has suffered a series of potentially debilitating splits based
largely on personal ambition. The ruling Liberal party in Honduras is
now split into at least five factions and the Christian Democratic
party of El Salvador barely weathered a leadership struggle prior to
the 1984 presidential elections between José Napoleon Duarte and

his heir apparent, Fidel Chávez Mena. The tendency toward party factionalism is not perhaps as extreme as in other Latin American countries such as Bolivia, where a reported 323 political parties have competed for power since 1958.[21] But factionalism is nonetheless a major problem because it directs political competition inward rather than outward. One Honduran analyst has suggested that there is greater intraparty competition in Honduras than interparty competition.[22] Moreover, factionalism reinforces the tendency toward internal competition and conflict resolution, rather than on purpose and problem solving. In this context, payoffs (political favors, jobs, unequal access to limited resources such as foreign exchange) are related back to groups competing for power, not forward to their consequences for society. While Charles Tilly has noted that the formation of national states and widespread popular involvement in them in Europe emerged inadvertently as the result of "small groups of power hungry men" fighting off numerous rivals and great popular resistance in the pursuit of their own ends, the model hardly seems to be reassuring for Central America.[23]

But there is a larger issue. Are parties capable of incorporating newly emerging sectors into the ongoing political fabric? Many of the region's Christian and Social Democratic leaders were originally members of more traditional parties. They believed that these parties could not or would not expand beyond their own more narrow and traditional interests to accommodate the newly emerging middle class created by post-World War II economic expansion. As Mario Solorzano has indicated, "Agricultural diversification, the industrialization process and the massive entry of foreign capital had an important impact with relation to the economy's modernization, generating the appearance of new business groups, expanding the size of the middle sectors and catalyzing the appearance of urban and rural proletariat."[24]

While some parties could not adapt, others were quickly forming to capture the political space left unprotected by the less responsive political parties. The efforts of these emergent parties have had very high costs. In Guatemala, key leaders have been assassinated. In El Salvador they have been exiled and/or assassinated. In Honduras they have been marginalized. In Nicaragua, both before and after Somoza, they have been harassed and menaced. Where minority parties have emerged in Costa Rica, they have either been successful in articulating their interests through the unicameral national assembly or they have joined, in coalition, with one of the parties. With few exceptions, no party in Central America has been able to fashion a meaningful and lasting relationship with any of the region's major labor unions.

These problems are related to another one. With the exception of the Sandinistas, particularly during their first two years in power, few parties have had the skills or the wherewithal to mobilize large groups of people. Central America has had no Perón, Haya de la Torre, Vargas, or Cárdenas. This absence of dominant political figures is made even more complicated by the fact that Central America's military establishments and the left- and right-wing death squads have made open political mobilizing quite dangerous. The rights of assembly and speech exist in every constitution of the region, but in practice they are subject to the particular correlation of forces and sentiments in force at the time.[25]

A far more important tactic for the establishment and maintenance of power, if not for democracy, may be for the dominant political forces, especially parties, to seek accommodation with one another. The most common form of public accommodation in Latin America has come about through the articulation of "pacts" between parties and other political groups. These pacts are agreements on how the spoils of power will be used. They have been essential elements in the evolution of social peace and democracy in Colombia and Venezuela,[26] and have had their equivalents in Central America: in Nicaragua and Honduras in the early 1970s and in El Salvador most recently. While such pacts may be political devices which actually enshrine expediency and "ad-hocism," they may also be essential to achieving the currently fashionable concept of "democracy as the second-best option," particularly where no one group has hegemonic power and can impose its political will on the rest.[27]

Effective Suffrage, No Reelection

Weiner's third characteristic of democracy points to the importance of an elected government's willingness to yield power if defeated in an election. As Mexicans learned under Díaz, this was no simple matter. Díaz's tenacity helped galvanize the revolutionary forces in their efforts to topple the dictator. In Central America, in fact, there has been very little *continuismo*, the forty-year Somoza dynasty notwithstanding.

The key to understanding political relations in Central America can be found in the armed forces and their relations to civilian groups. Thus, while it is true that Guatemala has had periodic electoral changes, as table 9.1 shows, behind the scenes in every crucial decision were the armed forces of that country. In El Salvador, the military directly dominated each government, beginning with the Hernández-Martínez dictatorship (1931), while in Honduras the armed forces play the decisive internal political role. Nicaragua's Sandinistas are increasingly relying on military power to maintain their control, and it is this dependence that may be tipping the balance of control internally with the ruling front.

The permanency of the military in power, either formally or informally, is what has prompted Solorzano to describe Central America as a region of "facade democracies" (*democracias de fachada*). Thus, while there has been very little *continuismo* in strict terms, few presidential candidates have taken public office in Central America without the military's expressed support. Indeed, elections have recently been held in the region where the candidates with the most number of votes did not take power. Dealy explains this phenomenon by pointing to the fact that Latin Americans prefer "guided" elections. The alternative—transferring power based on "uninhibited voting"—suggests a community without collective goals and a theory of equality, both of which Latin Americans deny.[28]

In practice, the predominance of the armed forces throughout Central America reflects a number of problems. First, the military as a group have very little confidence in civilian political leadership. This lack of confidence derives from a larger sense among the military and their allies that civilians cannot be trusted. This distrust is compounded by what Wynia calls the military's "craving" for control over things that affect them, "a trait that may be wise in war but is counterproductive in constitutional politics."[29] Second, this situation is compounded by the fact that at least three of the region's military establishments consider themselves to be fighting insurgencies of significant proportions. The Guatemalan rebellion has been a continuing dimension of civil-military relations since the early 1960s, virtually guaranteeing the armed forces of that country an extraordinary role in political life. In El Salvador, the insurgency is now in its fifth year and gives the Salvadoran military less motivation to bring their own much criticized security forces into greater order. And in Nicaragua, the *contra* maneuvers in the north and south of the country give the Sandinistas a crucial resource whereby to justify their policies limiting political freedoms. The growing military sophistication of the Honduran armed forces gives the region a "garrison-state" complexion that only further undermines the weakened base of civilian politics.[30]

The armed forces' predominance in the region reflects a third problem. In many instances, civilian politicians would rather deal with the military than with other civilians. While José Nun captured the essence of this relation several years ago with his essay on the "middle-class military coup," he underemphasized the extent to which this type of alliance inevitably erodes a range of civilian institutions beyond simply upholding civilian rule as a norm.[31] The region's legal systems have been hostage to the privilege and exclusiveness which the military and their nonuniformed coalition partners have insisted upon. The fact that few military officers have been brought to trial for human rights abuses in Guatemala and El Salvador illustrates the extent to which the region's legal systems are evaded by those with power and privilege. Thus their power and privilege have not only undermined the possibilities for a broad-based civilian landscape, but as importantly have undercut the parallel institutional systems vital to the creation of public legitimacy and efficacy.

While Weiner specifies as an essential feature of democracy that "governments defeated in an election step down," he shows little sensitivity to the fact that many governments at best share power with other powerful institutions. This will be a problem in the four Central American countries for the foreseeable future. The military will play a decisive role. Ultimately, for the armed forces to be controlled, parallel organizations will need to change and penetrate them. Two options are available: in Mexico and Tanzania, the military are subordinate to noncommunist ruling parties. On the other hand, in communist countries, the military are subordinate to the ideologically based party. In Central America, the Salvadoran model seems the most likely. In this situation, it is the United States that supports the party in power, giving that party extraordinary leverage over the military. While this support is important at a symbolic level, it may be more apparent than real, given the current party's inability to effect basic structural reforms in the legal system.

What is clear is that the military will continue to be the major force for political accountability in the region's political systems. This notion runs counter to Weiner's fourth characteristic of democracy, to be discussed below.

"I Obey but I Do Not Comply" (*"Obedezco pero no cumplo"*).

The issue of accountability is essential to prospects for the long-term success of democracy in Central America. Like other components of democracy, accountability has a number of elements that deserve analysis. Traditionally there has been little public accountability for those who wielded power in Central America. Rather, leaders catered privately to either the military, the oligarchy, the private external financial interests with investments in the country, or some combination of these groups. Only in Costa Rica has some tradition of accountability been established, largely through the electoral system, and to a lesser extent through the courts.

In rare instances, political leaders have been forced to be accountable to a wider audience. Public demonstrations brought down governments in Guatemala and El Salvador in 1944, and almost did so in Costa Rica in 1947. The Sandinista rebellion of 1979 could not have been successful without a multiclass movement to oust the dictatorship. Growing Catholic church militancy has provoked a greater consciousness about the importance of government responsiveness and has contributed to the rise in public demands in El Salvador, Guatemala, Honduras, and Nicaragua. But church militancy has also sparked a counter-response, particularly from conservative evangelicals seeking to eschew the disorder inherent in liberation theology teachings.

The thrust of Ebel's analysis is to question the real power that any Central American government has. To be accountable to the larger public, a government has to have resources so that it is not dependent on private interests. If, as Ebel suggests, the Central American city-state is penetrated by a series of vertical, corporatively organized interest associations, then accountability could take on a new dimension in Central America. Yet perhaps it is just this particularized accountability that explains why governments appear to do so little in the region. The minorities to which Dahl refers have captured and cannibalized the state to such an extent that it really is incapable of being accountable to any large audience. The presence of the military helps ensure the continuity of that system.

Another aspect of the accountability issue is the availability of both human and material resources. The limited economic productivity of the region, coupled with its shortage of skilled and semiskilled labor, contribute to further undermine any responsiveness that a government may desire. Thus even when there is a genuine effort to respond to some public need, the capability simply may not be there. A recent study of the National Agrarian Institute (INA), charged with land management in Honduras, revealed the following:

> The current INA management inherited a motor vehicle pool which theoretically contained about 400 vehicles. . . . Virtually all of these vehicles are deadlined; in fact, most of them are junk; . . . in all of INA, including the seven regional offices, there are twenty-four vehicles running.
> However, there are problems in every area of administrative support. There is no personnel system other than a small office which handles the paperwork; all office space is poorly assigned, poorly furnished, overcrowded and clearly demoralizing. Supplies and equipment are in short supply.[32]

Thus, while the old saying "*Obedezco pero no cumplo*" ("I obey but I do not comply") has been interpreted to mean that the colonial administrator *chose* not to comply with orders received from Spain, in the modern version, its meaning can be expanded to suggest that the administrator *cannot* comply simply because the human and material resources are unavailable.

Is This Central America's Democratic "Moment"?

One recent analysis on redemocratization in the Andean countries asserts that Latin America is entering a new "democratic cycle," and that we should watch for the emergence of "democratic moments within the historical process of Latin America."[33] If Central America's "moment" has arrived, as Seligson suggests in his examination of the region's sociocultural and economic conditions, this is not reflected in the structural arrangements that characterize the political organization of most Central American countries. As Dahl suggests, "What we ordinarily describe as democratic 'politics' is merely the chaff. Prior to politics . . . is the underlying consensus on policy that usually exists in the society among a predominant portion of the politically active members."[34]

There are at least four preconditions necessary for the emergence of consensus in Central America. These will be described below.

1. The region's economy will have to reverse its downward spiral and return to the secular growth patterns characteristic of the 1960s and 1970s. However, as Booth and others have shown, the cost of this growth cannot be unilaterally imposed on the Central American working classes as it was in the previous growth era.[35] Even in Brazil, as Robert Kaufman points out, the lesson there with authoritarianism is that "both the economic and political 'successes' were achieved . . . because of (rather than in spite of) the willingness of authorities to tolerate debates and to play the political game in ways that sometimes diverged sharply from their own anti-democratic mentalities."[36] If economic growth is to occur, it will have to respond to the basic needs of Central America's burgeoning population, which by the year 2000 will have almost doubled to about 42 million people. In this context, it is clear that growth cannot occur just in the area of nontraditional exports, but as well in the production of basic grains so that the population can feed itself. At present, the prospects for significant economic growth during the remainder of this decade and for the next are not good—particularly given the continued destruction of the region's infrastructure as well as the lack of investable surplus.

2. Leadership must at least be able to negotiate its way through the veritable "living museum" of interests in the region. It must have a capacity to accommodate the vast and complex political spectrum while nurturing and protecting the evolution of civil politics. This can indeed emerge as the "second-best" option because there are no "winnable" first options for any group. Moreover, the leadership must be able to resist the temptations of power, which often make them the first to abuse the democratic systems which they presumably want to create and maintain. In Honduras, the current president has egregiously weakened the nascent democracy there through interminable partisanship. In El Salvador, the Christian Democratic leadership has overzealously disregarded the laws passed by its own conservative congress, thereby directly violating the constitution. Even democrats have to practice being good democrats. Strong and decisive leadership in the region must articulate a larger democratic political project and organize and mediate the debates on issues that provide opportunities for participation while leaving space for incremental changes.

3. Armed insurgency and civil war must be stopped. In the Southern Cone, Kaufman suggests that "the maximalism of the extreme left merely fed the fears that contributed to the brutal authoritarian lurches to the right."[37] In Central America, there is good evidence that this relationship has worked in the other direction: the extremism of the far right led to the brutal (if not more episodic) response of the extreme left. As Gabriel Zaid has more than once persuasively argued for El Salvador, "That dirty trick of tampering so arrogantly with an election [of 1972] merely goaded on the rebels, the coup makers, the death squads."[38] The results for Central America has been what Zaid calls "armed pluralism."

The situation of "armed pluralism" has three important dimensions. First, with the exception of Costa Rica, the region's armed forces are paramount political actors in each Central American country. This is not likely to change, particularly given the new environment of "low-intensity conflict."[39] Some formula must be sought to minimize the political influence of the military. Such a formula is unlikely under conditions of insurgency. Kaufman remarks of the Southern Cone that "one of the striking uniformities of otherwise very different liberalization experiences in contemporary Argentina, Brazil and Uruguay has so far been the absence of such insurgencies."[40] He further argues that "guerrilla activities have been counter-productive" as a means by which to accelerate the disintegration of bureaucratic-authoritarian regimes What he is less clear about, however, is how to keep the military at a meaningful distance from the political arena.[41]

In Central America, this dilemma is complicated even more by the fact that many civilians, as elsewhere, are often more comfortable with the military than with other civilians. This attitude is not simply at the elite level, however. The 1984 Salvadoran elections gave dramatic evidence to the drawing power of a conservative, nonreformist political formula. There, as elsewhere in the region (Guatemala, Honduras, Costa Rica), the contradictions created by the desire for modernization despite the inability to achieve it, the strength of conservatism as expressed through religious values, and current patterns of political organization, suggest the need to learn a lot more about the region's mass political values and their modes of political expression.[42]

It is unrealistic to believe that Central America's military leaders will "return to the barracks" in the foreseeable future. Indeed, for those searching for some formula to depoliticize the military, the search will most likely be fruitless. Incrementalist solutions will probably depend more on changes in nonmilitary facets of political life and the emergence in the military of strong leadership that chooses to be more democratic.

The other two dimensions of "armed pluralism" are as intractable as the first. As stated earlier, the presence of "extremist" parties is but a reflection of a larger problem in Central America. Fed by patterns of mistreatment inherited from the colonial period, a culture of violence dominates the area.[43] Official violence, whether emanating from Guatemala's secret police or from the *turbas divinas* (divine mobs) in Sandinista Nicaragua, are now quasi-institutionalized forms of political control. Distinctions between the two types of violence suggested here can be made. "Rightist" violence attempts to maintain the existing political system by eliminating those who would challenge it. "Leftist"-inspired violence is oriented at creating a new system by eliminating those opposed to change. Tactics within each group vary, as does ideology. The results seem to be the same. The region's "blood tax" gets higher and higher.[44] Within this context, the procedural norms and the consensus critical to democracy have little opportunity to prove themselves.

Finally, it is clear that a critical element in Central America's search for democracy will continue to be the United States. Strong U.S. support is a necessary but not a sufficient condition for democracy in the region. Without U.S. support, the region's democrats are not strong enough to maintain their struggle. They are defenseless against both right and left extremists and sectors within the military as well. To support democracy, however, the United States must develop confidence in democratic forces and in the almost ineluctable necessity of broad-based popular support. The development of this support will require human, material, and symbolic resources—all of which have been in short supply in the region's past. Given the current scarcities and the unprecedented internationalization of the conflict in Central America, the United States may be facing an almost insurmountable task if it pushes democracy too hard and too fast. This will be particularly true if American policymakers maintain too rigid a view of what constitutes democracy and allow themselves to disregard the U.S. legacy in the region.

Notes

1. See Donald E. Schulz and Douglas H. Graham, *Revolution and Counter-revolution in Central America and the Caribbean* (Boulder, Colo.: Westview Press, 1984); Steve C. Ropp and James A. Morris, *Central America: Crisis and Adaptation* (Albuquerque: University of New Mexico Press, 1984); Thomas P. Anderson, *Politics in Central America* (New York: Praeger, 1982); and Martin Diskin, ed., *Trouble in our Backyard: Central America and the United States in the Eighties* (New York: Pantheon, 1983).

2. Roland H. Ebel, "Governing the City-State: Notes on the Politics of the Small Latin American Countries," *Journal of Inter-American Studies and World Affairs* 14, no. 3 (August 1972).

3. See Roland H. Ebel, "The Development and Decline of the Central American City-State," in *Rift and Revolution: The Central American Imbroglio*, ed. Howard Wiarda (Washington, D.C.: American Enterprise Institute for Public Policy Research, 1984), pp. 70–104.

4. Ebel, "Governing the City State," p. 335.

5. See chapter 8.

6. Ibid.

7. See Douglas A. Chalmers, "Parties and Society in Latin America," in *Friends, Followers and Factions: A Reader in Political Clientelism*, ed. Stefan W. Schmidt et al. (Berkeley: University of California Press, 1977), pp. 401–21.

8. Howard J. Wiarda, "The Origins of the Central American Crisis," in *Rift and Revolution*, ed. Wiarda, p. 11.

9. See Robert A. Pastor, "Our Real Interests in Central America," *Atlantic Monthly*, July 1982.

10. Piero Gleijeses, "The Elusive Center in Central America," *Working Papers*, November–December 1981, pp. 30–37.

11. Gabriel Aguilera, "Las perspectivas de la crisis en Centroamérica," presented at the Sixth Central American Congress of Sociology in Panama, March 1985.

12. Ibid., p. 13.

13. Ibid., pp. 13–14.

14. Myron Weiner, "Empirical Democratic Theory," in *Competitive Elections in Developing Countries*, ed. Myron Weiner and Ergun Ozbudun (Washington, D.C.: American Enterprise Institute, forthcoming).

15. Robert Dahl, *A Preface to Democratic Theory* (Chicago: University of Chicago Press, 1956), pp. 132–33.

16. Eldon Kenworthy, "Coalitions in the Political Development of Latin America," in *The Study of Coalition Behavior*, ed. Sven Groennings et al. (New York: Holt, Rinehart and Winston, 1970), p. 104.

17. Glen Dealy, "Pipe Dreams: The Pluralistic Latins," *Foreign Policy* 57 (Winter 1984–85): 118.

18. Dahl, *A Preface to Democratic Theory*, p. 132.

19. Robert Leiken, "The Salvadoran Left," in *Central America: Anatomy of Conflict*, ed. Robert Leiken (New York: Pergamon Press, 1984), p. 112.

20. Jorge Mario García Laguardia, "Partidos políticos, orden jurídico y cambio social en Guatemala: La cuadratura del círculo," in *Centroamérica: desafíos y per-*

spectivas, ed. Ignacio Sosa and Jorge Mario García Lagurdia (Mexico City: UNAM, 1984), pp. 14–15.

21. Raul Rivadeneira Prada, "Partidos políticos, partidos taxi y partidos fantasma: la atomización de los partidos en Bolivia," *Nueva Sociedad* 74 (September/October 1984): 75–95.

22. Edgardo Sevilla Idiaquez, "The Limits of Democracy in Honduras," in *Honduras Confronts its Future: Contending Perspectives on Critical Issues*, ed. Mark B. Rosenberg and Philip L. Shepherd (Boulder, Colo.: Lynne Rienner Publications, 1986).

23. Charles Tilly, ed., *The Formation of National States in Western Europe* (Princeton: Princeton University Press, 1975), p. 635.

24. Mario Solorzano, "Centroamérica: democracias de fachada," *Polémica* 12 (November–December 1983): 46.

25. See Jorge Mario García LaGuardia, *La defensa de la constitución* (Guatemala: Universidad de San Carlos, Facultad de Ciencias Jurídicas y Sociales, 1983).

26. See Harvey F. Kline, "The National Front: Historical Perspective and Overview," in *Politics of Compromise: Coalition Government in Colombia*, ed. Albert Berry et al. (New Brunswick, N.J.: Transaction Books, 1980), pp. 59–87; and Bruce Michael Bagley, "The National Front and Beyond: Politics, Public Power and Public Policy in an Inclusionary Authoritarian Regime" (Washington, D.C.: SAIS, Central American and Caribbean Program, June 1984).

27. See Dankwart Rustow, "Transitions to Democracy: Toward a Dynamic Model," *Comparative Politics* 2, no. 3 (April 1970): 337–65; and Robert R. Kaufman, "Lessons from the Southern Cone"; and Terry Karl, "Democracy by Design? The Christian Democratic Party in El Salvador," both presented at the Seminar on Transitions to Democracy in Central America, San José, Costa Rica, 1984.

28. See Dealy, "Pipe Dreams," pp. 118–19.

29. Gary Wynia, "Militarism Revisited," *Journal of Inter-American Studies and World Affairs* 25, no. 1 (February 1983): 115–16.

30. Mark B. Rosenberg, "Nicaragua and Honduras: Toward Garrison States," *Current History* 83, no. 490 (February 1984): 59–62, 87.

31. José Nun, "The Middle Class Military Coup," in *The Politics of Conformity in Latin America*, ed. Claudio Veliz (London: Oxford University Press, 1967), pp. 66–118.

32. Jack Vaughn et al., *Final Report: An Administrative Analysis of the National Agrarian Institute of Honduras* (Arlington, Va.: Development Associates, Inc., 1983), pp. 7–8.

33. James M. Malloy and Luis Abugattas, "Redemocratization in Latin America: The Andean Pattern," unpublished, Department of Political Science, University of Pittsburgh, p. 2.

34. Dahl, *A Preface to Democratic Theory*, pp. 132–33.

35. John A. Booth, " 'Trickle-up' Income Redistribution and Development in Central America During the 1960s and 1970s," in *The Gap Between the Rich and the Poor*, ed. Mitchell A. Seligson (Boulder, Colo.: Westview Press, 1984), pp. 351–64.

36. Kaufman, "Lessons from the Southern Cone," p. 13.

37. Ibid., p. 12.

38. Gabriel Zaid, "Salvadorans go to the Ballot Box," *Dissent*, Fall 1984, p. 457.

39. Caesar D. Sereseres, "Central America's Low Intensity Conflict Environment: Security Implications for the United States," presented at the Conference on Security Perspectives and Prospects: Central America and the Caribbean in the 1980s, Claremont-McKenna College, 1984.

40. Kaufman, "Lessons from the Southern Cone," p. 22.

41. Ibid., p. 22.

42. Anthony P. Maingot, "The Caribbean: The Structure of Modern Conservative Societies," in *Latin America, Its Problems and Promise: A Multidisciplinary Introduction*, ed. Jan Black (Boulder, Colo.: Westview Press, 1984).

43. Jim Handy, *Gift of the Devil: A History of Guatemala* (Toronto: Between the Lines, 1984), pp. 21–22.

44. Zaid, "Salvadorans Go to the Ballot Box," p. 454.

IV Conclusions and Prospects for the Future

IV. Conclusion and Prospect for the Future

Cole Blasier

10 The United States and Democracy in Latin America

Presidents of the United States have engaged in prodemocratic rhetoric from the Monroe Doctrine in 1823 up to President Reagan in 1985. But do these statements represent sincere goals or were they simply a way to conceal other objectives? More important, has U.S. official behavior sought to promote or retard democratic development in the Americas? Answers to these questions may be found by studying U.S. relations with authoritarian as well as with democratic leaders and regimes.

From such studies, one can begin to draw conclusions about the extent to which the United States has fomented democratic development. Has the United States actually advanced the cause of democracy in the hemisphere and should it be expected to do so? If not, what should U.S. policy about democratic practice in the hemisphere be? Or, to raise an even broader question, to what degree can one country help build democracy in another?

U.S. Rhetoric

American presidents have expressed their dedication to democracy and explained their policies throughout most of the history of their relations with the region. In 1823, in his famous dictum about Latin America, President Monroe distinguished the republican New World from the monarchical Old World. President McKinley justified the war with Spain in 1898 as a means of stopping "oppression at our very doors,"[1] not as a means of expanding U.S. territory or power.

Of all American presidents, none was probably a more fervent advocate of democracy than Woodrow Wilson. In his speech of

219

March 11, 1913, Wilson set forth the rules for U.S. relations with Latin America:

> Cooperation is possible only when supported at every turn by the orderly processes of just government based upon law, not upon arbitrary or irregular force. We hold, as I am sure all thoughtful leaders of republican government everywhere hold, that just government rests always upon the consent of the governed, and that there can be no freedom without order based upon law and upon the public conscience and approval. We shall look to make these principles the basis of mutual intercourse, respect and helpfulness between our sister republics and ourselves. We shall lend our influence of every kind to the realization of these principles in fact and practice, knowing that disorder, personal intrigues and defiance of constitutional rights weaken and discredit government and injure none so much as the people who are unfortunate enough to have their common life and their common affairs so tainted and disturbed. We can have no sympathy with those who seek to seize the power of government to advance their own personal interests or ambition. We are the friends of peace, but we know that there can be no lasting or stable peace in such circumstances.[2]

Wilson's statement constituted a high-water mark in American democratic idealism, official ignorance, and diplomatic condescension. It was also a harbinger of the high tide of U.S. imperialism in Latin America, with U.S. armed forces occupying Nicaragua, Haiti, the Dominican Republic, Cuba, Mexico, and Panama during his presidency.

There is no particular reason to doubt these presidents' preference for democracy as an abstract concept, nor as a political model. But there are grounds to doubt that democratic goals were the primary motive for their policies. Monroe's main objective, for example, was to keep France and Russia, not to mention England, from acquiring new possessions in the Americas. With Spain's control of Cuba crumbling, McKinley wanted to make American interests dominant on the island. Wilson sought to protect the United States from disorders in Mexico that spilled across the border and from German interference in the Caribbean. In order to keep others away, the United States seized or dominated these lands for itself.

The democratic values of the United States continued to be a thread in U.S. policies toward Latin America after 1945. In announcing the Alliance for Progress, President Kennedy laid heavy stress on democratic institutions as the best framework for achieving economic progress and social justice.[3] In 1965, President Johnson described the armed intervention in the Dominican Republic as a timely action "to preserve freedom."[4] In the Chilean presidential campaign of 1970, Henry Kissinger explained U.S. purposes "to promote a clear-cut popular choice between the democratic and totalitarian forces."[5] His statement had the effect of masking U.S. covert participation in the campaign against Allende as a counter to communist support for him.

President Carter's main emphasis was on human rights, rather than democracy per se, but he did express his support for "political systems that allow their people to participate freely and democratically in the decisions that affect their lives."[6] Unlike most other postwar presidents, Carter did not intervene covertly or militarily in Latin America. But, as indicated below, he did exert pressure on various governments for human rights purposes.

President Ronald Reagan and Secretary of State George Shultz have repeatedly stressed their support in Central America for democratic freedoms threatened in the face of communist totalitarianism. In calling for continued financial support for U.S. covert operations against the Sandinistas, the president has urged U.S. backing for "freedom fighters,"[7] a term he has used to describe the U.S.-backed contras operating mainly out of Honduras. Similarly, the Reagan administration has justified its programs for economic and military support of the Duarte administration in El Salvador as a means of standing by "our friends" in their struggle for freedom.[8]

As in U.S. official rhetoric before 1945, Washington's assertions about its democratic motives often warrant skepticism at the very least. What is perhaps more important is that democratic goals were only part of these purposes, and probably not the main purpose. President Kennedy may always have wished to promote democracy in Latin America, but it was not until the rise of Castro that Washington put together the Alliance for Progress to combat communism in the hemisphere. President Johnson's military occupation of the Dominican Republic appears to have been more an effort to prevent "another Cuba" than to promote Dominican democracy. The Nixon administration's covert operations in Chile appear to have been designed to eliminate a nonconforming Marxist government than promote democracy there. The same might be said for the Reagan administration's policies towards Nicaragua. Democratic rhetoric appears frequently to have been more an adornment to than the substance of U.S. policy.

U.S. Behavior

The U.S. record with respect to democracy in the hemisphere can be better determined by what Washington did, then what it said. Has Washington implemented its rhetoric by supporting democratic regimes? Part of the problem is agreeing on which regimes are democratic. It is easy to rule out authoritarian regimes at political extremes—Trujillo's and Castro's, for example—but there is disagreement about some governments in between, such as those of Arbenz and Allende. So, we will examine U.S. behavior with respect to regime types. The assignments of governments to one group or another are, of course, open to discussion.

Right-wing regimes. This group includes the old-style Latin dictators like Trujillo, Batista (except for 1940–1944), the Somozas, and the modern-day dictator, Pinochet.

Trujillo and Somoza used their positions as heads of the local armed forces during the U.S. military occupation of their countries in the 1920s and 1930s as the springboard to dictatorship. Both gained total power after U.S. forces had left Nicaragua and the Dominican Republic. The United States was blamed for their regimes because it gave them both a start. Also, carrying out the precepts of the Good Neighbor Policy, Washington refused to interfere against them in their rise to power. Batista gained his military position in Cuba in the revolt of the sergeants in 1933, but Washington's hands-off policy later worked to Batista's advantage in the consolidation of his power.

The three Caribbean dictators received relatively little U.S. economic assistance. Batista received $40 million total and Trujillo less than $3 million. The Somozas received nearly $300 million, but support fell off sharply under the Carter administration as the Somozas' end neared.[9]

Military aid to Batista, never high, was cut back in his last year. Military aid toward the end was minimal for Trujillo, too, as it was for the Somozas. U.S. military assistance probably had primarily political rather than military significance; it signaled to any opposition forces that Washington approved the incumbent dictators.

After displaying harsh opposition to the Allende government in Chile, U.S. leaders hoped to establish close relations with the successor government. Washington initially provided the Pinochet government with economic and military aid, but as his human rights excesses became better known, Congress cut off all military aid in the mid-1970s.[10]

Except for Brazil, U.S. assistance to these authoritarian regimes was not great, but it did constitute a burden on the U.S. taxpayer and entangled U.S. diplomacy politically and morally with their regimes. In the three Caribbean Basin cases, the United States withdrew its aid toward the end of these regimes, and this constituted one of many factors in their downfall.

The United States seemed to be caught on the horns of a dilemma; it could maintain relatively normal ties with dictatorships or be forced to break relations entirely. Trade, financial, political and other ties were formed that gradually deepened U.S. links to the incumbent regimes. To the extent that these were mutually beneficial relationships, they had the effect of bolstering the reigning dictatorship. Moreover, if the United States had made it a policy to refuse trade and diplomatic relations with Latin American dictatorships, in some years there would have been few U.S. missions in the Americas.

Centrist regimes. Washington has tended to support democratic centrist regimes in such countries as Colombia and Venezuela. And it has long maintained good relations with the quasi-democratic regime in Mexico. If anything, traditional U.S. policies toward these countries have tended to either promote or at least not greatly to hinder their democratic development.

Revolutionary regimes. U.S. leaders have tended to characterize revolutionary regimes in Latin America as antidemocratic. Often discrediting revolutionary regimes as oppressive and totalitarian appeared necessary in order to justify U.S. sanctions against the governments concerned. In any case, the Castro regime in Cuba cannot be considered democratic by any American standards. Nor could the Bishop regime in Grenada.

But the determination of that issue with respect to the Allende government in Chile and the Sandinistas in Nicaragua is not so easy. Allende was a constitutionally elected president. A full spectrum of political parties were functioning, and Parliament had authority throughout his administration. Civil liberties, though occasionally violated, were protected most of the time. And the Allende period was more democratic and less abusive of human rights than the Pinochet regime that followed.

The Sandinista regime in Nicaragua never was and is not, of course, a typical Western-style democracy. In the first place, since the fall of Somoza, there has been no realistic prospect of turning out the Sandinista leadership by elections. The form of the regime has been established by Sandinista fiat. Nevertheless, Nicaragua has some incipient democratic elements, quite unlike the socialist governments of Eastern Europe. Opposition parties, though controlled, exist. The range of opinion and dissent in the press and in public debate is far wider than in most dictatorships. Opposition elements can influence policy through minority positions in the Parliament. Though socialist in style, the Nicaraguan economy is more than half private. All these things mean that in 1986 Nicaragua may be just as democratic as Mexico, maybe more so.

By a variety of sanctions, Washington has sought to overthrow both regimes. In the case of Allende, the pressures were primarily economic; Chile's huge debts to the United States began to fall due in large installments as Allende came into office. The Nixon administration took steps to reduce sharply Chile's sources of foreign exchange. Also, the Central Intelligence Agency provided financial support to his domestic opponents. When the Chilean military fell under the control of elements hostile to Allende, it was not difficult to overthrow his government. The Reagan administration has used many of the same sanctions against the Sandinistas but has included, in addition to economic measures, support for paramilitary forces, operating mostly against the Sandinistas from Honduras. Unlike Allende, however, the Sandinistas are in firm control of their armed forces.

By these sanctions against Allende and the Sandinistas, the United States may well have contributed toward snuffing out democratic tendencies in both countries, tending to militarize both regimes. Judging democracy in Chile by a high standard is realistic, given the nation's heritage. But not in Nicaragua, where the Sandinista regimes may be closer to democracy than that nation has usually ever come. The effect of U.S. sanctions in both cases has been to radicalize domestic politics, handicapping domestic elements seeking democratic solutions. As U.S. sanctions against the Sandinistas have grown, Soviet and Cuban influence has mounted, too.

Reformist regimes. Perhaps the ultimate test of the U.S. capacity to promote democracy in Latin America may be found in its relations with reformist regimes. Reformist regimes have tended to be relatively moderate, often democratic. While Washington has traditionally been slow to pressure right-wing dictatorships, it has often reacted quickly and with hostility to the reformists.

In reformist regimes, there usually have been incumbent political leaders struggling for reform against right-wing military coups and against left-wing insurrection. In such conflicts, the incumbent reformists and opposition rightists vie for the support of the United States. Ordinarily nationalist in character, such governments seek reform not only in domestic politics but also in strengthening national independence. Inevitably, this brings them into conflict with the United States. Not unexpectedly, reform may threaten some vested U.S. interests: investors, traders, dedicated anticommunist ideologues, labor organizers, U.S. diplomats. The political struggle of these regimes is reflected in controversy in the United States. In the end, indecision in the United States, such as that between Congress and the executive, may paralyze U.S. support for reform and contribute to punitive policies.

The Arévalo government (1945–1951) sought to gain Guatemalan control over some of the United Fruit Company lands, foreign-owned railroads, power and communications companies, and to prevent U.S. penetration of the labor movement in Guatemala. Considering the defense of U.S. business interests his first duty, the U.S. ambassador opposed the government persistently. Eventually, Arévalo charged him with plotting with Guatemalans to overthrow his government.[11] The ambassador was ordered back to Washington. Although far from perfect, the Arévalo government was more democratic than most previous Guatemalan governments, having a multiparty political system, a functioning parliament, a fairly open press, and only occasional violations of civil liberties.

The United States is usually criticized for complicity in the fall of the Goulart government in Brazil, which, whatever its shortcomings— and it had many—was more democratic than the military governments that followed it. U.S. officials deny complicity in the coup. Whether U.S. officials actually participated in the plot appears less important than what the military conspirators knew about what the U.S. reaction would be in advance. Washington's hostility to Goulart was widely known, and there was no doubt that Washington would welcome Goulart's fall. Washington sent in elements of the U.S. fleet on the eve of the coup. That was all the signal from the United States the Brazilian military plotters needed, and they proceeded forthwith to overthrow him.[12]

Similarly, Washington gave economic and military assistance to the military regime in Brazil in 1964 after it overthrew the constitutional president, João Goulart. Brazil was ruled for twenty years thereafter by an authoritarian military government, which did not move definitively toward democratic rule until the 1980s.

Juan Bosch had in some ways a similar experience while he was president of the Dominican Republic (1963). His proposed reforms were not as comprehensive as Arévalo's, and there was far less U.S. investment on the island because Trujillo had reserved almost all business opportunities for himself and his family. But, whereas Arévalo had the backing of important segments of the army, Bosch was virtually at the mercy of Trujillo's generals when he took power. By refusing to back Bosch against the military, the American ambassador, John Bartlow Martin, was in a position to mediate between competing factions, and sometimes to call the political tune. Also nationalistic, Bosch tried to maintain Dominican national integrity in the face of critical U.S. sugar, oil, land, labor, and congressional interests. In the end, when Bosch faced a military coup, the American ambassador instructed his military attaché, pressured by conspiring generals, "to let him [Bosch] go."[13]

Two of the best-known instances of the United States' direct exercise of power, the threat of the use of military force, occurred in the Dominican Republic. The first of these was in 1961, when President Kennedy called the American fleet to the horizon around Santo Domingo, to insist that Trujillo's political heirs, the "wicked uncles," not restore the dynasty to the island. These naval maneuvers helped achieve the elections in which Juan Bosch was elected president. But as we have seen above, the incumbent military outmaneuvered Bosch, and he was overthrown. A similar episode occurred in 1978, when President Carter sent a high-level delegation and the commanding general of the Southern Command to the inauguration of the recently elected president, Antonio Guzmán. American officials told the long-entrenched president, Joaquín Balaguer, that he was not to attempt to overthrow the electoral verdict.[14] These two actions, and especially the second, appear to be among the rare cases of successful U.S. intervention on behalf of democracy. Since Dominican democracy is so fragile, however, it remains to be seen how long the present Dominican regime can last when it is so dependent on United States support.

U.S. efforts to support the reformist regime of Eduardo Frei in Chile (1964–1970) are perhaps the best known of all. Here a Christian Democratic leader sought reforms throughout Chilean society that would not create insoluble disputes with the United States. In arranging for the Chilean purchase of substantial participation in the copper industry, Frei largely achieved that goal. The United States provided extensive assistance to his government, except for the last part of his term.

Frei's problem was not Washington opposition, but excessive help. CIA operations were massive in supporting him and opposing the opposition candidate, Salvador Allende, in the 1964 elections. Again, in 1970, the CIA repeated its electoral interference against Allende, this time unsuccessfully. In the end, U.S. aid and U.S. interference were unable to save the Christian Democrats or Chilean democracy.

In these cases—Arevalo, Bosch, and Frei—the United States failed to promote democratic government effectively.

Human Rights

Human rights may be divided into three broad categories: (1) security of the person, including freedom from summary execution, torture, and arbitrary arrest; (2) basic needs, including food, clothing, shelter, health care; and (3) political rights, including freedom of speech, press, religion. It is the third category that comes closest to incorporating traditional concepts of democracy. But the Carter administration judged that the most flagrant abuses of human rights were those in the first category, that is, against security of the person. Thus it was to this category of violations that Carter turned his government's main efforts.

Four policy instruments were at hand to get the leverage necessary to promote human rights: military aid, bilateral economic aid, multilateral development bank loans, and private economic transactions. Although by the late 1970s military aid to Latin American governments had already fallen to low levels, the Carter administration did impose restrictions on such aid to Argentina, Bolivia, El Salvador, Guatemala, Haiti, Nicaragua, Paraguay, and Uruguay[15] because of the gross violations in human rights occurring in those countries. In his last year in office, however, Carter retreated, raising military aid to El Salvador. As to bilateral economic assistance, it was at such low levels by the late 1970s that it was not a potent tool for promoting human rights or any other policies.[16]

The Bureau of Human Rights and Humanitarian Affairs established in the Carter administration was able to inject human rights issues into U.S. consideration of loan applications to various multilateral development banks. Although no loans were denied because of U.S. opposition, this policy, and its incorporation into the Department of State's decision-making process, had the effect of deterring loan applications from Latin America's most repressive governments.

Another potential avenue for exerting foreign policy influence in favor of human rights was private economic transactions. Although government officials have in the past, on rare occasions, been able to persuade U.S. business leaders to take action in support of particular policies, they did not do so with respect to human rights under Carter. That, for example, would have been helpful in Chile, where private bankers picked up the slack when foreign economic assistance declined under Pinochet. Moreover, U.S. investment in Chile also began to grow again in the late 1970s, while official policies toward Pinochet hardened on human rights grounds. As it turned out, the Carter administration was either unable or unwilling to persuade business to go along on human rights in Chile or in most other places in Latin America.

The Carter administration's public condemnation of human rights and its political interventions related thereto, however, saved lives in several countries, especially Argentina.[17] Influenced by human rights considerations, U.S. policy towards Somoza in Nicaragua appears to have hastened his fall. Perhaps the most lasting contribution of Carter's human rights policy is not what it accomplished in Latin America, but rather what it accomplished in the United States. Human rights considerations now play an established, if often unsuccessful, role in pressure-group politics and government decision making in the United States. Whereas the Nixon-Ford administration had been able to sweep most human rights consideration under the rug, the Reagan administration found it necessary to face Carter's human rights policies head on and retain the Bureau of Human

Rights and Humanitarian Affairs at its high level in the Department of State.

When Reagan came into office, U.S. legislative restrictions on economic and military assistance to governments that were identified as gross violators of human rights were an obstacle to the new administration's aim to improve relations with the military dictatorships in such countries as Chile, Guatemala, and El Salvador. Some way had to be found around this legislation and the likely public outcry if the U.S. government were to resume assistance to regimes that arrested, tortured, and executed its own citizens without due process. In 1979, Jeane Kirkpatrick, later U.S. ambassador to the United Nations, accused the Carter administration of following a double standard in dealing with totalitarian (Castro) and authoritarian (Pinochet, Videla, Somoza) regimes.[18] Secretary of State Alexander Haig later urged that terrorism rather than human rights violations be made the target of the administration.[19] Also, early in the Reagan administration, the Department of State attempted to direct public attention toward democracy as the main element in human rights, thereby attempting to reduce the emphasis on sanctions against torture, murder, and arbitrary detention. In his certifications to effect U.S. military assistance to El Salvador, the president did not show that gross violations of human rights had ceased, but rather that there were fewer of them.[20] In his public speeches, Reagan emphasized the regime's progress toward democracy, often defined mainly in terms of "free" elections. The rationale for this apparent attempt to defuse public indignation about police state brutality was to facilitate U.S. cooperation with military dictatorships considered "friends" for strategic and economic reasons. Yet the Reagan administration never made clear how better relations with the dictatorships in Guatemala and Chile, for example, were in the U.S. interest.

On balance, the Carter administration's rhetoric about human rights and its genuine sincerity about seeking to protect them did have global reverberations and, in particular cases, appears to have had constructive results. The one tool it did sharpen for use against abuses was the denial of military aid. Its use of the other diplomatic weapons described above had only marginal results at best. Reagan attempted to reverse U.S. policy completely by attempting to rebuild relations with military governments that the Carter administration had criticized for violations. At the same time, he shifted rhetorical emphasis to the campaign against terrorism. The upshot of all of this is that the United States and the world are probably more aware of human rights violations than we were before Carter, but Reagan has turned the U.S. government away from the protection of human rights as operative policy.

Washington's Record

The dominant tendency in U.S. behavior has been to oppose changes in the status quo in Latin America. This is the usual way in which political and economic structures protect themselves. In this sense, U.S. behavior can be explained better by systemic rather than ideological reasons.

When dictatorial regimes have predominated in Latin America, U.S. actions have often been interpreted as antidemocratic, dealing as Washington usually has done with the regimes it finds in the region. But just as the United States has seemed to support dictatorship, so too has it supported incumbent centrist regimes, many of which have been democracies.

But the pro–status quo bias has tended to guarantee that the United States opposes most revolutionary regimes, as Washington so often does. Revolutionary regimes are labeled antidemocratic—as they are or may become—and U.S. policies are defended as pro-democratic. What seems more likely is that the democratic issue is not paramount; strategic and economic issues are.

The test of U.S. behavior towards democracy in Latin America is probably best found in relations with right-wing and reformist regimes. With respect to the former, Washington has usually provided enough economic and military assistance to be implicated in such regimes' crimes but not enough to have had much material impact. When the dictators begin to lose their grip on power, and association with them becomes a liability, Washington usually abandons them. At that point, Washington has sought—in the cases of Cuba in 1959 and Nicaragua in 1979—to prevent radicals from seizing power by installing moderates. These efforts failed in both countries. Now even the Reagan administration appears concerned about the brutality and unpopularity of the Pinochet regime in Chile. Fearing a radical revolutionary successor to Pinochet, Washington has been maneuvering for a moderate outcome.

Washington has had its best opportunity to influence political development in a democratic direction with respect to the reformist regimes. Even the reforms favored by Arévalo and Bosch adversely affected so many U.S. vested interests that Washington soon became an enemy. The reformist regime of Frei in Chile was smothered with overt and covert U.S. assistance, and was succeeded by a socialist revolutionary regime.

The United States has resorted increasingly to economic and military assistance, covert political and military action, and armed intervention intended to affect political outcomes in Latin America. Such actions, aimed at determining who rules a particular country, constitute brazen hegemonic interference or intervention.

Such hegemonic behavior is incompatible with democracy as a form of popular sovereignty. Democracy, presumably, is a political system in which the people determine their political system and leadership. Foreign governments, however well-meaning, are not supposed to interfere. If they did successfully, the countries would not be democracies, but colonies. A striking inconsistency in U.S. policy was revealed during the El Salvadoran elections, heralded as a great forward step toward democracy. The *New York Times* openly discussed subsidies channeled through the CIA of millions of dollars to back the candidates Washington hoped would win.[21] The record shows that the United States has not been consistently capable of promoting democracy in Latin America.

What, Then, Should Washington Do?

U.S. policies with respect to democracy in other countries must be based on realistic principles. No government has the obligation or the right to establish democracy in foreign countries any more than socialist governments have such rights with respect to socialism. More important, no government has the capability of establishing democracy in a foreign country. By definition, that can be achieved only by a nation's own citizenry. Even in Japan and Germany, democracy would not have been possible without a receptive leadership and people.

The United States should not be expected to and cannot establish democracy in other countries. As quoted above, Woodrow Wilson was well-meaning, but unrealistic about Latin America. But his assumption that, in general, democratic regimes suit U.S. long-term interests in Latin America better than authoritarian regimes of either the right or left was correct. What constructive steps, then, can the United States take in the light of its limited capabilities to pursue its interests?

First, the U.S. government should continue to collect and publicize evidence of human rights violations everywhere. Torture and murder are universally condemned and, as a principle, arbitrary arrest is, too. U.S. officials should not hesitate to speak out about them. Who speaks, when, and how, will depend on particular situations.

Second, the U.S. government should extend no bilateral economic or military assistance to governments that are gross violators of human rights. It is not easy to justify such assistance to any government, much less to human rights violators. One reason is that brutal regimes eventually are overthrown, and the U.S. government must then pay on top of the original dollar costs the political costs for its association with them.

Third, the U.S. government should respect private interests. While it could provide counsel to U.S. private interests in Latin American countries that are flagrant violators of human rights, it should not expect to sacrifice them to policy purposes. That applies particularly to relations with the Soviet Union where official sanctions, such as the grain embargo, appear to have hurt U.S. interests more than Soviet interests.

Fourth, Washington should not interfere in the domestic politics of other nations "to promote democracy." If this were a workable proposition, it might be worth considering. In fact, it is not. U.S. leaders and political systems are unsuited for such a role, and almost always botch such efforts. What is more likely to happen is that "the promotion of democracy" will simply be a self-serving excuse to advance a variety of U.S. special interests.

By speaking out forthrightly on human rights issues, and by denying public funds to gross violators, the U.S. government can dissociate itself from crimes against humanity. By not interfering or intervening directly, it helps such nations defend the independence necessary for building democracy. Each country must do that on its own. Above all, the U.S. leaders can be most effective to these ends by working to perfect and defend democracy at home, without which little can be expected of U.S. influence in this respect anywhere else.

Notes

1. *Speeches and Addresses of William McKinley from March 1, 1897 to May 30, 1900* (New York, Doubleday and McClure, 1900), p. 134.
2. *New York Times*, March 12, 1913, p. 1.
3. *Public Papers of the Presidents: John F. Kennedy, 1961* (Washington, D.C.: GPO, 1962), p. 171.
4. *Public Papers of the Presidents: Lyndon B. Johnson, 1965*, vol. 1 (Washington, D.C.: GPO, 1966), p. 466.
5. Henry A. Kissinger, *White House Years* (Boston, Little, Brown, 1979), p. 677.
6. *Public Papers of the Presidents: Jimmy Carter, 1978*, vol. 1, (Washington, D.C.: GPO, 1979), p. 1145.
7. See President Reagan's televised address to the nation of May 9, 1984, *New York Times*, May 10, 1984, p. 6.
8. Ibid.
9. The aid figures for Batista, Trujillo, and Somoza are found in *U.S. Overseas Loans and Grants, July 1, 1945 to September 30, 1981* (Washington, D.C.: USAID, 1982) p. 44 (Batista), p. 45 (Trujillo), p. 54 (Somoza).
10. Aid figures for Pinochet are found in ibid., p. 41.
11. Cole Blasier, *The Hovering Giant: U.S. Responses to Revolutionary Regimes in Latin America* (Pittsburgh, Pa.: University of Pittsburgh Press, 1983), p. 61.
12. The role of the United States in the overthrow of Goulart, as well as U.S. hostility to Goulart, are detailed in Phyllis R. Parker, *Brazil and the Quiet Intervention, 1964* (Austin: University of Texas Press, 1979).
13. John Bartlow Martin, *Overtaken by Events: The Dominican Crisis from the Fall of Trujillo to the Civil War* (New York: Doubleday, 1966), p. 573.
14. *New York Times*, May 18, 1978, p. 14, May 19, 1978, p. 11.
15. Lars Schoultz, "The Carter Administration and Human Rights in Latin America," *Human Rights and Basic Needs in the Americas*, ed. Margaret E. Graham (Washington, D.C.: Georgetown University Press, 1982), pp. 321–23. This section relies heavily on Schoultz.
16. Ibid., p. 324.
17. Charles Maechling, Jr., "The Argentine Pariah," *Foreign Policy*, Winter 1981–82, p. 75; Charles Maechling, Jr., "Human Rights Dehumanized," *Foreign Policy*, Fall 1983, p. 129.
18. See Jeane Kirkpatrick, "Dictatorships and Double Standards," *Commentary*, November 1979, pp. 34–45.
19. Haig's remarks on terrorism can be found in "Secretary Haig's News Conference of January 28, 1981," *Department of State Bulletin*, February 1981, p. G-K (special section); "Interview for Spanish Television, March 30, 1981," *Department of State Bulletin*, May 1981, pp. 7–9.
20. *New York Times*, July 28, 1982, p. 1, 4.
21. *New York Times*, May 12, 1984, p. 6; *New York Times*, May 13, 1984, p. 12. According to the reports, the CIA gave $960,000 to Duarte and $437,000 to Francisco José Guerrero of the National Conciliation party.

James M. Malloy

11   The Politics of Transition in Latin America

The revival of democracy in Latin America in the late seventies and early eighties has posed a new challenge to our understanding of the region's political dynamics. In most areas of study, theoretical developments are "colored by the events of the day," and this has been particularly true with the analysis of the Latin American political systems. Theoretical developments have been strongly influenced by short-term events and theories are soon discarded when confronted with a more enduring reality. In the fifties and early sixties, the main concern in the study of Latin American politics was the evaluation of the socioeconomic requisites for democracy. Interpretations of the regions' political systems assumed, in essence, a unidirectional tendency in political development, with democratic government as the natural outcome. According to this view, military interruptions of democratic procedures were perceived as pathological and as a symptom of political immaturity. Expectations that the time for democracy had finally come were soon shattered, however, by the wave of military takeovers that swept through Latin America, beginning with the 1964 Brazilian coup d'état. Before the decade was over, most of the region was under military rule.

The new militarism of the mid-sixties and the seventies generated a revisionist trend among students of Latin American politics. The wisdom of the past was soon discarded, and novel interpretations were advanced about the nature of the region's political systems. This revisionist trend followed different lines, but, in general, it stressed the authoritarian and corporatist nature of Latin America and/or the structural constraints produced by dependent capitalism, and discounted the possibility of democracy in the area.

235

In the eighties, events in Latin America challenged the theories once again. Just as most observers and analysts of the region were beginning to feel comfortable with a theoretical understanding of Latin American authoritarianism, a democratic tide swept through the region. At the time of this writing, most Latin American countries have functioning democracies. In those countries still under military rule (with the probable exception of Paraguay and Cuba), there are strong democratic pressures that will likely accelerate the democratization process. Even Central America, which, except for Costa Rica, had been largely immune from the prior cycles of democratization, has elected regimes in all five republics. Scholarly interest, as a result, has shifted from the military overthrow of civilian regimes and Latin American authoritarianism toward the prospects and processes of redemocratization.

Current analyses of the redemocratization of Latin American politics have focused on the short-term dynamics of regime change. That is, starting from situation A, of so-called bureaucratic-authoritarian rule, these studies focus on why and how a given regime broke down and made the transition to situation B, democratic rule. Recent experiences as well as earlier redemocratization processes have been analyzed from this perspective. This line of analysis is useful, but we must avoid being overcome, once again, by short-term events and losing track of the long-term trends in Latin American political development.

A potentially more valuable approach to the political evolution of most of the Latin American countries should begin by accepting what by now must be surely axiomatic—that there is no unilinear tendency toward democracy or toward authoritarian rule. Rather, the predominant pattern is cyclical, with alternating democratic and authoritarian "moments." Furthermore, both tendencies are rather strong in the area. Therefore, there is no justifiable reason to view either democracy or authoritarianism as anomalous modes of rule incompatible with some natural predisposition toward one or the other. The understanding of the political dynamics in Latin America demands the analysis of both modes of rule and of the transitions from one to the other. Our research agenda, besides the current interest in the movement from authoritarian to democratic government should include the study of the underlying forces that historically have generated the alternation between them in most Latin American polities. Current examinations of redemocratization are important steps in that direction. Once sufficient case studies on the demise of authoritarian regimes have been accumulated, and those experiences contrasted with the breakdown of democratic regimes, we will be in a better position to advance some generalizable hypotheses about long-term trends in Latin American politics.

This concluding chapter looks at several recent transitions to democracy in Latin America against the broader historical backdrop of cyclical developments and the constraints of national and international economic forces. The connection between these factors is mediated by conflicting political movements whose demands for political and economic participation challenge these societies' capacity for constitutional engineering and their capacity to form public policy capable of satisfying these conflicting demands.

From this perspective, one can see that the chapters in this volume point toward at least two observations. First, whatever general processes are going on, the wide diversity from case to case precludes the development at this point of broad general models or theories of the shifts between authoritarian and democratic modes of governance in Latin America. We must be content with tentative conclusions of varying degrees of generality, few of which will hold without qualification for the entire region. Second, the link between certain recurring economic issues and regime shifts, while real, is by no means a deterministic one; the same is true of cultural or institutional predispositions in these societies. Rather, economic issues have mainly posed problems to be solved while limiting the options for their solution.

Conditioning Factors in Political Transitions

Changes in regime are significantly influenced by the decisions of the political leaders who have frequently sought total control of the state. If this assertion is correct, there is obviously a key voluntary dimension to the process that not only makes it difficult to formulate a general theory but also precludes neat deterministic theories based on general laws. This is particularly true if we try to predict the longevity of the new democratic regimes that have been established in Latin America. The best we can come up with is an approach that allows us to produce rationally plausible explanations of past dynamics that hold for as many cases as possible and to project from them a set of ongoing constraining situations and "prudential" rules of action that will indicate certain trends. It should also be remembered that at each step of the way decisions regarding the political responses to groups and movements as well as constitutional structure are always as important in shaping outcomes as economic factors.

The bulk of the recent scholarship on the "new authoritarianism" in Latin America, as well as on transitions to democracy indicates that in analyzing cycles in regime shifts, we should begin with the 1930s. The Great Depression was a watershed in Latin America that shaped a number of key and recurring problems in the region's political economy.

At the risk of oversimplification, we can reduce those problems to three basic issues. First, establishing successful *models of economic development* involved the need to reorganize the economies of the region as a result of the exhaustion of the export model that had hitherto been predominant. Second, viable *institutional structures* had to be created capable of incorporating newly mobilized social sectors, particularly organized labor, into the political process. Third was the need to form viable *ruling coalitions* to sustain regimes capable of addressing the first two issues.

Since the 1930s, most of the countries of South America have experienced demonstrable cyclical shifts between authoritarian and democratic modes of government. Within these fluctuations, neither authoritarian nor democratic regimes have been able to establish any fundamental base of legitimacy. Democracy has, in the main, been the clearly stated ideal, but at critical moments many social groups not only have proved willing to accept authoritarian regimes but also have encouraged them. However, such regimes have usually been viewed as exceptions; authoritarian regimes have been given "authority" because they are seen as temporary interregnums on the way back to some more perfect form of civil democratic rule.

The problem of establishing the legitimacy of a regime is a complex theoretical issue that is beyond the scope of this chapter.[1] However, in the Latin American context, at least two historical realities are worth noting. First, the legitimacy of democratic modes of governance has been undercut not so much by the "immaturity" of the broad populations of these countries, as many have argued, but rather by the concrete behavior of critical civil leaders. One of the key problems in establishing democratic legitimacy is the behavior of the political elite. Another factor is that over the years both democratic and authoritarian leaders in Latin America have been unable to solve key issues of public policy. Indeed, the shift from one type of regime to another usually occurs because of the failures of the pre-existing regime. In other words, one regime emerges in response to the incapacity of another.

In a practical sense, then, since the 1930s the problem has been to found a government capable of solving key economic problems. The issue of regime type has thus been secondary to establishing an effective decision-making center, regardless of form. The structural problems of political economy in Latin America can be reduced to a duality that many have argued has been the key contradiction besetting modern capitalist societies, whether of the advanced industrial center or the less developed periphery. These dilemmas are produced by the underlying tension between the imperative to accumulate capital for economic development and the need to build legitimacy to sustain political stability. In practical terms, this translates into an ongoing contradiction between accumulating an investable surplus through—at least in part—curtailing levels of consumption relative to production, and building political support for specific governments (and by extension regime types) by meeting the demands of key social groups for increased levels of consumption.

This dilemma has been particularly severe in Latin America because of the constraints on both political and economic options produced by the region's dependent position in the international capitalist system. The recurring political question in all of these countries concerns who is going to bear the costs of any given economic strategy. A related question is what kind of government can answer the question of distributing those costs? Both of these questions are particularly urgent today because of the domestic and international economic crisis exemplified by the foreign debt that, in one way or another, bedevils all the countries of the region. The new language of debt negotiations and economic packages, in fact, addresses old problems that are becoming more severe because neither authoritarian nor democratic modes of rule have yet solved them.

Another cycle runs parallel to the cycle of shifting regime types—namely, that between populism and antipopulism. Since the 1930s, populist political movements of one form or another have linked economic and political imperatives because they articulated strategies for dealing with both. An explicit assumption of all populist approaches has been that regimes could simultaneously spur development, incorporate many sectors of the society in the political system, and broadly distribute the surplus. As most of the cases treated in this volume demonstrate, the populist premise was not only resisted by entrenched elites but also defeated when populist governments, in either authoritarian or democratic guise, came up against the intractable realities of a dependent economy. As in the case of Peru, the populist/antipopulist cycle has been played out not only as a result of the resistance of an entrenched elite but also when populist governments themselves have been forced by circumstances to shift to antipopulist policies. Thus populist governments have taken both authoritarian and democratic forms. Indeed, one central conclusion that seems to emerge is that since the 1930s the dynamics of the populist/antipopulist cycle has been the main motor pushing the alternating cycles of authoritarian and democratic regimes. The evidence clearly suggests that the two are intimately linked.

While populism sought, and to a large extent achieved, a multiclass base of support, the key support group for populism has been organized labor. Indeed, populism, whether championed by political parties like APRA in Peru and the MNR in Bolivia or leader-centered movements like those of Perón in Argentina or Vargas in Brazil, successfully undercut the classic Marxist parties of the left and became the main vehicle through which labor made its claim for incorporation into the existing systems of governance and distribution. As a result, labor in Latin America has not, in the main, been a revolutionary force but one demanding an entree into the existing political game.

As we look back, it is evident that one of the key issues affecting regime type and stability in Latin America has been the relationship between organized labor and other social groups and classes as mediated by the state. As numerous analysts have pointed out, labor was incorporated politically in Latin America mainly through a process of state-centered co-optation. This pattern had a number of consequences that probably have, over the years, undercut any predispositions on the part of labor leaders and other elite groups to give primacy to democratic modes of rule.

The co-optive pattern did not imply that labor did not receive benefits. On the contrary, the benefits were substantial. However, the pattern entailed the integration of labor into a clientelistic bureaucratic framework where labor in effect traded off certain modes of political power and "political rights" of citizenship in return for particularistic economic benefits expressed as "social rights" of citizenship.

However, as recent studies of Latin American social security systems have demonstrated, the co-optive pattern in Latin America undercut the development of universal notions of political and social rights such as those of the more social democratic systems of some of the industrialized nations. Instead, a more qualified concept of citizenship was substituted in which social benefits came as particularized legal privileges defined and enforced by the state.[2] As one observer puts it: "Rather than a right inherent to citizenship, welfare protection under the co-optive pattern becomes a legal provision available to particular functional strata defined by the state."[3]

The co-optive pattern of incorporating labor both reflected and reinforced the tendency of Latin American society to be organized into diffuse vertical hierarchies of patron-client networks. These reflected patriarchal and patrimonial systems of authority more than modern rational-legal systems. The co-optive system emphasizes access to the central mechanisms that control the flow of particular benefits and privileges rather than broad-based citizen participation. As many have pointed out, this pattern is a corporatist one that links individuals to the state less as citizens than as members of legally reorganized groups with privileged access to their own pieces of the state. In the case of labor, these linkages are mainly to ministries of labor and social security institutes.

This pattern has had crucial consequences for the problem of establishing a democratic regime. As we have seen, the key issue for labor leaders was not the democratic or authoritarian nature of the regime but rather whether they had access to benefits that they could use as patronage for their union members. Labor leaders often had as much if not more access to such benefits under authoritarian governments as they did in democracies. In short, organized labor over most of the period did not develop a primary commitment to democracy as either a principle or as a specific way of distributing the surplus.

As Charles A. Anderson argued some years ago, the core of the co-optive pattern is the willingness of the established elite to foster a controlled incorporation of new power contenders into the political game so long as each new group can accept the game as such.[4] This then, becomes an additive process of incorporation that emphasizes distribution rather than political form. The result is that the demand load on the distributable surplus inevitably increases and the emphasis in the system leans toward the politics of distribution through formal bureaucratic channels organized de facto in patron/client networks that undercut formal rationality. The size of the state bureaucracy expands even as organizational rationality declines. Moreover, the formal clash between parties and programs is less relevant than a pragmatic struggle between ins and outs defined in terms of factional coalitions that often bridge party lines.

The upshot is that there is often a disjuncture between formal electoral and parliamentary politics and the practical process of governance through bureaucratically organized distributive nets. As Chalmers notes, elections and parliamentary manuevers often do not really resolve key issues of power and distribution.[5] And they seldom produce viable parliamentary-based coalitions to support the government, especially regarding innovative programs. In the end, intrabureaucratic and patrimonially focused factional politics are often more important than electoral, parliamentary, or programmatic politics.

Historically, populist parties and movements have been ambivalent toward these patron-client structures. At one level they have proved adaptable to the bureaucratically focused clientelistic game, sought access to it, and in the end reinforced it. The cases of Argentina and Brazil stand out in this regard. However, populist movements have also demonstrated a clear hegemonic intention: they seek to monopolize the game to the detriment of other players. The model for many populist movements in this regard has long been Mexico, where behind a formal democratic facade the PRI monopolizes politics by monopolizing the patronage flow within the party. This pretension to hegemony has given populist movements an air of illegitimacy in countries like Peru, producing a deep resistance to the APRA party. But all of these cases show that, if unable to realize their hegemonic intentions, populist leaders will settle for access to the distributional game especially in key areas like labor and social policy.

The co-optive incorporating approach fosters a politics of "bureaucratic turf" model that has had multiple effects. It pushes for a steady expansion of the role and size of the state so as to increase the distributive patrimony of the state. At the same time the state tends to be colonized into a multiplicity of turfs under the control of elites associated with different interest groups and political organizations. This fact in turn fosters a behavioral orientation among groups and parties to first gain access to turf but second to protect acquired turf. The orientation becomes particularistic and defensive and all groups become more oriented to vetoing initiatives perceived as threatening to turf rather than producing innovative policy thrusts.

As a result, the decision-making process that emerges focuses on technical elites formed around executives who are usually disconnected to either party or interest-group structures. The pattern has tended to be one in which technical policy leaders have proposed policy while defensively oriented, particularistic, group-based elites have executed it, often negatively. As Chalmers puts it: "The relations between the technicians and the organized groups in society tend to be one in which the latter play a defensive and opportunistic role."[6]

Historically there has been a tendency in Latin America to view the state as an entity set off against society to be either captured, in whole or in part, and/or to be defended against. The co-optive model brought considerable stability to some systems. However, the additive nature of the approach eventually runs up against the limits of the distributional capacities of the state, fostering the idea that politics is essentially a zero-sum game of "ins" and "outs." The objective becomes getting into the distributional game through direct access to the executive apparatus, regardless of the niceties of electoral outcomes and democratic procedures. Moreover, once entrenched, the "ins" tend to defend acquired turf and access to power by blocking rival elites and organizations—again, through any means available. In short, this type of system does not necessarily reward democratic behavior and often rewards its opposite. Groups like organized labor quickly learned in many Latin American societies that they can advance themselves better under authoritarian regimes than under democratic ones.

In addition to these structural tendencies, there were two other substantial consequences. First, the co-optive distributional model fostered a steady increase in politically mediated consumption in these societies. Levels of consumption have often weighed heavily on the productive capacities of these societies, especially at times of economic crisis produced by fluctuations in the international system. Populist-oriented policies have been particularly important in this regard. The co-optive distributional model has often brought to the fore the underlying tension between economic and political imperatives.

At the same time, the defensive posture of entrenched interests has fostered a blocking style of group politics that is often at odds with objectively produced needs for innovative decision making. In short, there is in the classic co-optive model a marked tendency toward political immobilism that renders these systems increasingly ineffective, especially during economic crises. The tendency toward immobilism can manifest itself in a variety of regimes. However, democratic regimes seem to be particularly susceptible and vulnerable to paralysis.

This helps to explain the alternating pattern of regime change in Latin America. Political systems dominated by the co-optive model tend to become trapped by an internal immobilism: problems accumulate until a crisis reveals the need to break the stalemate, by force if necessary. Immobilism, often most pronounced in democratic regimes, heightens the crucial necessity of finding an effective and authoritative decision center from which to grapple with the key issues of development—namely, capital accumulation and sharing the costs of development.

The most recent authoritarian cycle initiated by the military uprising in Brazil in 1964 was a consequence of different versions of civil democratic immobilism in many of these countries. In a number of cases, military and civil leaders were predisposed to intervene because of the fear of leftist revolutionary subversion.

Post-1964 Authoritarian Moments

As we noted in the introduction, the authoritarian regimes that emerged after 1964, while part of a historical cyclical pattern, also manifested elements of linear evolution. Analysts of the region, led by O'Donnell, identified them as a new regime type, the bureaucratic-authoritarian (B-A) regime.[7] In retrospect, it seems clear that only Brazil and Argentina conformed closely to the B-A model. Other regimes in Ecuador and Peru, while falling short of the model pattern, exhibited many B-A characteristics and represented significant organizational advances over previous military regimes. Bolivia made an attempt to emulate other regimes, but because of internal weaknesses, most of the nation's institutions, including the military, disintegrated. In Chile, B-A characteristics have been evident, but they are submerged in the neopatrimonial patterns of General Pinochet's personalistic rule.

Thus, while the post-1964 regimes were part of a general cycle, there were important differences among them in organization and institutional development. The Brazilian regime seems to stand out as the most significant evolutionary advance, from an organizational point of view, and in many respects came to set the standard for regimes in other countries. In any event, understanding how these regimes differed from earlier types as well as among themselves is necessary for an understanding of the later transitions to democracy. The nature of any given authoritarian regime clearly shapes the return to democracy.

Whatever the organizational differences among them, the post-1964 authoritarian regimes followed similar policies toward populism, particularly capital accumulation and development. One important difference from earlier military-backed regimes was the pretension that the new leaders would bring about political and economic changes so as to resolve the key dilemmas besetting Latin America since the 1930s. Above all, the new regimes sought to restructure the relationship between the state and organized labor.

With the exception of Ecuador and Peru, the new authoritarian regimes from the outset followed antipopulist development strategies. Capital accumulation took precedence over general levels of consumption and the costs of the process were allocated most directly to organized labor and other popular sectors. To make these allocations stick, the regimes moved to break the power of organized labor and push it out of the political process. The co-optive model of incorporation was replaced by an exclusion model based on coercive control. Indeed, crushing the ideological left and the repression of traditional labor organizations became the hallmark of the regimes in Brazil, Argentina, Uruguay, and Chile.

In Ecuador and Peru the new authoritarian regimes began as attempts to realize the populist promise of development and distribution, but simultaneously to control political mobilization, especially with regard to labor. Fairly early, however, both regimes came up against the basic contradictions generated by populism in a context of dependent capitalist development. Hence, both soon shifted to a more antipopulist stance in which, under the guise of "austerity" programs, the state sought to emphasize accumulation over consumption. However, the level of repression in these states never reached those of Brazil, Argentina, and Chile. Bolivia, in turn, experienced first one antipopulist military regime, followed by a military-populist interlude, and then a return to an antipopulist regime. In the Andean republics, the populist and antipopulist cycles occurred during the authoritarian epoch, but all ended in an antipopulist mode.

At their core, then, all of the new authoritarian regimes that came to power in South America after 1964 demonstrated a clear link between the cyclical pattern of alternation between democracy and authorianism and the populist/antipopulist cycle. All eventually followed antipopulist policies designed to dismantle the co-optive structures of previous regimes, to reduce the politically mediated consumption, and to assert some measure of control over organized labor. All came to rest their claims to authority on their ability to transform their respective societies and especially to promote rapid and sustained economic development. Finally, while all represented organizational advances over previous authoritarian regimes, as in Argentina and especially Brazil, few came close to the B-A regime type elaborated by O'Donnell.

However one views their economic performance, it is clear that in political terms the new authoritarian regimes were failures. As previous cycles have shown, most authoritarian regimes in Latin America seem incapable of winning anything other than a short-term, superficial level of popular acceptance. Never have they succeeded in sustaining long-term legitimacy and support for a strong central decision center expressing itself in an authoritarian mode of rule. Military-backed regimes can still justify themselves only as exceptions provoked by specific circumstances in which constitutional government can be temporarily abrogated. As chapter 3 shows, even the apparent quasi-legitimacy of the military regime in Brazil was short-term and predicated on the fact that, for most of its tenure, the regime presented itself as in transit to some nonauthoritarian mode of rule. The popularity of military regimes—as opposed to legitimacy—turns mainly on the proximity and gravity of the crises to which they respond or on short-term policy success, such as economic recovery.

Latin America's recent experiences with authoritarianism demonstrates that the argument for the existence of a powerful cultural predisposition to authoritarianism is quite wrong. At most, authoritarian propensities exist alongside equally powerful predilections for some mode of competitive politics in a constitutional framework. These cases show that as time puts distance from some specific precipitating crisis, justification for "rule by exception" decreases. Moreover, as policy success fades and economic problems develop, popularity based on a specific precipitating crisis evaporates. When this is accompanied by sustained repression of popular demands, support can be swiftly converted into intense opposition.

In retrospect, two further observations regarding the recent history of military rule in Latin America seem in order. Politically, populist-oriented military regimes are undermined by the problem of structuring and controlling the mobilization of the masses to which they are committed. Antipopulist military regimes, on the other hand, run the risk of becoming detached from and set against the society at large. This in fact was the situation these regimes found themselves in during the late 1970s, and this led, in my view, to their retreat from power.

A critical weakness of all these military governments was that they either did not or could not build institutional linkages to the rest of society—ties that could underwrite and sustain authoritarian rule over time. Hence, as problems mounted and frustrated demands built up in the society, an increasingly antagonistic polarization between state and society developed. And, by extension, this polarization was increasingly perceived as setting the armed forces against society as a whole. This was particularly upsetting to the military establishment because it had styled itself as embodying national unity and integrity. The situation was clearly threatening to the institutionalist forces in the military elite who were mainly concerned with the long-term legitimacy and corporate self-interest of the armed forces.

Institutionalist concerns were exacerbated by the proliferation of factions and by elite rivalry within the military establishment. The generals had in part justified their rule by the need to depoliticize civil society and submit it to some of the discipline and unity of the barracks. However, in suppressing politics in civil society, the military leaders effectively transferred the struggle over issues and power to the military institution itself. The longer they remained in power, the more politicized the military elite became and the more the institutional integrity and coherence of the armed forces were undermined. Politicization and fragmentation among the military advanced farthest in Bolivia, where institutional coherence all but disappeared.

The alienation of military-backed regimes from civil society demonstrates that suppressing social groups by excluding them in no way solves the underlying populist issue of the need to incorporate popular sectors, especially organized labor, into the state. Repression might solve an immediate economic problem, but it only creates further political problems. Moreover, all these cases show that while the "disciplining of labor" gains the short-term support of business, the necessary enlargement of a heavy-handed state apparatus, as well as continued labor restiveness, eventually provokes doubt and concern in the private sector as well. Moreover, concerns rise as business leaders realize that they have at best only erratic influence over government policy formed by closed sets of technicians directly dependent on the military elite. In short, private-sector interests quickly grasp that they have made a bad bargain in giving up the right to rule or to influence policy in return for the right to make money. At some point, all social groups seek to restore their right to regularly participate in and influence central decision making.

One thing is certain: none of the new authoritarian regimes solved any of the real underlying structural problems of guiding economic development, incorporating popular sectors, or resolving the tension between political and economic imperatives. Dependent capitalism imposes severe constraints on development, and authoritarian regimes have now demonstrated that they are as ineffectual in the face of these problems as are civil-democratic regimes. A sad but ironic note is that when the new authoritarians began to return power to civilian leaders, their nations were facing a worse version of the same economic crisis that laid democratic regimes low in the first place. After years of repression, during which problems deepened, the authoritarian regimes were able to divert attention from the economic crisis by offering to open the political process.

The Present Democratic Moment

Given the record of Latin America's authoritarian regimes, this is both the worst and best of times to try to establish (or reestablish) some viable pattern of civil democratic rule. It is the worst of times owing to the severe economic crisis assailing these countries, underlying structural problems, and constraints imposed by international actors such as the IMF. Each of these factors severely limits the options of the fledgling democratic regimes and their ability to grapple with these problems. It is the best of times because the authoritarian military and technocratic leaders have failed to solve the very problems that they had claimed justified their usurpation in the first place. Further, all sectors of society have learned that the best way to further their interests is through regular and predictable participation in central decision making. As the chapter on Brazil shows, the present context of crisis is rather different from that of the 1960s and early 1970s throughout the region and this fact helps buy time for the movement toward some mode of democratic governance.

However one looks at it, the present economic crisis obviously looms large as a major obstacle in the path toward the stability of democracy. Would-be democratic regimes must begin to bring this crisis under control. It is too much to hope that they can solve the crisis in any definitive way, but at least it must be seen that constructive action is being undertaken and that amelioration is possible in the not-too-distant future and at not too high a cost. Whatever the details, some positive thrust must be defined.

In this regard, the behavior of international actors will be crucial. The reality of Latin America's dependent situation is that many of the key variables in the economic crisis are not under local control. By extension, then, the move toward democracy is not purely a matter of domestic decision and negotiations. It is patent that external actors can help or hinder the process. Any professed desire to help must go beyond high-blown rhetoric to concrete economic policies that take some of the acute pressures off of these embryonic democratic regimes.

Current international policies toward the debt problem, for example, as manifested by the IMF, are undermining the democratic transition. They escalate the amount and kinds of costs that these governments must impose on their respective populaces—especially on those who have been carrying the burden under the military regimes and who looked to democracy as an escape. Present economic policy belies the prodemocratic rhetoric because, among other things, it demands decision-making centers able to impose policies resisted by almost all segments of society. This is a task that prior cycles show is beyond the capacity of open democratic regimes in Latin America. This seems to confirm what many Latin Americans have argued all along: when it comes to tension between their perceived short-term economic interests and their stated political values, international actors like the United States and other industrial powers will pursue the former at the expense of the latter.

International actors have an impact on the process mainly by closing or opening options to domestic policymakers. Such actions obviously help shape the flow of events, but in the end, the outcome of the transition and eventual regime formation will be determined by the decision and behavior of social groups and political leaders within each of these countries. In each case, the outcome will be different.

However, it would still be useful to try to tease out some general theme of transition on which the processes in specific countries will be variations. Central America, as a specific case in point, illuminates the larger developments occurring throughout Latin America.

The Politics of Transition in the 1980s and 1990s

Political development in Central America generally has lagged behind that of South America, largely because of Central America's slower socioeconomic evolution. For example, the late development and small scale of the industrial sector have retarded the development of organized labor. Yet, upon closer examination, many of the same forces at work in the more advanced South American cases can be seen in Central America, albeit on a small scale. In Costa Rica and Guatemala, as early as the 1940s, populist, reformist government came to power, although the United States' intervention in Guatemala terminated that experiment in 1954. In the early 1970s Honduras experienced a reformist military government modeled in part after the regime of Peru's General Velasco. The Sandinistas in Nicaragua overthrew one of the oldest extant personalist dictatorships in Latin America and have made a concerted effort to modernize the country. In El Salvador, the power of the traditional landed aristocracy seems to have been reduced as a result of land reform and open elections— both of which have come about as a fairly direct result of the guerrilla war raging there.

Central America is also experiencing many of the same economic strains that are affecting the South American cases treated in this volume. All of the Central American economies have suffered a sharp downturn in the 1980s. This decline has resulted in an increased tension between Central America and other major international actors because the growing foreign debt of the former has become so large relative to the size of their economies. This is especially true of Costa Rica, where the stability of this long-vaunted democratic system is being questioned as a result of the protracted failure of government leaders to resolve the debt problem. International pressures have become even more intrusive in Central America than in South America because of the United States' heightened interest in Nicaragua and El Salvador. In short, the Central American cases are not nearly as unique and unrelated to the main currents of Latin American political development as they once seemed to be.

This volume leads to a rather obvious but nonetheless important conclusion. While one can look back over past processes and identify, for analytical purposes, structural situations and conditions that made certain turns in the cycle of regime transformation seemingly inevitable, there are no such readily identifiable structural parameters that allow us to project—let alone predict—the outcomes of this transition process. The best one can do is identify issues, problems, and trends with which concrete actors will have to contend, and speculate on the possible consequences of this or that course of action. The present situation in Latin America is in fact a fluid and volatile one in which no actor or group of actors is in control of the key variables. Hence, we confront a situation in which the best laid plans of all political groupings will probably come up short in the face of a reality that will test the creative abilities of political leaders and groups to seize upon serendipitous opportunities and improvise their way into something new.

The point is that we are not apt to see in the short term any definitive solutions to the question of regime types. Moreover, in all likelihood we shall not witness a nice neat linear movement from one clear-cut regime type (authoritarian) to some other type (democratic). Linear movements, oscillations between poles, and cyclical turns are analytical devices that we impose on events. The metaphors we use often reflect the limited time horizons we employ. The experience of Latin America since at least the 1930s would suggest that we project for the medium term (twenty years) a process of movement and countermovement, of progress and regression, in which at any point particular regimes will not conform neatly to any of our theoretical or practical models of authoritarian and democratic regimes.

Internally the primary task confronting the political player is one of constitutional engineering that has both institutional and behavioral dimensions. As chapter 7 shows, one of the key institutional problems in Ecuador is that there is a marked disjunction between electoral/parliamentary politics and the executive-based process of governance. Elections do not tend to produce total governments with executive and legislative faces, but rather dualized governments in which there is a marked tendency toward standoffs between legislatures and executives. To avoid immobilism, executives are often tempted or inclined to govern around or over legislatures, often bending or ignoring the democratic rules of the game in the process.

Behind this institutional dilemma is a further disjunction between political parties and the key groups that make up civil society. Parties in Latin America historically have not been the main vehicle for representing civil society to the state and thereby providing an ongoing infrastructural link between state and society that can legitimate specific regime types.

Although this institutional structural problem has many sources, a major one is the predisposition of these societies toward a patrimonial social structure. They are formed around diffuse vertical hierarchies that link central structures to the people by means of ascending and descending patron-client ties. As Chalmers (among others) has noted, this deep structural tendency helps account for the fact that while class and interest-group dynamics exist in these societies, they are often overridden or blunted by vertical cross-class and status-group clientelistic dynamics.[8]

This underlying dynamic has a number of politically relevant consequences. The first is that key groups look to the state as the patrimonial source of privileges. Group strategy, as we saw, is used mainly to directly penetrate the state through the executive apparatus to extract specific concessions. Parties and legislatures are not the preferred vehicle for interest representation. Nor is there an interest in producing broad-based legislation for universal application. Rather, the inclination is to capture executive sources of benefits that flow more as patronage and privileges than as universal rights.

The upshot is that in periods of democratic rule interest groups target the executive for primary positive action and usually operate through parties and legislatures only to defend achieved privileges. This fact reinforces the institutional tendency to view the executive as the main source of positive action and rule and legislatures as negative blocking instruments. Moreover, most groups and factional leaders have shown over and over that the main issue for them is access to the executive lodestone and not formalized democratic procedures of rule making and conflict resolution. Hence, they are equally, if not more disposed to authoritarian regimes that guarantee their lines of access as they are to democratic rule.

In the end, access to power and control over distributable goods is the name of the game, not forms of regimes. The present movement by civilian interests away from the new authoritarianism springs mainly from the economic failures and the exclusionary tendency of these regimes. The state's forceful exclusion of labor was all too obvious. However, many of these regimes also acted as closed circles of military and technocratic decision makers that denied regularized channels of access to other groups as well. Hence, many groups that originally supported the new authoritarian regimes turned against them because of the erratic patterns of access offered to them and the impact upon them of policies that were formed with little or no counsel from them. Party leaders as well as some leaders of other social groups, even when they were formally identified with the regime, have pressured the regime to "decompress" so as to open more access to patronage.

The past record would indicate, then, that many groups, parties, and factions support a return to democracy not out of a primary commitment to liberal government, but as a result of concrete negative experience with the alternative. Democracy in contemporary Latin America, as in other historical contexts, will probably emerge as a result of negative consensus in which democracy is a second-best option in relation to absolutism.[9]

This fact does not necessarily augur ill for democracy. It merely reminds us that most democratic formulas spring from negotiations among key elite groups that provide for the ongoing access of all key players. This will have to occur in Latin America if democracy is to prevail. Moreover, ways must be found to convert electoral and legislative action into channels of access to power such that legislatures, elections, and parties can articulate and represent interests of civil society.

At present there are two significant examples of how structural problems have been overcome to produce stable regimes. One is Mexico, where the Partido Revolucionario Institucional (PRI) has established its hegemony as the singular vehicle of interest representation and government support. However, the result is a facade democracy that masks a civilian authoritarian system. Most of Latin America's populist political movements took their inspiration from Mexico, and, if they had been successful, would probably have followed the Mexican model.

The other relevant case is Venezuela where a populist party was forced to seek accommodation with its main civil opponents organized in parties. The resulting competitive democracy, with an excellent track record for longevity in Latin America, was based on a negotiated compromise among party leaders. The agreement included the following basic elements: parties would be the main contenders for power; losers in electoral contests would not be excluded from the game; and regardless of electoral outcomes, the winning party would share executive patronage with the principal losing party. In addition, military strongmen were all but bought off with large budgets to buy hardware and substantial concessions in salaries, pensions, etc. In short, there were plenty of incentives for key leaders to enter the game for the long haul, regardless of specific electoral outcomes. Another factor of some significance in Venezuela is that organized labor was integrated into the regime through the party system rather than direct influence with the executive branch. It is significant that at this moment a labor leader is emerging as a major contender for the nomination as its presidential candidate by one of the major parties, Acción Democrática (AD).

Constitutional engineering must go beyond the role and functions of political parties per se to confront the crucial problem of integrating key social groups into the new democratic systems. Since the 1930s, no group has been more crucial to the success of any regime than organized labor. The central dilemma is that previous modes of incorporating labor into the government have occurred in co-optive corporatist structures that were as compatible with authoritarian regimes as with democratic ones. Moreover, the quest for particular privileges undercut universal notions of citizenship crucial to modern democratic systems. As a result, state policies contributed to politically mediated increases in expenditures at the expense of capital accumulation.

This is not meant to imply that labor is the key culprit to explain the political instability of Latin America. Rather, the point is that the co-optive corporatist mode of incorporation created a structure of rule based on an accretion of power contenders who also generated demands and then "colonized" pieces of the state, their patron. This approach steadily increased state spending and policies that increase consumption even as it diminished the capacity of the state, especially in democratic form, to act. The reason was mainly that political support was contingent on acquired patronage and sources of benefits thereby fostering a defensive orientation among admitted groups. Finally, the co-optive style of incorporation was—and probably still is—as adaptable to an authoritarian government as to a democratic one, if not more so.

The issue of labor brings us back to the populist cycles and the costs of development. In capitalist systems, costs tend to be apportioned more heavily toward the mass consuming power of popular sectors, and especially labor. Hence, since the 1960s all regimes, authoritarian and democratic alike, have found themselves in confrontation with labor over who should bear the burden of development. Most regimes have moved to shift those costs by curtailing or eliminating the political power and participation of labor.

The new democratic regimes have not been able to escape this dilemma. Indeed the populist/antipopulist cycle has not only taken a new turn but in a sense has come full circle. In the current scene, democratic regimes often headed by the original populist parties and personalities have found themselves pursuing antipopulist cost-allocating policies that bring them into conflict with labor. Should conflict turn into persistent confrontation, the propensity of these states to move into a more authoritarian mode will increase. Indeed, as the case of Peru under Belaúnde shows, a civil democratic regime that follows antipopulist policies begins to adopt aspects of an authoritarian decision-making style.

Herein perhaps lies the key to the future of regime types in Latin America in the near future, at least. As we have argued throughout, most of the key dilemmas that have bedeviled both democratic and authoritarian regimes since the 1930s not only persist but also in the present international context are actually more acute. All things being equal, this does not augur well for democracy. However, at the moment the record of recent authoritarian regimes clearly helps buy some time for democracy. However, when push comes to shove the central question of whether democratic regimes can make and enforce key decisions in such matters of cost allocations is inescapable. Moreover, recent history shows that attempts to grapple with these issues encourage the compression of power at the center, to overcome the tendency toward immobilism built into more open participatory decision procedures.

Many scholars have commented on the cyclical patterns in Latin American history. The real underlying cycle might be the movement from diffuse participatory structures to compressed, minimally participatory structures. Behind this may lie the fact that, in a context of dependent capitalist development, the state is perforce pushed into the role of primary mediator with international actors and coordinator of the domestic development process. Even in Chile, where the state pushes an open market model, the state remains the main enforcer of the cost allocations implicit in that model. Whatever the rhetoric, it is clear that all parties, both international and domestic, look to the state as the primary definer and resolver of these dilemmas. Witness the fact that all international actors look to the respective states to solve the debt crisis (by, among other things, standing responsible for all debts both public and private) and that the central politics of the day is the politics of "economic packages."

The basic problem, then, is finding a basis for an ongoing stable system of governance. Regimes have in fact oscillated around this issue; neither classic democratic nor authoritarian regimes have provided a base for stability. Democracy has tended to lapse into immobilism, while authoritarianism has fostered a rupture between the state and society that has threatened the coherence of all key institutions, including the armed forces.

One possibility—in fact, a probability—is that the basic cyclical swing between authoritarian and democratic modes will continue. Perhaps the region is trapped. Political participation and respect for civil liberties inevitably diminishes the central decision center. When situations arise that demand immediate action and the state is unable to respond adequately, there is a call for greater centralization. Yet compressed power brings short-term decision power at the cost of alienating the central state from society as a whole.

However, there may also be some linear movement in the cyclical process. We might well see the emergence in Latin America of new regime types that do not conform neatly to our classic notions of either democracy or authoritarianism. Mexico resolved its revolution through the emergence of such a new regime. It is highly unlikely that any of these societies will emulate the Mexican system as such, but it may well give us some clues as to where they might go.

The recent political transitions also offer some intimations. In Brazil the lines between regime types have been blurred. In a sense, the fluid, ongoing transition process itself has become a kind of de facto regime type. We might not see any neat definitive solutions to either the question of defining the regime dilemma or economic problems, but rather an ongoing process of negotiation and renegotiation of policies and who makes them. Like Bolivia, we may have to start thinking not of definitive solutions to political and economic issues but rather a series of *salidas* or short-term resolutions of specific problems. New regimes may well emerge more as a result of the accumulation of serendipitous *salidas* rather than any great constitutional designs or sharply defined economic models.

The recent experience of Peru with Belaúnde's "authoritarian democracy" may also provide some clues. Within the unfolding transition process, the direction of the *salidas* might be to contain the movement toward compression and decompression of power within a single outward judicial form rather than oscillation between outward forms by means of coups d'état. We may then see the development, in some of these societies, of hybrid regimes that assure democratic political participation and maintain civil liberties, while giving the executive quasi-authoritarian power in times of crisis. As some of the chapters in this book suggest, the oscillations between compression and decompression within such a regime would reflect cycles of socioeconomic crisis and the perceived need to make hard decisions that are apt to be resisted by key social groups. In the near term, this cycle will continue to pivot around questions of accumulation versus distribution, populism versus antipopulism, and the relationship of the state with popular sectors, especially organized labor.

For such a process of hybridization to continue, areas of "constitutional engineering" will be crucial. First, the electoral process will have to be meaningfully related to governance by means of legislative coalitions that can underpin strong executive power. Political parties must mediate between socioeconomic groups and the executive apparatus of the state. Second, military and civilian leaders will have to compromise and form de facto coalitions so that the military find it in their own interest to back a strong civilian regime in moments of crisis.

Given the recent experiences of authoritarian rule in Latin America, it is likely that most critical leaders, including the military, will seek *salidas* within some kind of formalized democratic regime. The question now turns on the ongoing creativity of the key players and whether the international system will help by expanding the economic space within which *salidas* can be found or whether they will restrict options so much that only a highly compressed authoritarian regime will be able to enforce the measures required for debt payments. At the moment, these remain the best and worst of times for democracy in Latin America, and its future development is far from certain.

Notes

1. For the empirical issues, see Mitchell A. Seligson and Edward N. Muller, "Political Support under Crisis Conditions: Costa Rica, 1978–1983," *International Studies Quarterly*, forthcoming.

2. For an overview, see James M. Malloy, "Statecraft and Social Security Policy and Crisis: A Comparison of Latin America and the United States," in *The Crisis of Social Security and Health Care: Latin American Experiences and Lessons*, ed. Carmelo Mesa-Lago (Pittsburgh, Pa.: Center for Latin American Studies, University of Pittsburgh, 1985), pp. 19–51.

3. Sergio H. Abranches, "The Politics of Social Welfare Development in Latin America," Instituto Universitario de Pesquisas do Rio de Janeiro, Serie de Estudos, October 1982, p. 8.

4. Charles W. Anderson, *Politics and Economic Change in Latin America* (Princeton, N.J.: Van Nostrand, 1967).

5. Douglas A. Chalmers, "Parties and Society in Latin America," in *Friends, Followers and Clients: A Reader in Political Clientelism*, ed. Steffen W. Schmidt et al. (Berkeley and Los Angeles: University of California Press, 1977), pp. 401–21.

6. Ibid., p. 410.

7. O'Donnell's writings on this subject are many. The basic formulation is in Guillermo A. O'Donnell, *Modernization and Bureaucratic Authoritarianism: Studies in South American Politics* (Berkeley, Calif.: University of California Institute of International Studies, 1973).

8. Chalmers, "Parties and Society in Latin America."

9. Dankwart A. Rustow, "Transitions to Democracy: Towards a Dynamic Model," *Comparative Politics* 2 (1970): 337ff.

Notes on Contributors

Luis A. Abugattas is professor of political science at the Universidad del Pacífico in Lima. He has published on the political economy of Peru and is currently involved in a major study of the role of the private sector and economic policymaking in Ecuador, Peru, and Bolivia.

Cole Blasier is research professor of political science and Latin American studies at the University of Pittsburgh. He has published extensively on the relations of the United States and the Soviet Union with Latin America. He was elected 1986–1987 president of the Latin American Studies Association.

Silvia T. Borzutzky is a principal research assistant at the University Center for International Studies at the University of Pittsburgh. She has done extensive work in social policy in Latin America, with an emphasis on Chile.

Catherine Conaghan is assistant professor of political science at Ohio State University. She has recently completed a major study of industrialists and political reform in Ecuador.

Silvio R. Duncan Baretta is research associate in sociology at the University of Pittsburgh. He has published articles on contemporary Brazil and has finished a book-length study of politics in nineteenth-century Rio Grande do Sul.

Eduardo A. Gamarra is assistant professor of political science at Florida International University. He has recently completed a book-length work on the role of the national legislature in contemporary Bolivia.

James M. Malloy is professor of political science and chairperson of the department of political science at the University of Pittsburgh. He has published extensively on revolution, social policy, and authoritarianism in Latin America.

John Markoff is associate professor of sociology at the University of Pittsburgh. He has published articles on Brazil and recently completed a major sociological study of the French Revolution.

Mark B. Rosenberg is professor of political science and director of the Latin American and Caribbean Center at Florida International University. He has published widely on Central America and on social policy.

Mitchell A. Seligson is professor of political science and director of the Center for Latin American Studies at the University of Pittsburgh. His extensive publications include studies of the political economy of Latin America and the developing world.

Aldo C. Vacs is assistant professor of political science at Skidmore College. He has published on Soviet-Argentine relations and recently completed a comparative study of the political economy of external debt in Brazil and Argentina.

Index

Adelman, Irma, 180
Aguilera, Gabriel, 199–200
Alfonsín, Raúl, 31, 32, 36
Allende, Salvador, 221, 222, 223, 224, 227
Alliance for Progress, 221
Anderson, Charles A., 241
Aramburu, Pedro, 16
Arévalo, Juan José, 225, 226, 231
Argentina: authoritarianism in, 9, 16–21, 44–45, 246; Catholic church in, 32–33; Central Bank of, 25–26, 35; clientelism in, 242; cyclical pattern of democracy in, 44–45; economy of, 16, 18, 20, 22–27, 29–30, 35, 41n8; elections in, 16, 32, 34–35; and foreign banks, 33, 35–36; foreign debt of, 35; General Confederation of Labor of, 28, 34; human rights violations in, 228; and the IMF, 33, 35–36; interest groups in, 19; labor unions in, 28, 30, 32, 37, 40, 245; law of national pacification in (1983), 30; and the Malvinas War (1982), 26, 28–29, 32; military of, 15, 16–21, 25, 28–31, 33, 37–38; Multipartidaria coalition of, 27; Isabel Perón regime of, 21; Juan D. Perón regime of, 16, 32, 240; Peronists in, 16, 19, 21, 27, 29, 30–32, 240; political culture of, 17, 19–20, 36, 39, 122, 123; political parties in, 18–19, 27, 37, 38; Radical party of, 16, 19, 27, 30, 31–37; redemocratization of, 15–21, 40, 172, 200; Revolución Argentina of, 16, 22; Revolución Libertadora of, 16; socioeconomic levels in, 7; state terrorism in, 21, 28, 30; Unión Cívica Radical of, 31–32; universities of, 40
Armed forces. See Military
Arosemena, Carlos Julio, 154
Arosemena, Otto, 154
Authoritarianism: in Argentina, 16–24; in Brazil, 43–44; cycle of in Latin America, 235–37, 238, 246; and Latin American political culture, 10, 246; and

U.S. support for, 222–23. See also individual countries

Baca, Raúl, 149, 152
Balaguer, Joaquín, 226
Banco de Chile, 78
Banco Español (Chile), 78
Bánzer Suárez, Hugo, 102–11, 113
Barrientos Ortuño, René, 97–99
Batista, Fulgencio, 222
Belaúnde Terry, Fernando, 122, 135, 138–41, 255, 256–57
Best, Michael, 185
Bignone, Reynaldo, 29
Bishop, Maurice, 223
Bolivia: ADN of, 111; asamblea popular of, 100, 101; Bánzer regime of, 102–11; bureaucracy in, 106; as B-A regime, 244; Central Labor Confederation ot (COB), 94–95, 100, 101, 115, 116, 118; Confederation of Private Entrepreneurs of, 115; Congress of, 112–14, 117; Constitution of, 97; co-optation in, 95–99, 103, 104–05; economy of, 8, 94–96, 97, 98, 100, 101, 102–08, 111, 114–16; elections in, 96, 97, 108, 110–12, 113; Falange Socialista Boliviana of (FSB), 103; foreign debt of, 113, 115; human rights in, 228; and the IMF, 113, 115, 116; inflation in, 116; labor unions in, 99, 100; Left Revolutionary Movement ot (UDP), 111, 115, 116; military of, 99–101, 109–10, 114, 247; military coups in, 96–99, 102, 110, 112, 113; "military populism" in, 99, 103, 105; mining industry in, 106; Movimiento Nacionalista Revolucionario of (MNR), 93–98, 100, 101, 103, 111, 240; Nationalist Democratic Action of (ADN), 111; neopatrimonialism in, 98–99, 104–08, 109; peasants of, 101; political chaos in, 93, 101, 114–16, 118, 256; political parties in, 94–98, 100–02, 103, 111, 116, 204;

Pitt Latin American Series
Cole Blasier, Editor

The United States and Cuba: Hegemony and Dependent Development, 1880–1934
Jules Robert Benjamin

MEXICO
Essays on Mexican Kinship
Hugo G. Nutini, Pedro Carrasco, and James M. Taggart, Editors

The Mexican Republic: The First Decade, 1823–1832
Stanley C. Green

The Politics of Mexican Oil
George W. Grayson

Voices, Visions, and a New Reality: Mexican Fiction Since 1970
J. Ann Duncan

US POLICIES
Cuba, Castro, and the United States
Philip W. Bonsal

The Hovering Giant: U.S. Responses to Revolutionary Change in Latin America
Cole Blasier

Illusions of Conflict: Anglo-American Diplomacy Toward Latin America
Joseph Smith

Puerto Rico and the United States, 1917–1933
Truman R. Clark

The United States and Cuba: Hegemony and Dependent Development, 1880–1934
Jules Robert Benjamin

The United States and Latin America in the 1980s: Contending Perspectives on a Decade of Crisis
Kevin J. Middlebrook and Carlos Rico, Editors

USSR POLICIES
Discreet Partners: Argentina and the USSR Since 1917
Aldo César Vacs

The Giant's Rival: The USSR and Latin America
Cole Blasier

OTHER NATIONAL STUDIES
Barrios in Arms: Revolution in Santo Domingo
José A. Moreno

Beyond the Revolution: Bolivia Since 1952
James M. Malloy and Richard S. Thorn, Editors

Black Labor on a White Canal: Panama, 1904–1981
Michael L. Conniff

The Origins of the Peruvian Labor Movement, 1883–1919
Peter Blanchard

The Overthrow of Allende and the Politics of Chile, 1964–1976
Paul E. Sigmund

Panajachel: A Guatemalan Town in Thirty-Year Perspective
Robert E. Hinshaw

Peru and the International Monetary Fund
Thomas Scheetz

Rebirth of the Paraguayan Republic: The First Colorado Era, 1878–1904
Harris G. Warren

SOCIAL SECURITY
The Politics of Social Security in Brazil
James M. Malloy

Social Security in Latin America: Pressure Groups, Stratification, and Inequality
Carmelo Mesa-Lago

OTHER STUDIES
Adventurers and Proletarians: The Story of Migrants in Latin America
Magnus Mörner, with the collaboration of Harold Sims

Authoritarianism and Corporatism in Latin America
James M. Malloy, Editor

Authoritarians and Democrats: Regime Transition in Latin America
James M. Malloy and Mitchell A. Seligson, Editors

Constructive Change in Latin America
Cole Blasier, Editor

Female and Male in Latin America: Essays
Ann Pescatello, Editor

Latin American Debt and the Adjustment Crisis
Rosemary Thorp and Laurence Whitehead, Editors

Public Policy in Latin America: A Comparative Survey
John W. Sloan

Selected Latin American One-Act Plays
Francesca Colecchia and Julio Matas, Editors and Translators

The State and Capital Accumulation in Latin America: Brazil, Chile, Mexico
Christian Anglade and Carlos Fortin, Editors

Transnational Corporations and the Latin American Automobile Industry
Rhys Jenkins